THE INSECURE WORLD OF HENRY JAMES'S FICTION

The Insecure World of Henry James's Fiction

Intensity and Ambiguity

Ralf Norrman

St. Martin's Press   New York

ISBN 0–312–41863–9

Library of Congress Cataloging in Publication Data

Norrman, Ralf.
  The Insecure World of Henry James's Fiction.

  Includes bibliographical references and index.
  1. James, Henry, 1843–1916—Style. I. Title.
PS2128.N6   1982   813'.4   81–50017
ISBN 0–312–41863–9   AACR2

For E-L

Le style est l'homme même
(Buffon)

Contents

Foreword

Though published only now, this book was written several years ago. In the time that has passed since then my thinking on James has developed. I have now become firmly convinced that the most important key to an understanding of the psychomorphology of James's thinking is the nature and function of the rhetorical figure of *chiasmus*, which, in the present study, is dealt with only in the fifth chapter, which is the last. James was what I would like to term a *chiasticist*: his use of chiastic thinking was habitual and compulsive.

Chapter 5 of the present work is therefore the most important of all chapters, and impatient readers may want to begin with that rather than Chapter 1.

I could of course have rewritten this book, laying more stress on chiasmus, and structuring the text around what is now Chapter 5. However, I decided to let it stand, and to return to James's use of chiasmus in another context.

Meanwhile, I would like to refer any readers who become interested in the nature and function of chiasmus to a book on the subject that I am at present writing, and which I hope will be published in the near future. The preliminary title is *Samuel Butler and Chiasmus: A Study of an Ambilateralist Mind*. This study will use the works of Samuel Butler (1835–1902) as source of examples but the results will be applicable to Henry James as well, and it is actually astonishing how similar James and Butler were in their ways of thinking. The similarity is accounted for by the fact that both were addicted to one particular pattern of thought – chiasmus.

Oxford   Ralf Norrman
December 1980

Acknowledgements

I am grateful to Dr Larzer Ziff of the University of Pennsylvania (formerly of Exeter College, Oxford) for reading drafts of the first two chapters and making a number of helpful comments and suggestions.

I am very grateful for financial assistance from the H.W. Donner Fund.

I wish to thank my wife Eva-Liisa for typing and proof-reading and for a number of discussions that brought forth new ideas and helped to put old ones into perspective.

While writing this study I was at Linacre, and for a short time at Queen's. I am grateful to these Oxford colleges, and to the Finnish Academy, for academic hospitality and financial support.

Chapter 1 and an early version of Chapter 2 of this book have appeared as articles in periodicals: 'Referential Ambiguity in Pronouns as a Literary Device in Henry James's *The Golden Bowl*', *Studia Neophilologica*, vol. 5 (1979), no. 1, pp. 31–71; 'End-Linking as an Intensity-Creating Device in the Dialogue of Henry James's *The Golden Bowl*', *English Studies*, vol. 61 (June 1980), no. 3, pp. 236–51. Some of the material in the present fifth chapter appeared earlier in my essay 'Chiastisk inversion: Ett mönster hos Henry James', in *Pegas och Snöbollskrig: Litteraturvetenskapliga studier tillägnade Sven Linnér*, Publications of the Research Institute of the Åbo Akademi Foundation, no. 44 (Åbo Akademi, 1979), ss. 209–25. I thank the editors for permission to reprint.

Every effort has been made to trace all copyright holders but if any have been inadvertently overlooked the publishers will be pleased to make the necessary arrangement at the first opportunity.

Introduction

The guiding principle of this study is the belief that the style reflects the man. Each of the chapters following will deal with a specific feature of Henry James's style, and in each case the contention is that the nature of the stylistic device reveals an essential aspect of James's fictional world.

Taken together the chapters also present a picture of that world. It seems that the picture could be summed up in one single word, and that word is *uncertainty*.

One very characteristic feature of James's prose is referential ambiguity in pronouns. If it is true that style is a microlevel reflection of the thematic macrolevel, then this confusion in pronominal reference suggests that uncertainty about identities characterizes James's universe. It is not clear 'who is who'.

Another stylistic device which is highly characteristic of James's prose is what I call 'end-linking', i.e. the linking of the end of one linguistic unit to the beginning of the next. One variety of end-linking is the figure of anadiplosis. Another, on the textual level, is rheme-to-theme repetitional linking of sentences. This type of intersentence link, which is a favourite in James's textual grammar, is a resumptive, backward-looking device, which testifies to the insecurity of a mind which could never regard anything as finished. Nothing is ever final in James. Therefore the sentence he puts down on paper when writing often raises more questions than it answers and James feels obliged to let it grow, through the resumptive link of rheme-to-theme repetition, into an addition, modification, qualification, or even contradiction, in the next sentence. End-linking stylistically presents to us the extraordinary spectacle of James dancing a strange dance with his subject: one step forward, two steps backward. In the James universe there is always and forever *something else*: 'One can never be ideally sure of anything. There are always possibilities', as Fanny Assingham puts it in *The Golden Bowl* (p. 101).[1] James can always think of more questions than answers, and this at times tends to make his writing an

1

exercise in the kind of infinite regression of which 'end-linking' is a tell-tale sign. James's writing comes to resemble the process of nuclear fission in a breeder-reactor – the process produces more fuel than it consumes.

Yet another idiosyncrasy, which gives James's dialogues their inimitable authentic ring, is the use of 'emphatic affirmation'. By emphatic affirmation I mean the type of affirmation that relies on an emphatic word for word repetition of the whole question, rather than, for instance, on the use of the word 'yes'. The preference for the emphatic form of affirmation is an intensity-creating device. It may seem strange to argue that emphatic affirmation too reveals a sense of insecurity, since, on the face of it, intensity and emphasis may seem antithetical to ambiguity and uncertainty. In reality, however, intensity and ambiguity are only different sides of the same coin. It is precisely in a universe where most things are uncertain and ambiguous that, if anything is to be asserted at all, it has to be asserted with special intensity and emphasis. Furthermore, since it is in the nature of the case that insistent and emphatic intensity is used in life primarily in those situations where it is most needed – which is in contexts characterized by uncertainty and ambiguity – the device itself, with another turn of the screw, may also become a case of 'over-much protesting', counteracting its own purpose and thus contributing further to ambiguity and uncertainty rather than alleviating or allaying existing doubts.

Another relevant Jamesian mannerism is what I shall call the 'finding a formula'-formula, which involves a tendency on the part of James's characters to half-believe in a magic power of language over reality, so that if only something can be formulated in the right way the magic inherent in words will mysteriously make reality conform to language. James's characters are primitives who make use of euphemisms, spells and incantations. They long for a world governed by a special brand of William James's pragmatism – i.e. a world in which things become true when you say them. To create reality by verbal magic is however the monopoly of the privileged literary artist. In life, alas, reality tends to remain reality and language language. James was proud of his own powers of verbal invention and believed in art as a self-sustained and self-sufficient thing: 'It is art that *makes* life, makes interest, makes importance'.[2] Many of James's characters are little replicas of their creator – the 'artist-figure' is a well-known type in James's fiction. But when James's solipsistic 'artist-figure' characters try to govern reality through language they are never quite sure that it is possible. Thus the 'finding a formula'-formula also reveals the insecurity of James's world.

Oxymoron and antithesis are favourite Jamesian figures. That self-contradictory combinations are frequent and significant in James's style indicates an uncertainty about values in his world. Antonymic opposition, or the juxtaposition of antagonistic forces, is frequent in James. Particularly important, however, in connection with antithetic structuring is James's characteristic tendency towards a lability which allows the most extraordinary changes of positions. This quite often results in a pattern which I shall call 'chiastic inversion'. Just as referential ambiguity in pronouns reveals uncertainty about identities, so chiastic inversion reveals uncertainty about *roles*. Referential ambiguity in pronouns suggests doubts as to 'who is who'; chiastic inversion suggests doubts as to 'who does what'.

The method of literary scholarship which attempts to illuminate the created 'world' of a writer through analysis of his style is highly controversial. When Count Buffon produced his famous dictum he did not mean quite the same as his words have since been taken to imply, and the word 'style' at that time was used in a wide sense. The idea that the style reflects the man has given rise to a great variety of critical approaches, all of which have not been equally rewarding or respectable.

Despite the excesses that have given the method a bad name in some quarters I think there is nevertheless a sufficient degree of truth in the idea to justify a study such as the present one. The applicability of the idea that 'the style reflects the man' naturally varies from man to man, since it is sometimes pertinent to ask whether a certain author has a style of his own at all. James's style, however, is unmistakeably idiosyncratic, which should support my claim for the legitimacy of this study.

A further complication is that there are several James styles: early and late; or first, second and third manner; and thus one might ask whether there are also several men – several Jameses. During my earlier investigations of James's technique I have become convinced that most, if not all, of the idiosyncrasies of the late style exist in embryonic form in the early style. It could therefore be argued that James – the same James – is at his most characteristic late in his career. Accordingly I have decided to concentrate on that period and take my examples mainly from *The Golden Bowl*.

For a sub-title I have chosen 'Intensity and Ambiguity'. Readers will hardly find my choice of these two words a surprising novelty. Critics have always regarded 'intensity' and 'ambiguity' as apt words to characterize James's works.

The word 'intense' has been found useful in descriptions of the nature of the dialogue in *The Golden Bowl*. Even in the early reviews of the novel the word 'intense' appeared,[3] and it has remained a favourite with commentators. One critic recently used it four times in the opening paragraph of his chapter on *The Golden Bowl*.[4] In particular critics resort to the word when they wish to describe the atmosphere of James's conversations.

The term 'ambiguity' is by now a commonplace in James criticism. James's ambiguity was noted from the very beginning; in 1934 Edmund Wilson's article on James's ambiguity started a tradition which continues today as vigorously as ever, and a number of excellent works have been published on the subject of James's ambiguity.[5] These include interpretative works such as Jean Frantz Blackall's *Jamesian Ambiguity and* The Sacred Fount,[6] evaluative works such as Charles Thomas Samuels's *The Ambiguity of Henry James*[7] and theoretical treatises such as Shlomith Rimmon's *The Concept of Ambiguity – the Example of James*.[8]

There is thus a wide consensus on the two epithets 'intense' and 'ambiguous'. Naturally this does not guarantee that thereby the essential truth about James's prose has been revealed. But on the other hand 'the fact that a lot of people have been saying something does not necessarily mean it is not true' – as the old maxim has it – and acting on the wide consensus on the two terms *intensity* and *ambiguity* I hope I shall be able in this study to explore some of the ways in which the effect of intensity and ambiguity is created.[9] My view of the case, however, is not only that there exists ambiguity, and that there also exists intensity, in James. In my opinion the two are closely related, and deserve to be dealt with together. It is a case not only of intensity *or* ambiguity, nor even of intensity *and* ambiguity, but often quite definitely of *ambiguous intensity* or *intense ambiguity*.

Let me finally say a few words about the relation between the present study and my earlier book on James, *Techniques of Ambiguity in the Fiction of Henry James: With Special Reference to* In the Cage *and* The Turn of the Screw (Åbo: Åbo Akademi, 1977). Though the present work is self-contained and can be read on its own, there are some respects in which the two are complementary. I have repeated only as much of earlier arguments as was necessary to make the present chapters able to stand on their own feet.

1 Referential Ambiguity in Pronouns

The Golden Bowl is a game of combinations. It is a prime example of James's love for abstractions, diagrams and various forms of neat symmetry.[1] In some works, such as *The Other House* or *The Sacred Fount*, this tendency in James produces bloodless or perverse results; in others like *What Maisie Knew*, although the growth of combinations runs totally amok, the result is nevertheless satisfying because the absurdity is made thematic. *The Golden Bowl* carries on a tradition in James that started very early and was already mature in *Confidence* and *The Europeans*. Of all James novels that diagram easily *The Golden Bowl* seems the best because the combinations are an integrated part of the whole and, although James has great fun playing with his combinations, the switches of partners are not an artificial element in the novel – they *are* the novel.

'Once I had fallen in love with the beautiful symmetry of my plan' (p. 322) says Fanny Assingham who engineered not only the marriage between Maggie and the Prince but that between Adam and Charlotte as well. James, too, obviously had fallen in love with the beautiful symmetry of his plan. The symmetry is basically two marriages, plus two other emotional attachments (father and daughter; stepmother and son-in-law) and the resulting six possible coupling combinations. The formula is

$$\frac{n^2 - n}{2}$$

which yields three combinations for a triangular drama, six for a *Vierpersonenkonstellation* and fifteen for a game involving six participants.

The Golden Bowl is a game *à quatre*. A triangular drama is well enough but a *Vierpersonenkonstellation* is much better because it doubles the number of possible combinations. Two basic switches are possible and there is the additional interest of the

6

relationships between the persons of the same sex. In *The Golden Bowl* all the possibilities are exploited.² It is a *situation nette* (pp. 295, 298) in more than one sense.

Where does the *Vierpersonenkonstellation* lead us to? Let us start with Fanny Assingham's analysis in Chapter IV.

'All their case wants, at any rate,' Bob Assingham declared, 'is that you should leave it well alone. It's theirs now; they've bought it, over the counter, and paid for it. It has ceased to be yours.'

'Of which case,' she asked, 'are you speaking?'

He smoked a minute; then with a groan: 'Lord, are there so many?'

'There's Maggie's and the Prince's, and there's the Prince's and Charlotte's.'

'Oh yes; and then,' the Colonel scoffed, 'there's Charlotte's and the Prince's.'

'There's Maggie's and Charlotte's,' she went on – 'and there's also Maggie's and mine. I think too that there's Charlotte's and mine. Yes,' she mused, 'Charlotte's and mine is certainly a case. In short, you see, there are plenty. But I mean,' she said, 'to keep my head.'

'Are we to settle them all,' he inquired, 'to-night?' (92–3)

As readers we may find it hard to keep our heads sometimes in *The Golden Bowl*, keeping track of all the cases, of which there are, in truth, plenty, but without any claims to settle them all in this chapter nor in this study as a whole, let us look at them methodically from the beginning.

To start with there are three relationships between people who are lovers in what we may call the technical sense. These are Amerigo–Maggie, Adam–Charlotte, and Amerigo–Charlotte. Of these three the first two are 'legitimate' and the third 'illicit'. To set off the illicit relationship between Amerigo and Charlotte there is the strong paternal – filial relationship between Adam and Maggie – or perhaps it would be better to call it the filial–paternal relationship between Maggie and Adam, since Maggie often seems to be the more active partner. This relationship is necessary for the symmetry, to set off the bond between Amerigo and Charlotte. 'A necessary basis for all this must have been an intense and exceptional degree of attachment between the father and daughter – he peculiarly paternal, she passionately filial', wrote James, when he jotted down the idea for *The Golden Bowl* in his *Notebooks* for the first time.[3]

The relationship between Adam and Maggie is not directly 'illicit' since paternal and filial affection must be regarded as normal, but nevertheless the relationship is a good counter-weight to Amerigo–Charlotte, because it is unnatural. After her marriage Maggie's attachment to her father could have been expected to be superseded by her attachment to her husband. In every way the coupling Maggie–Adam is on a level with the coupling Charlotte–Amerigo. This can be seen for instance in the relation of the two couples to the central symbol of the novel, the golden bowl. When Charlotte and Amerigo have their surreptitious outing on the eve of his marriage and go into the shop in Bloomsbury they are thinking of each other to such a degree, and so little of Maggie, that the shopkeeper afterwards, distilling the essence of the visit, says that they (i.e. Amerigo and Charlotte) wanted to give each other presents.[4] When Maggie, later on, accidentally comes to the shop and buys the bowl she is out hunting for a birthday present for her father. Thus, in connection with the bowl, the Prince is unfaithful to his (future) wife with Charlotte, and Maggie is unfaithful to her husband with her father.[5] In the novel Maggie openly and repeatedly discusses being 'married' (p. 163)[6] to her father; a metaphor which is meant to suggest that the relationship Maggie–Adam is as strong as Charlotte–Amerigo.

By making the balancing 'illicit' relationship in his paradigm a father–daughter relationship James intensifies our interest. If the relationship had been a more conventional one, between people not kin to each other, Charlotte's and Amerigo's griev-ance would have become more pronounced and their conduct more defensible in a technical sense. The combinations would then have been more trivial and the reader would have begun to expect innumerable exits and entries, and much hiding in closets, as with the *Vierpersonenkonstellationen* of much French farce.

By choosing to make Adam and Maggie father and daughter James became able to tap the thematic interest of many springs of *motifs*. Not only did he gain access to the dramatic interest of the clash of loyalties for a person torn between affections of different kinds (family bonds and loyalties incurred through marriage), the 'divided duty' that has been the theme of so much world literature – of medieval Germanic literature, for instance. He also made us intensely interested in Maggie's process of growing up from daughterhood into wifehood. In fact there is a strong element of 'the fortunate fall' in the novel. James reverted to type and became more American as he grew older.

Doubtless, if a certain kind of combination-happy modern author could have laid hands on the idea of *The Golden Bowl* he would not only have made the relationship between Maggie and Adam incestuous but would also have managed a homo-erotic subplot Adam–Amerigo and a lesbian interlude Charlotte–Maggie. Well, James is not far behind, for at least as far as the interest of these relationships can contribute to the plot the relationships *are* there. Amerigo complains in the very first conversation that he cannot make out his prospective father-in-law and his interest in studying Adam becomes more and more absorbing as the narrative progresses. That Charlotte and Maggie love each other, or at least that Maggie loves Charlotte, is stressed repeatedly.

> Something in Charlotte's eyes seemed to tell him this, seemed to plead with him in advance as to what he was to find in it. He was eager – and he tried to show her that too – to find what she liked; mindful as he easily could be of what the friendship had been for Maggie. It had been armed with the wings of young imagination, young generosity; it had been, he believed – always counting out her intense devotion to her father – the liveliest emotion she had known before the dawn of the sentiment inspired by himself. (76)[7]

The order here of Maggie's preferences is Adam, Amerigo, Charlotte, and since, in the hierarchies of the others, the three top places are also always taken by various combinations of the remaining three members of the quartet, this tightly knit pattern of devotion contributes greatly to intensity. Everybody loves everybody else in this *ménage à quatre*.[8]

Once the basic situation was given James needed some intensifying device to dramatize the successive stages in the development of the plot. A device that very naturally suggested itself was referential ambiguity.[9] This ambiguity usually occurs in some form of misunderstanding in a dialogue.

Misunderstandings occur frequently in actual conversations.

They are usually disambiguated through an interrupting query and a clarifying, expanded re-take of the ambiguous part of the preceding utterance. Usually when authors imitate this aspect of life they leave out misunderstandings in their dialogues. To put in misunderstandings that are cleared up would be to include an unnecessary deviation from the straight path of the dialogue towards its purpose.[10] To include misunderstandings in a dialogue in a literary text you usually need a stronger reason than a mere wish to be 'lifelike'. Misunderstandings are normally included only if they fulfil some more definite artistic purpose.

James sometimes used misunderstandings that are *not* cleared up as an ambiguity-creating device to achieve interest through mystification. But he also used referential ambiguities which are sorted out as a surface device in his text to remind the reader regularly of the combinations and relationships in *The Golden Bowl*. Referential ambiguities occur both in the dialogues and elsewhere. In particular these referential ambiguities are ambiguities of pronouns, since James's four-person set-up, with the Assinghams as observers, afforded him such endless possibilities of making use of this device.

In a conversation between Maggie and Charlotte any 'he' is in theory potentially ambiguous (could refer either to Adam or to Amerigo). And since Maggie, despite her marriage to Amerigo, is in fact almost more attached to her father; and since Charlotte, despite her marriage to Adam is in fact more interested in Amerigo, the ambiguity often does not remain potential but is activated and regularly has to be disambiguated by queries and clarifications. In a conversation between Adam and Amerigo any 'she' is in theory potentially ambiguous. And since the case with the men is exactly symmetrical to that of the women these ambiguities too are often activated.

In a conversation between the Assinghams any 'he' or 'she' is ambiguous. In addition any 'they' is ambiguous; if 'they' refers to two people it is sextuply ambiguous (Maggie+Charlotte; Maggie+Amerigo; Maggie+Adam; Adam+Amerigo; Adam+Charlotte; Amerigo+Charlotte), but naturally it could also refer to three people; or to all four; or to various combinations of these possibilities. In different types of conversations the number of alternative ways that a 'we' could be ambiguous, depending on the participants, can be calculated mathematically, and the design of the plot is such that almost all the combinations that are possible in theory are also actually there in practice.

'You' naturally has the same number of possible combinations as 'we', but in addition there is the ambiguity inherent in this pronoun in the English language, i.e. is it second person singular or plural?

There is not space here to go through all the possibilities of potential pronominal referential ambiguity; instead let us trace the main pattern of the occurrence of actual *activated* ambiguity in the dialogues and their contribution to the effect of intensity in the novel.

Our first example comes in Chapter II in a dialogue between the Prince and Mrs Assingham.

'It isn't a question of everything, but it's a question of anything that may particularly concern me. Then you shouldn't keep it back. You know with what care I desire to proceed, taking everything into account and making no mistake that may possibly injure *her*.'

Mrs Assingham, at this, had after an instant an odd interrogation. ' "Her"?'

'Her and him. Both our friends. Either Maggie or her father.'

'I *have* something on my mind,' Mrs Assingham presently returned; 'something has happened for which I hadn't been prepared. But it isn't anything that properly concerns you.' (64)

Mrs Assingham's odd interrogation here functions as a foreshadowing of Charlotte. As early as in the first conversation between Fanny and Amerigo it is suggested to the reader that there is more than one 'she' in Amerigo's life.

James used referential ambiguity for foreshadowing in several works. The most famous case, and the most difficult to explicate, is the passage in *The Turn of the Screw* where an unexplained referential ambiguity is brought into a conversation between the governess and Mrs Grose.

'The last governess? She was also young and pretty – almost as young and almost as pretty, Miss, even as you.'

'Ah then I hope her youth and her beauty helped her!' I

recollect throwing off. 'He seems to like us young and pretty!'
'Oh he *did*,' Mrs Grose assented: 'it was the way he liked
every one!' She had no sooner spoken indeed than she caught
herself up. 'I mean that's *his* way – the master's.'
I was struck. 'But of whom did you speak first?'
She looked blank, but she coloured. 'Why of *him*.'
'Of the master?'
'Of who else?'
There was so obviously no one else that the next moment I
had lost my impression of her having accidentally said more
than she meant; and I merely asked what I wanted to know.[11]

In the conversation between Mrs Assingham and the Prince the
obscurity is soon cleared up when Fanny announces, a few
interchanges later, that Charlotte Stant is in London. Nevertheless the referential ambiguity was not a superfluous Jamesian
eccentricity. The intensity of Fanny's 'odd interrogation' pre-
pares the reader for the drama of the introduction of Charlotte's
name. The dramatic force of this again is dependent on the
reader being able to perceive the Prince's excitement and also
that the Prince tries to hide this excitement. Therefore the
referential ambiguity had to precede the introduction of Charlotte's name. If the order had been the reverse the dramatic
effect of the introduction of Charlotte's name would have been
weakened; there would have been no mystery about the referential ambiguity, only uncertainty and the reader's attention
would not have been so closely captured.
    In Chapters III and V–VI the Prince and Charlotte are
already in fact planning their adultery – which is fast work
indeed; both on James's part and on that of the two lovers
(Charlotte and Amerigo). In Chapter III the Prince hopes that
Charlotte will marry, that she will marry some 'capital fellow'
(80). This pun (which, by the way, James was fond of – he used
it also for instance in *The Wings of the Dove*) foreshadows Mr
Verver and his millions and, in the direction of the past, the
common experience of Charlotte and the Prince who would have
married if they had had enough money. Meanwhile the conversation bristles with innuendo, usually of such a blatant nature
that every reader must get the point – at least on a second
reading.
    As in other conversations as highly charged with intensity as

this in *The Golden Bowl* a type of referential ambiguity that occurs is the euphemistic replacing of a name with another.

> 'The position of a single woman to-day is very favourable, you know.'
> 'Favourable to what?'
> 'Why, just *to* existence – which may contain, after all, in one way and another, so much. It may contain, at the worst, even affections; affections in fact quite particularly; fixed, that is, on one's friends. I'm extremely fond of Maggie, for instance – I quite adore her. How could I adore her more if I were married to one of the people you speak of?' (80)

Here 'Maggie' simply means the Prince. Charlotte makes the case over-obvious through her addition of 'for instance'. Charlotte is putting herself forward, offering herself to the Prince and this is the real motive of their discussion of the married and single state. Charlotte wants to continue their love-affair and her view of the state of single women was brought out for this reason. The Prince however has a different idea, which the pair (Charlotte and the Prince) get successively closer to until the climactic ending of Chapter VI (which is also the end of Part I) reveals the whole idea. Charlotte is to marry and *then* they will carry on their affair.

> He had signalled – the cab was charging. She put out no hand for their separation, but she prepared to get in. Before she did so, however, she said what had been gathering while she waited. 'Well, I would marry, I think, to have something from you in all freedom.' (127)

The play of combinations in the novel creates considerable suspense when the two basic sets of relationships (either Adam+Charlotte and Maggie+Amerigo or Adam+Maggie and Amerigo+Charlotte) are at different times strengthened or weakened. The reader's interest in this is enhanced through James's play with appearance and reality.

Often when a certain relationship should be growing stronger in fact its opposite is. This is the case in Part I (Chapters I–VI) where the relationship Amerigo–Maggie should be strengthening since they are about to be married whereas in fact the bond between Charlotte and Amerigo is growing stronger – so strong that they decide that she must marry someone for his (Amerigo's) sake and for the sake of the future of their liaison.

The foundations of Amerigo's role are well laid in Part I, but so are those of Charlotte's, and, indeed, of Adam's. It is established that Charlotte will marry to please the Prince, which is necessary for the symmetry of a later stage in the novel when Adam will marry to please Maggie, i.e. this part of the game strengthens the set-up Maggie+Adam/Amerigo+Charlotte.

Generally the play of illusion and reality in the first part is based on an ostensible pairing Maggie+Amerigo/Charlotte+Adam and a real, solid one Charlotte+Amerigo/Maggie+Adam. Towards the end of the novel illusion and reality becomes a much more sophisticated issue. Then the illicit relationships begin to break up and the legitimate ones to reassert themselves – or really 'assert' themselves since they have seemed somehow unreal until now. But also a new variable is thrown into the game of combinations, namely deception, which again doubles possibilities and more than doubles them if you work out different possibilities for each individual.

Then not only do you have a real and false relationship – which may be either of the two possible ones, and a different one at different stages in the novel – but you may have a person pretending to be carrying on either of them whereas in fact he is drawn to the other etc. It is a tremendous merry-go-round.

To return to Chapter III we may note that the foreshadowing of the relation Amerigo+Charlotte has a parallel foreshadowing of the future relationship Charlotte+Adam.

> But he had another word for Charlotte. 'I dine to-night with Mr Verver. Have you any message?'
> The girl seemed to wonder a little. 'For Mr Verver?'
> 'For Maggie – about her seeing you early. That, I know, is what she'll like.' (81)

This is no more than a mechanical foreshadowing of the link Adam+Charlotte which James planted since he had a convenient occasion. Naturally the confusion also functions to dramatize the relations between the two women – Charlotte, after all, comes uninvited.

Chapter IV includes a long conversation between the Assinghams and here we find some of the first instances of the main role of referential ambiguity; to function as a dramatization of the combinations and thereby create intensity.

> She was high, she was lucid, she was almost inspired; and it was but the deeper drop therefore to her husband's flat common sense. 'In other words Maggie is, by her ignorance, in danger? Then if she's in danger, there *is* danger.'
>
> 'There *won't* be – with Charlotte's understanding of it. That's where she has had her conception of being able to be heroic, of being able in fact to be sublime. She *is*, she will be' – the good lady by this time glowed. 'So she sees it – to become, for her best friend, an element of *positive* safety.'
>
> Bob Assingham looked at it hard. 'Which of them do you call her best friend?'
>
> She gave a toss of impatience. 'I'll leave you to discover!' But the grand truth thus made out she had now completely adopted. 'It's for *us*, therefore, to be hers.'
>
> ' "Hers"?'
>
> 'You and I. It's for us to be Charlotte's. It's for us, on our side, to see *her* through.'
>
> 'Through her sublimity?'
>
> 'Through her noble, lonely life.' (100)

There are two mix-ups here, with one explicit disambiguation-question from the Colonel ('Which of them ...') and one momentary disambiguation-request ('"Hers"?'), a repetition-query with typographic ambiguity-signals (quotation-marks). In addition *us* is ambiguous (with the typographic ambiguity-signal of italicization – which at the same time signals intensity). Mrs Assingham disambiguates the referential ambiguity of 'hers' and *us* after they have done their work as pointers to remind us of the situation, but 'which of them is her best friend' she leaves open, for the Colonel and for the reader. The word 'friend' in English is well suited for the referential ambiguity since it could refer to either a male friend or a female.[12] The Colonel with his 'realistic' views of morality presumably means to suggest the former.

In this example, as in our first quotation above, the referential ambiguity was lodged in a pronoun ('hers'). As we noted there are, in James's *Vierpersonenkonstellation*, endless possibilities of confusion over 'them' (their etc.), 'we' (us, our etc.) and 'she' (her etc.) or 'he' (him etc.), and it is therefore natural that James should make the most of the possibilities of referential ambiguity precisely in connection with pronouns. But, in addition, we may note that James's play with pronouns is highly sophisticated in every respect throughout his career. Pronouns are used as euphemisms, overused or avoided all according to the demands of James's purpose.[13] Finally, quite apart from the artistic success of James's use of pronominal ambiguity, this study as a whole will, I hope, reveal that he was temperamentally attracted to the device.

In his dissertation 'A Study of the Style of James's Late Novels' Robert Johnson makes some observations on James's use of pronouns:

> Also important in this paragraph is another stylistic technique of James's late style: distant, obscured or ambiguous pronoun reference. It was seen in Chapter II that James made a greater quantitative use of pronouns in his late style. A comparison of propositions to original sentences in the late style reveals something of how these increased pronouns are used. It will be noticed that the paragraph begins with two unidentified personal pronouns. This is a very typical usage in the late style of Henry James. Often, as in the case here with 'her', one or more of the personal pronouns is never given a referent in the paragraph. Often, too, pronouns (as is the case here with masculine pronouns) represent two or more males or females in a single paragraph.
>
> The unidentified personal pronoun(s) that begins a James paragraph in the late style may have its referent as many as five pages before. James sets a scene, peoples it, and develops it without constantly – or even, in some cases, occasionally – reminding his reader which characters are involved. Where personal pronouns are concerned, this has the effect, first, of making the reader doubly alert to speakers and reflectors, and, second, of blending together the various perceptions of two or more characters. The ambiguity that develops through distant and infrequent reference is added to by the ambiguity developed by similar pronouns. In this paragraph, Maggie's husband and father blur in the sentence:

> It had been strange that the most natural thing of all to

say to him should have had that appearance; but she was more than ever conscious that *any* appearance she had would come round, more or less straight, to her father, whose life was now so quiet, on the basis accepted for it, that any alteration of his consciousness, even in the possible sense of enlivenment, would make their precious equilibrium waver.

The final 'their' must be ultimately read as referring to Maggie and her husband, but the 'his' reference to her father that occurs immediately before it suggests at first that 'their precious equilibrium' is Maggie's and her father's. The effect of this ambiguity is, as so often in the late style of James, to include inferentially all possible referents while specifying only one. The strong internal identification on Maggie's part of her father with her husband is here suggested, as in the broader implication that all parties to a personal and social situation are equally involved in its intricacies. The vivid sense of 'society' present in the late work of James owes much to this device of inclusive ambiguity.[14]

There are several interesting points here. Johnson's quantification corroborates one's impression that James uses pronouns more frequently in his late period. That James should use pronouns frequently in works such as *The Golden Bowl* where the design of the plot should have compelled him *not* to use them if he wanted to avoid ambiguity is a significant indication of James's purpose and preference. In a work where he ought to have cut down on pronouns he actually increases his use of them.

One can hardly avoid the conclusion that this overall tendency in James's use of pronouns is either intentional or inevitable, or both. This has consequences for the analysis of James's odd use of 'their' in the passage that Johnson quotes. I think we can take Johnson's comments further. Johnson writes that Maggie's husband and father blur in the sentence, and that 'the final "their" must ultimately be read as referring to Maggie and her husband'. This suggests that the ambiguity should be sorted out, and *can* be sorted out, and slightly works against Johnson's praise of James for his 'inclusive ambiguity'. In other words, it is as if James's 'inclusive ambiguity' were achieved by the way.

Maybe we should temporarily shake off all the prejudices that normative grammar, which sees ambiguity in a pathological light, has given us. Let us assume that in this case the ambiguity is intentional or inevitable and the difficulty more important than its solution.[15]

The term 'inclusive ambiguity' is in a sense very appropriate but in another slightly misleading because the ambiguity is a 'which one'-ambiguity. It is a primitive ambiguity which exists simply as a device to create binary suspension of the type 'will she or won't she', or in this case, 'is she linking up with Adam or Amerigo'. The question 'whom does "their" refer to' reminds the reader of all the necessary thematic questions at this point in the novel. Who creates and upholds the equilibrium of pairings? Charlotte and Amerigo? Adam and Maggie? And which equilibrium? Maggie+Adam/Charlotte+Amerigo? Or Maggie+Amerigo/Charlotte+Adam? Or Maggie+Charlotte/Amerigo+Adam?

James planted these obscurities to create hesitation, confusion and dramatic interest. Rational grammar gives us rules to sort out the antecedents that pronouns refer to. But language is not always rational. And sometimes authors make use of irrational language. The drift of interpretative criticism is often towards some sort of monistic goal because it is meant to help the reader past difficulties towards what the critic offers as the 'correct' interpretation. But in this case maybe it is legitimate to be less interested in 'what' (what does the pronoun ultimately refer to) and pay more attention to 'how' (i.e. the ambiguity itself).[16]

As I said the conversation between the Prince and Charlotte during their secret visit to the shop in Bloomsbury bristles with innuendo. But the narrative prose between the conversations is so full of ambiguities too that I wish to present one here. The following passage is part of the Prince's reflections.

> That was accordingly, in fine, how they had come to where they were: he was engaged, as hard as possible, in the policy of not magnifying. He had kept this up even on her making a point – and as if it were almost the whole point – that Maggie of course was not to have an idea. Half the interest of the thing at least would be that she shouldn't suspect; therefore he was completely to keep it from her – as Charlotte on her side would – that they had been anywhere at all together or had so

much as seen each other for five minutes alone. The absolute secrecy of their little excursion was in short of the essence; she appealed to his kindness to let her feel that he didn't betray her. There had been something, frankly, a little disconcerting in such an appeal at such an hour, on the very eve of his nuptials: it was one thing to have met the girl casually at Mrs Assingham's and another to arrange with her thus for a morning practically as private as their old mornings in Rome and practically not less intimate. (106–7)

The focal point here is the phrase '... didn't betray her'. 'Her' is ambiguated through the semantic nature of the neighbouring 'betray' and through the comment that explicitly draws attention to the idea ('there had been something, frankly, a little disconcerting ...').

Assuming that we first take 'her' to apply to Charlotte, which is grammatically natural, we are shocked to find the word 'betray' used in connection with Charlotte. We are then reminded of the question whether Amerigo's relation to Charlotte is as strong a tie as his relation to Maggie. Finally, through the explicit comment ('... disconcerting ...') we are reminded of the ultimate motive for the presence of the word 'betray' in the text. Its mere presence serves to suggest that the Prince's behaviour is a betrayal of Maggie's trust. James almost forces the reader to formulate the sentence 'he's betraying her' (Maggie) through putting the word ('betray') spatially, though not logically, next to a sentence concerned with Amerigo's marriage.[17] It is a pointed verbality outside the main run of the text. One is reminded of the technique in Hogarth's etchings, for instance in *Harlot's Progress*, where, in the first picture, he makes the face of the girl a parallel with the face of the goose so that one is mentally forced to exclaim 'she is a silly goose', or, in a later picture in the same series 'heightens the cliché' of 'to stab someone in the back' by a trick of perspective so that the secret lover's scabbard seems to touch the back of the man who 'keeps' the girl.

In the seven Chapters that constitute Part Second (Chapters VII–XIII) the set-up Charlotte+Amerigo/Maggie+Adam is strengthened throughout, all appearances to the contrary notwithstanding. The arrival of the Principino on the stage could have been expected to strengthen the bond between Maggie and

Amerigo but it strengthens the mutual attachment between daughter and father as well.

> It was of course an old story and a familiar idea that a
> beautiful baby could take its place as a new link between a
> wife and a husband, but Maggie and her father had, with
> every ingenuity, converted the precious creature into a link
> between a mamma and a grandpapa. (151)

Charlotte's marriage to Adam could have been expected weaken the Charlotte–Amerigo tie but Chapter XIII makes it very clear that Charlotte marries Adam to please the Prince and Adam marries Charlotte to please Maggie. There is a semantic mix-up in Chapter XII to equate the words 'daughter' and 'wife' and to suggest that in the semantic word-picture of Adam (and Maggie) they come to the same.

> 'Oughtn't we,' she asked, 'to think a little of others? Oughtn't
> I, at least, in loyalty – at any rate in delicacy – to think of
> Maggie?' With which, intensely gentle, so as not to appear too
> much to teach him his duty, she explained. 'She's everything
> to you – she has always been. Are you so certain that there's
> room in your life – ?'
> 'For another daughter? – is that what you mean?' She had
> not hung upon it long, but he had quickly taken her up.
> (200)[18]

Chapter XIII completes James's peopling of his scene, when Charlotte joins the family, having had her telegram from the Prince. The merry-go-round can now be speeded up, and James loses no time. Even before the end of the chapter the disastrous effects of Maggie's and Mrs Assingham's mistake are already imminent.[19] The conversation between Charlotte and Adam at the end of the chapter is full of foretelling, prophetic utterances, cruel dramatic irony and double meanings. Especially Charlotte's remarks are loaded with private meaning.

> 'Well, what then? Isn't our situation worth the little
> sacrifice? We'll go back to Rome as soon as you like *with*
> them.'
> This seemed to hold her – as he had previously seen her

held, just a trifle inscrutably, by his illusions to what they
would do together on a certain contingency. 'Worth it, the
little sacrifice, for whom? For us, naturally – yes,' she said.
'We want to see them – for our reasons. That is,' she rather
dimly smiled, '*you* do.'

'And you do, my dear, too!' he bravely declared.

'Yes then – I do too,' she after an instant ungrudging
enough acknowledged. (207)

The superfluously wide semantic coverage of 'we', 'them' and
'our' must be pared down here by the reader, following
Charlotte's suggestion, to singulars, i.e. Adam wants to see
Maggie, and Charlotte wants to see the Prince, which is the real
situation, and the ostensible singular-meaning which is that
Charlotte wishes to see Amerigo *and* Maggie, or Maggie.

This ambiguity is reinforced shortly afterwards:

The manner of it operated – she acknowledged with no
great delay this natural possibility. 'No – nothing is incredible
to me of people immensely in love.'

'Well, isn't Amerigo immensely in love?'

She hesitated but as for the right expression of her sense of
the degree – but she after all adopted Mr Verver's. 'Immensely.'

'Then there you are!'

She had another smile, however – she wasn't there quite
yet. (208–9)

James creates referential ambiguity ('With *whom* is Amerigo
immensely in love? – 'with Charlotte') here by giving promi-
nence to the passage in a number of ways. There is repetition
(immensely – immensely – immensely); there is the hesitation
before the second repetition – a typical Jamesian ambiguity-
creating technique; and there is the Jamesian number one
favourite index to draw attention to an ambiguity, the phrase
'there you are', which in this case finally is itself heightened by
being commented upon (' – she wasn't there quite yet'.).

Charlotte agrees that Amerigo is immensely in love, her
private meaning being that he is immensely in love with *her*, and
just as the 'immensely'-passage showed Amerigo suspended
between Charlotte and Maggie a passage a few pages later shows

Charlotte suspended between Amerigo and Adam.
Charlotte receives her longed-for telegram.

> She broke the envelope then in silence, and for a minute, as
> with the message he himself had put before her, studied its
> contents without a sign. He watched her without a question,
> and at last she looked up. 'I'll give you,' she simply said, 'what
> you ask.'
> The expression of her face was strange – but since when had
> a woman's at moments of supreme surrender not a right to be?
> (213)

The cover-up decent sense here is surrender to Adam but the
real sense is surrender to Amerigo.

The state of combinations in Part Second is symbolically
expressed through the two telegrams. Maggie wires Adam;
Amerigo wires Charlotte. 'When Mr Verver buys Charlotte for a
wife', wrote one early critic, recapitulating the plot, 'the fat is
conspicuously in the fire'.[20] In Part Third (Chapters XIV–
XXIV) it is already sizzling rather furiously. Maggie partly
moves in with her father, usurping her stepmother's rooms, and
taking her carriage, so that Charlotte has to go around the town
in a cab, which is degrading, but also happens to be convenient
for her plans. Charlotte and Amerigo meet, kiss and seal their
understanding. They decide to shed the Assinghams. They carry
out their adulterous plans after staying at the appropriately
named Matcham under the pretence of seeing the tomb of the
likewise appropriate Gloucester. Fanny Assingham realizes her
mistake; worries and predicts that Maggie will see her through.
All of these developments are dramatized with the aid of
referential ambiguity in conversations.

The Assinghams are at this stage increasingly brought in by
James. In Chapter XIV Mrs Assingham couples the Prince and
Charlotte in an ambiguous 'You' which could mean Charlotte
but is easily stretched to include the Prince.

> 'And what reason is there, in the world, after all, why he and I
> shouldn't, as you say, show together? We've shown together,
> my dear,' she smiled, 'before.'
> Her friend, for a little, only looked at her – speaking then
> with abruptness. 'You ought to be absolutely happy. You live

with such *good* people.'
    The effect of it, as well, was an arrest for Charlotte; whose face, however, all of whose fine and slightly hard radiance, it had caused, the next instant, further to brighten. (224)

This is the beginning of a process in Part Third in which pronouns stabilize to a large extent so that in the conversation of the Assinghams 'they' means the Prince+Charlotte or Maggie+Adam and 'you' as here in a dialogue with Charlotte means Amerigo+Charlotte.
    But there are also ambiguities similar to the one that Johnson quoted, for instance the following (Chapter XVI, dialogue between the Assinghams):

She knew he never cared what she said, and his neglect of his chance to show it was thereby the more eloquent. 'Leave it,' he at last remarked, 'to *them*.'
    ' "Leave" it – ?' she wondered.
    'Let them alone. They'll manage.'
    'They'll manage, you mean, to do everything they want? Ah, there then you are.'
    'They'll manage in their own way,' the Colonel almost cryptically repeated. (244)

Who are 'they'? Fanny thinks of Charlotte and Amerigo because the pairing arrangements at this stage have made that coupling natural, but the Colonel's repetition (cf. Maggie's 'for love', below) also suggests the possibility of Maggie and Adam. Actually Maggie+Amerigo/Charlotte+Adam is also possible (every theoretical combination is in fact possible) and in addition there is the strong possibility that 'them' refers to all four.
    At this stage Charlotte and Amerigo are thrown more and more together and the result of this is that the reader is exposed to a constant bombardment of 'they's, meaning Maggie+Adam, and 'we's, meaning Charlotte+Amerigo (e.g. p. 248). The pair-bonding process between Amerigo and Charlotte naturally includes some playful use of pronouns, even if it is only in the mental speculations of one of the characters (Charlotte), as in the following case where James explicitly comments on it:

All men were brutes enough to catch when they might at such

chances for dissent – for all the good it really did them; but the Prince's distinction was in being one of the few who could check himself before acting on the impulse. This, obviously, was what counted in a man as delicacy. If her friend had blurted or bungled he would have said, in his simplicity, 'Did we do "everything to avoid" it when we faced your remarkable marriage?' – quite handsomely of course using the plural, taking his share of the case, by way of a tribute of memory to the telegram she had received from him in Paris after Mr Verver had despatched to Rome the news of their engagement. (248)

The act of adultery is focused in pronouns. The Prince and Charlotte have to commit a pronominal union first, and this is the real point at which they slip into sin; the fact will follow. They will unite pronominally and the collectivism of the first person plural is imperative if they are to share the guilt of the crime.

Therefore Charlotte violently protests against Amerigo's attempts to slip out of the bracket that the first person plural constitutes.

> 'Oh, they've a great deal of idea,' said the Prince. And nothing was easier than to mention the quantity. 'They think so much of us. They think in particular so much of you.'
> 'Ah, don't put it all on "me"!' she smiled.
> But he was putting it now where she had admirably prepared the place. (260)

Charlotte insists on 'us', the 'us' that already unites them linguistically. Maybe the fact that it is the Prince who tries to cheat is important. It indicates that Charlotte is the more active partner in the affair; she forestalls his pronouns just as she anticipates his concern with the practical arrangements for the adultery at Matcham–Gloucester. And the Prince's repeated attempts to dissociate himself from the first person plural foreshadows his future readiness to leave Charlotte for Maggie.

> They treated the matter not exactly with solemnity, but with a certain decency, even perhaps urgency, of distinctness. 'It would probably have been better,' Charlotte added. 'But

things turn out – ! And it leaves us' – she made the point – 'more alone.'

He seemed to wonder. 'It leaves *you* more alone.'

'Oh,' she again returned, 'don't put it all on me!' (261)

Charlotte wants to implicate the Prince to the same degree as herself but it is really she who takes the lead. Even in this paragraph it is Charlotte who goes on to reflect on how they must give the same version of their meeting – another mating-oriented idea, since their complicity over a meeting about which they have nothing to hide is a good dress rehearsal for the future case when they *will* have something to hide.

'They' in the sense of Mr Verver and Maggie is now so ingrained in the vocabulary of Charlotte and Amerigo that the pronoun has to be disambiguated if it refers to any other persons as in the following example where it refers to Maggie and the Principino.

She immediately passed, at any rate, to another point. 'I can't help wondering when you must last have laid eyes on them.' And then as it had apparently for her companion an effect of abruptness: 'Maggie, I mean, and the child. For I suppose you know he's with her.'

'Oh yes, I know he's with her. I saw them this morning.' (258)

The conversation becomes more and more electric – it is after all the conversation that leads up to the kiss; a scene which critics have been surprised to find one of the most erotic passages in English literature.

Charlotte describes the situation in Eaton Square. Maggie and Adam 'feel a confidence' – they are ripe to be betrayed. Charlotte has tested out the technicalities of movement and she has found that she can go around freely in a cab, and she has returned to the place repeatedly without Maggie and Adam noticing.

'So I had but to slip in, each time, with my cab at the door, and make out for myself, without their knowing it, that Maggie was still there. I came, I went – without their so much as dreaming. What do they really suppose,' she asked,

'becomes of one? – not so much sentimentally or morally, so t¢
call it, and since that doesn't matter; but even just physically
materially, as a mere wandering woman: as a decent harmless
wife, after all; as the best stepmother, after all, that really eve¹
was; or at least simply as a *maîtresse de maison* not quite withou
a conscience. They must even in their odd way,' she declared
'have *some* idea.'

'Oh, they've a great deal of idea,' said the Prince. An¢
nothing was easier than to mention the quantity. 'They thin]
so much of us. They think in particular so much of you.'

'Ah, don't put it all on "me"!' she smiled. (259–60)

'Decent', like 'capital' is another word that James likes to pla}
around with. Here it is used in 'decent, harmless wife' as a basi
for the expansion to *maîtresse de maison* in a paragraph of suc]
obviously cheeky Jacobean language that the reader hardl}
needs to feel ashamed if *maîtresse* puts him more in mind of ¿
Mme de Maintenon or some other example of one meaning o
mistress than the idea of the sense 'superior female in comman¢
of a household' and if 'maison' leads his thoughts to, fo¹
instance, the 'Maison de Tellier' rather than to the dull Englis]
house in Eaton Square. The Prince said in Chapter I that whe]
he speaks worse he speaks French. It seems that Charlott¢
imitates him.

'Them' in this climactic chapter is repeated again and agai]
as meaning Maggie and Adam (or Charlotte and Amerigo, too
in James's comments). Examples are so numerous that it i
difficult to choose a passage, but this, for instance, is a typica
exchange:

'And really, my dear,' Charlotte added, 'Fanny Assingha]
doesn't matter.'

He wondered again. 'Unless as taking care of *them*.'

'Ah,' Charlotte instantly said, 'isn't it for us, only, to d¢
that?' She spoke as with a flare of pride for their privilege an¢
their duty. 'I think we want no one's aid.' (262)

In the 'erotic passage' James used 'their' as a sort of reflexiv¢
pronoun; a use which was objected to by Clara McIntyre a
inaccurate,[21] but which is really artistically necessary because i
is the logical climax of the preceding development in the use o

pronouns in the chapter.

> She could rise to the highest measure of the facts. 'And for which we must trust each other – !'
> 'Oh, as we trust the saints in glory. Fortunately,' the Prince hastened to add, 'we can.' With which, as for the full assurance and the pledge it involved, their hands instinctively found their hands. 'It's all too wonderful.'
> Firmly and gravely she kept his hand. 'It's too beautiful.'
> And so for a minute they stood together, as strongly held and as closely confronted as any hour of their easier past even had seen them. They were silent at first, only facing and faced, only grasping and grasped, only meeting and met. 'It's sacred,' he said at last.
> 'It's sacred,' she breathed back to him. They vowed it, gave it out and took it in, drawn, by their intensity, more closely together. Then of a sudden, through this tightened circle, as at the issue of a narrow strait into the sea beyond, everything broke up, broke down, gave way, melted and mingled. Their lips sought their lips, their pressure their response and their response their pressure; with a violence that had sighed itself the next moment to the longest and deepest of stillnesses they passionately sealed their pledge. (264–5)

They meet, they embrace, they kiss, they melt together and their bodily union of course had to have its corresponding pronominal union. '... *their* hands ... found *their* hands ...'; '*Their* lips sought *their* lips'; '*their* pressure *their* response and *their* response *their* pressure'. 'Their' is a possessive pronoun, and naturally they now possess each other. James could have said 'they possess each other' but that would have meant using one personal and one reciprocal pronoun and James instead bans all other types of pronouns except the possessive itself.

The pronoun in fact becomes more than possessive, it becomes somehow 'reflexive', a self-sufficient thing that turns in on itself and needs nothing else, just as they have become a couple whose union is self-sufficient and where even reciprocity (pronouns 'each other' or 'one another' – 'they grasped *each other's* hands') is no longer needed but where each part of body (hands, lips) seeks its counterpart, which is now in collective possession, so that it does no longer belong separately to one or the other of them, but is fused into one single relation, expressed in the reiterated 'their'. Their hands were theirs; their lips were theirs. They were theirs.

For the needs of James's artistic purpose of course grammatical norms had to be flouted – it is the licence of poets. If – as critics are surprised to find it – the passage is one of the most erotic in the English language, maybe one of the reasons for its effect is James's use of pronouns.

Of the various ways of reaching intensity through referential ambiguity the use of pronouns is a prominent one. Usually the intensity it creates is, however, much less glamorous than in the 'erotic' passage. Most often the role of the pronouns, as Vernon Lee pointed out, is simply a demand on the reader's attention:

> Circle about and among; for we penetrate between them (one almost forgets what *they* really are, feeling *them* merely as something with which one is playing some game – pawns? draughts? or rather adversaries?), finding them now as a nominative, now a possessive, now a dative. It is noteworthy that this shifting of the *case* of these pronouns gives the sentence an air of movement, more than would be given by the presence of verbs. In the two next sentences I have again the impression of an unusual abundance of pronouns, perhaps because of the two its: 'What could *it* be, he asked himself,' &c. and '*It* seemed somehow,' &c. Evidently the use of pronouns implies a demand on the reader's attention; he must remember what the pronoun stands for, or rather (for no one will consent to such repeated effort where only amusement is at stake) the reader will have to be, spontaneously, at full cock of attention, a person accustomed to bear things in mind, to carry on a meaning from sentence to sentence, to think in abbreviations; in other words he will have to be an intellectual as distinguished from an impulsive or image-full person.[22]

But the 'erotic' passage shows to what lengths James could let himself go in the sophisticated, poetic use of pronouns once a scene had been painstakingly prepared for.

Chapter XXIII is almost completely taken up with a conversation between the Assinghams, and it is very typical of their 'intercourse by misunderstanding' (p. 304). The pages are just loaded with confusion. Part of this, no doubt, is comic relief – we need a scene with jesters and fools after the intensity of the Matcham experience. But undoubtedly also we need a dramatization of the latest stage of combinations, now that the union between Charlotte and the Prince has been consummated.

'Well, shows that I'm right – for I assure you I had wandered far. Now I'm at home again, and I mean,' said Fanny Assingham, 'to stay here. They're beautiful,' she declared.

'The Prince and Charlotte?'

'The Prince and Charlotte. *That's* how they're so remarkable. And the beauty,' she explained, 'is that they're afraid for them. Afraid, I mean, for the others.'

'For Mr Verver and Maggie?' It did take some following. 'Afraid of what?'

'Afraid of themselves.'

The Colonel wondered. 'Of "*them*selves"? Or Mr Verver's and Maggie's selves?'

Mrs Assingham remained patient as well as lucid. 'Yes – of *such* blindness too. But most of all of their own danger.'

He turned it over. 'That danger *being* the blindness –?'

'That danger being their position. What their position contains – of all the elements – I needn't at this time of day attempt to tell you. It contains, luckily – for that's the mercy – everything *but* blindness: I mean on their part. The blindness,' said Fanny, 'is primarily her husband's.'

He stood for a moment; he *would* have it straight. 'Whose husband's?'

'Mr Verver's,' she went on. 'The blindness is most of all his. That they feel – that they see. But it's also his wife's.'

'Whose wife's?' he asked as she continued to gloom at him in a manner at variance with the comparative cheer of her contention. And then as she only gloomed: 'The Prince's?'

'Maggie's own – Maggie's very own,' she pursued as for herself. (306–7)

On the next page comes still another confusion.

The twist seemed remarkable for instance as she developed her indication of what had come out in the afternoon. 'It was as if I knew better than ever what makes them – '

'What makes them – ?' he pressed her as she fitfully dropped.

'Well, makes the Prince and Charlotte take it all as they do.' (308)

Edmund Nierlich thinks that the misunderstandings between the Assinghams are part of James's characterization of them and their international marriage – Bob is English; Fanny is American.

> Das Missverstehen zwischen den beiden bestätigt die Gestört-heit dieser heteronationalen Ehe, wie das Kuriose an ihnen sie nach der anfangs aufgestellten These bereits signalisierte. Über diese Gestörtheit darf nicht hinwegtäuschen, dass die beiden innerhalb der sie umgebenden Gesellschaft als ein unzertrennliches Paar auftreten und dass ihre heteronationale Verbindung von ihren Freunden als 'the happiest of its class' (L 35) angesehen wird.[23]

This may be so; nevertheless I believe that James's concern with plot and situation may be an even more important reason than his concern with the characterization of the Assinghams. What are the Assinghams anyway but *ficelles*, conveniences for James's unfolding of the plot, even if they are so vividly created that the reader wishes, as with Maria Gostrey in *The Ambassadors*, that James had made them more than *ficelles*?

If James is to dramatize through referential ambiguity at this stage it has to be through the Assinghams, because only with them is the full potential of confusion available. 'They', 'he' and 'she' is possible in all meanings in a dialogue between the Assinghams, whereas with any of the other characters one of the 'they's would be a 'we' etc. It therefore seems that an important reason why James brings in the Assinghams at this point is combinational economy. Also the others are so deep in the imbroglio by this time that the irreverence and irrelevance of confusion would have been even less suitable in their conversations than in those of the Assinghams – the Assinghams, after all, remain outsiders to some extent.

Fanny now says there is nothing (between the Prince and Charlotte). This baffles the reader for some time because it is quite obvious that there *is* something. The problem is solved when Fanny breaks down and cries at the end of the chapter. This type of crying in James means that the sense of what has just been said is to be reversed.

> 'Then you're no longer unhappy?' her guest urged, coming more gaily toward her.
> 'I doubtless shan't be a great while.'
> But it was now Mrs Assingham's turn to want more. 'I've convinced you it's impossible?'
> She had held out her arms, and Maggie, after a moment, meeting her, threw herself into them with a sound that had its oddity as a sign of relief. 'Impossible, impossible,' she emphatically, more than emphatically, replied; yet the next minute she had burst into tears over the impossibility, and a few seconds later, pressing, clinging, sobbing, had even caused them to flow, audibly, sympathetically and perversely, from her friend. (423)

In his paraphrase of *The Golden Bowl* Robert Gale writes that Maggie is temporarily relieved by Fanny's lying denial of any sense of suspicion.[24] This is perhaps not quite correct. Rather it seems to be the case that the characters admit the truth to themselves and to others through the communication of tears, but deny it in words. They preserve their manners and collectively uphold lies verbally, but when they act after some revelation through tears they act on the real truth and not on the one they pretend to believe in.

The semiotics of tears is so clear in James that he even uses the absence of tears as a sign that the sense of a scene is *not* to be reversed.

> He looked at her a minute longer, but his tone at last was right. 'About the way – yes.'
> 'Well then – ?' She spoke as for the end and for other matters – for anything, everything, else there might be. They would never return to it.
> 'Well then – !' His hands came out, and while her own took them he drew her to his breast and held her. He held her hard and kept her long, and she let herself go; but it was an embrace that, august and almost stern, produced, for its intimacy, no revulsion and broke into no inconsequence of

tears. (535)

Mrs Assingham and the Colonel primarily discuss Maggie. 'They' is usually Amerigo+Charlotte and 'she' is Maggie.

> 'Precisely. "Trust their own wit," you practically said, to save all appearances." Well, I've trusted it. I *have* left them to pull through.'
>   He hesitated. 'And your point is that they're not doing so?'
>   'I've left them,' she went on, 'but now I see how and where. I've been leaving them all the while, without knowing it, to *her*.'
>   'To the Princess?'
>   'And that's what I mean,' Mrs Assingham pensively pursued. (313)

Mrs Assingham is convinced that Maggie has now begun to miss her husband (ibid.). She has never really had him and now she begins to feel the need for him.

These views are historic because they are the first sign of a breaking up of the bond Maggie–Adam and the formation of a new one Maggie+Amerigo. Nevertheless the shift is to be gradual, slow and heroic and therefore another referential ambiguity immediately reinforces the tie Maggie–Adam.

> 'They'll have had to be disagreeable to make her decide to live.'
>   . . .
> He had thought of the response his wife's words ideally implied. 'Decide to live – ah yes! – for her child.'
>   'Oh, bother her child!' – and he had never felt so snubbed, for an exemplary view, as when Fanny now stopped short. 'To live, you poor dear, for her father – which is another pair of sleeves!' And Mrs Assingham's whole ample, ornamented person irradiated, with this, the truth that had begun, under so much handling, to glow. 'Any idiot can do things for her child. She'll have a motive more original, and we shall see how it will work her. She'll have to save *him*.'
>   'To "save" him – ?'
>   'To keep her father from her own knowledge. *That*' – and she seemed to see it, before her, in her husband's very eyes –

'will be work cut out!' With which, as at the highest
conceivable climax, she wound up their colloquy. 'Good
night!' (319)

Fanny still prophesies that Maggie's first allegiance will be to
her father. This is where the idea of deception comes in and it
complicates issues enormously. The uncertainties from now on
will be endless. If Maggie tries to win back the Prince, will she
then be doing it for his and her own sake or for the sake of her
father; in other words, which relation, that to Adam or that to
Amerigo will then be the stronger *in reality* quite apart from
Which one *seems* the stronger (to the reader, to other characters
etc.)? The obscurity as to the real state of the sets of combinations will from now on be one of the major intensity-creating
devices to capture our interest. One of the really interesting
questions in the rest of the novel will be the widening split
between Maggie's real feelings and the picture that comes out in
her pretence. The pretence stays the same throughout the novel
– in that version, which she uses to deceive Charlotte, she always
loves her father. But in her real affections Amerigo goes up and
Adam has to be superseded.

Many of the possibilities of the future development of the plot
are foreshadowed in the rest of the conversation between the
Assinghams and there are several cases of referential ambiguity.

'Charlotte, in her way, is extraordinary.'
He was almost simultaneous. 'Extraordinary!'
'She observes the forms,' said Fanny Assingham.
He hesitated. 'With the Prince – ?'
'*For* the Prince. And with the others,' she went on.
'With Mr Verver – wonderfully. But above all with Maggie.
And the forms' – she had to do even *them* justice – 'are two-
thirds of conduct. Say he had married a woman who would
have made a hash of them.' (322)

A little later on:

'It illustrates the misfortune,' said Mrs Assingham gravely, 'of
being too, too charming.'
This was another matter that took some following, but the
Colonel again did his best. 'Yes, but to whom? – doesn't it

rather depend on that? To whom have the Prince and
Charlotte then been too charming?'

'To each other, in the first place – obviously. And then both
of them together to Maggie.'

'To Maggie?' he wondering echoed.

'To Maggie.' She was now crystalline. (324)

Fanny brings out the idea that the Prince does not really care for
Charlotte.[25] This is the symmetrical companion-piece of the idea
that Maggie misses Amerigo. If one relationship (Maggie+
Adam) is beginning to crack up, its symmetrical twin (Char-
lotte+Amerigo) must begin to as well. Fanny also now gives a
lucid analysis of the movements of the merry-go-round (pp. 325–
6), the vicious circle that Maggie started.

The next mix-up concerns the role of Adam.

'This, for him, is what it *was* to have married Charlotte. And
they both,' she neatly wound up, 'help.'

' "Both"?'

'I mean that if Maggie, always in the breach, makes it seem
to him all so flourishingly to fit, Charlotte does her part not
less. And her part is very large. Charlotte,' Fanny declared,
'works like a horse.' (328)

The end of the Assinghams' conversation is also the end of the
chapter, the end of the part and the end of the book (the first half
of the novel). At the end of the conversation there is therefore a
very sophisticated referential ambiguity. It is a 'them', which
means Maggie+Adam, and is thus a reinforcement of the old set
of combinations, but it shows Maggie and her father together
with the harmony all gone, when the situation has soured on
them.

'Moreover *now*,' she said, 'I see! I mean,' she added, 'what you
were asking me: how I knew to-day, in Eaton Square, that
Maggie's awake.' And she had indeed visibly got it. 'It was by
seeing them together.'

'Seeing her with her father?' He fell behind again. 'But
you've seen her often enough before.'

'Never with my present eyes. For nothing like such a test –
that of this length of the others' absence together – has

hitherto occurred.'

'Possibly! But if she and Mr Verver insisted upon it – ?'

'Why is it such a test? Because it has become one without their intending it. It has spoiled, so to speak, on their hands.'

'It has soured, eh?' the Colonel said.

'The word's horrible – say rather it has "changed". Perhaps,' Fanny went on, 'she did wish to see how much she can bear. In that case she *has* seen.' (331)

At the beginning of the second half of the novel (Book Second: The Princess), the crack in the crystal of the old set of combinations (Maggie+Adam/Charlotte+Amerigo) has already become a perceptible fissure. It is now to be expected that the quartet will move to the new set of combinations, which is Maggie+Amerigo/Charlotte+Adam. However, neither Maggie on the one hand, nor Charlotte and Amerigo on the other, are quite ready for this step yet. Charlotte and Amerigo naturally do not want to be deprived of each other and Maggie still cannot face losing her father. Therefore the two hostile parties (Maggie; Amerigo+Charlotte) grope for a compromise and thus for a while the identico-sexual set of combinations dominates the scene (Amerigo+Adam/Charlotte+Maggie). For Amerigo–Charlotte this is a falling back to their next line of defence after Maggie has charged over the first. For Maggie it is a partial victory because if it leaves her frustrated – she can have neither Adam nor Amerigo undividedly – it leaves everyone else so as well.

To begin with the new equilibrium in this set of combinations – let us call it 'the compromise set' – is mostly of Amerigo's and Charlotte's doing. They want to cover up and by taking care of the other person of their own sex within the quartet they avoid going completely to the new set of relations which is Amerigo+Maggie and Adam+Charlotte – let us call this 'the legitimate set' and Adam+Maggie/Amerigo+Charlotte 'the illegitimate set' – and they can at least stay together even if the illegitimate set is at the moment technically impossible for them.

What had in fact promptly enough happened, she presently recognised, was that if her stepmother had beautifully taken possession of her, and if she had virtually been rather snatched again thereby from her husband's side, so, on the

other hand, this had, with as little delay, entailed some very
charming assistance for her in Eaton Square. When she went
home with Charlotte, from whatever happy demonstration,
for the benefit of the world in which they supposed themselves
to live, that there was no smallest reason why their closer
association shouldn't be public and acclaimed – at these times
she regularly found that Amerigo had come either to sit with
his father-in-law in the absence of the ladies, or to make, on
his side, precisely some such display of the easy working of the
family life as would represent the equivalent of her excursions
with Charlotte. Under this particular impression it was that
everything in Maggie most melted and went to pieces –
everything, that is, that belonged to her disposition to
challenge the perfection of their common state. It divided
them again, that was true, this particular turn of the tide – cut
them up afresh into pairs and parties; quite as if a sense for the
equilibrium was what, between them all, had most power of
insistence; quite as if Amerigo himself were all the while, at
bottom, equally thinking of it and watching it. (362–3)

But by and by the compromise set begins to strike Maggie as
interesting too. It gives her a chance of getting used in a gentle
way to the idea of losing Adam. She could not yet give him up to
her rival Charlotte, but she can give him up to Amerigo. And
then she gets the idea of testing the compromise set by
suggesting that it should be made more absolute – by geographi-
cal separation of the two couples (i.e. Amerigo+Adam and
Maggie+Charlotte). This will put Charlotte and Amerigo in a
tight spot. It will be quite like the time when Maggie and
Charlotte were at school together or at the beginning of Maggie's
and Amerigo's marriage, when Amerigo was always very
accommodating to Mr Verver.

'And leave,' the Prince asked, 'you and Charlotte alone?'
'Why not?' Maggie had also to wait a minute, but when she
spoke it came clear. 'Why shouldn't Charlotte be just one of
my reasons – my not liking to leave her? She has always been
so good, so perfect, to me – but never so wonderfully as just
now. We have somehow been more together – thinking, for the
time, almost only of each other; it has been quite as in old
days.' And she proceeded consummately, for she felt it as

consummate: 'It's as if we had been missing each other, had got a little apart – though going on so side by side.'
...
'Your taking the child down yourself, those days, and your coming, each time, to bring him away – nothing in the world, nothing you could have invented, would have kept father more under the charm. Besides, you know how you've always suited him, and how you've always so beautifully let it seem to him that he suits you. Only it has been, these last weeks, as if you wished – just in order to please him – to remind him of it afresh. So there it is,' she wound up; 'it's your doing. You've produced your effect – that of his wanting not to be even for a month or two, where you're not.' (376–7)

Maggie is slowly falling in love with her husband and during one wild moment she has the feeling that if he only proposed to her the legitimate set; that they (Maggie + the Prince) should go away together, she would yield (p. 378). She even puts this in words, skirting the abyss of proposing the legitimate set herself. But Amerigo instead reminds her of the illegitimate one, of her father.

'And there's of course always Charlotte to be considered. Only their going early to Fawns, if they do go,' she said, 'needn't in the least entail your and my going.'
    'Ah,' Amerigo echoed, 'it needn't in the least entail your and my going.'
    'We can do as we like. What they may do needn't trouble us, since they're by good fortune perfectly happy together.'
    'Oh,' the Prince returned, 'your father's never so happy as with you near him to enjoy his being so.' (379-80)

Amerigo is still sufficiently tied up with Charlotte to have to disambiguate his own first person plurals. This is the way the conversation continues:

'Well, I may enjoy it,' said Maggie, 'but I'm not the cause of it.'
    'You're the cause,' her husband declared, 'of the greater part of everything that's good among us.' But she received this tribute in silence, and the next moment he pursued: 'If Mrs

Verver has arrears of time with you to make up, as you say, she'll scarcely do it – or *you* scarcely will – by our cutting, your and my cutting, too loose.'

'I see what you mean,' Maggie mused. (380)

The compromise set is by now rather 'neutral' ground. The Prince fought against this by reminding Maggie of the illlegitimate set. But he then retreats and suggests instead the compromise set, and in the process unwittingly gives away how much he is involved with Charlotte, by having to disambiguate 'our' by the clarifying 'your and my'.

The same thing, only far more blatantly, happens a little later, where, of his two women, it is again Charlotte who comes first to the Prince's mind (or does 'I' refer to Maggie?).

'I might, for the time,' she went on, 'go to stay there with Charlotte; or, better still, she might come to Portland Place.'

'Oho!' said the Prince with cheerful vagueness.

'I should feel, you see,' she continued, 'that the two of us were showing the same sort of kindness.'

Amerigo thought. 'The two of us? Charlotte and I?'

Maggie again hesitated. 'You and I, darling.'

'I see, I see,' – he promptly took it in. (380–1)

Maggie is now fighting desperately within the neutral ground of the compromise set. Despite the fact that these sterile unions will be factually the same whether the Prince undertakes them for Charlotte's sake or Maggie's the fight is still important to Maggie because she is fighting for the initiative. If only she can make the Prince agree to do something *with* her – even if it means, paradoxically, separating, she will begin to get him into her power. This is the way with Amerigo in amorous matters. To get him to enter into a secret pact will be half-way to winning him back. (Later on Maggie succeeds when she persuades Amerigo to lie to Charlotte – in this novel a secret shared by two is the lead-in to a union.)

Amerigo wriggles out of the geographic variant of the compromise set by referring to the legitimate set – it would not do for him to break in between husband and wife (Adam and Charlotte) (p. 382).[26] Maggie has a revelation that the compromise set, her beautiful new harmony, does not work, and that the

only way of separating Charlotte and Amerigo is to separate
herself from her father:

> She was powerless, however, was only more utterly hushed,
> when the interrupting flash came, when she would have been
> all ready to say to him, 'Yes, this is by every appearance the
> best time we've had yet; but don't you see, all the same, how
> they must be working together for it, and how my very
> success, my success in shifting our beautiful harmony to a new
> basis, comes round to being *their* success above all; their
> cleverness, their amiability, their power to hold out, their
> complete possession, in short, of our life?' For how could she
> say as much as that without saying a great deal more? without
> saying 'They'll do everything in the world that suits us, save
> only one thing – prescribe a line for us that will make them
> separate.' How could she so much as imagine herself even
> faintly murmuring that without putting into his mouth the
> very words that would have made her quail? 'Separate, my
> dear? Do you want them to separate? Then you want *us* to –
> you and me? For how can the one separation take place
> without the other?' That was the question that, in spirit, she
> had heard him ask – with its dread train, moreover, of
> involved and connected inquiries. Their own separation, his
> and hers, was of course perfectly thinkable, but only on the
> basis of the sharpest of reasons. Well, the sharpest, the very
> sharpest, would be that they could no longer afford, as it were,
> he to let his wife, she to let her husband, 'run' them in such
> compact formation. (388)

The word 'jealousy' is now introduced and significantly it is
Maggie's potential jealousy of Charlotte with her husband (p.
390). Maggie is much more advanced in her private thoughts
and forebodings than she is in her conversation with Fanny in
Chapter XXX because in that dialogue it is still her father that
comes first to her mind in connection with jealousy. The
inarticulate is usually ahead of the articulate in James.

> Fanny's look had taken a peculiar gravity – a fulness with
> which it seemed to shine. 'Is what it comes to that you're
> jealous of Charlotte?'
> 'Do you mean whether I hate her?' – and Maggie thought.

'No; not on account of father.'

'Ah,' Mrs Assingham returned, 'that isn't what one would suppose. What I ask is if you're jealous on account of your husband.'

'Well,' said Maggie presently, 'perhaps that may be all.' (415)

At the end of the chapter, however, comes the crying scene which means that the intellect catches up with the emotions.

In this conversation comes the most celebrated of all referential ambiguities in *The Golden Bowl*:

'My dear child, you're amazing.'

'Amazing – ?'

'You're terrible.'

Maggie thoughtfully shook her head. 'No; I'm not terrible and you don't think me so. I do strike you as surprising, no doubt – but surprisingly mild. Because – don't you see? – I am mild. I can bear anything.'

'Oh, "bear"!' Mrs Assingham fluted.

'For love,' said the Princess.

Fanny hesitated. 'Of your father?'

'For love,' Maggie repeated.

It kept her friend watching. 'Of your husband?'

'For love,' Maggie said again.

It was, for the moment, as if the distinctness of this might have determined in her companion a choice between two or three highly different alternatives. (419–20)

Many critics cite this passage to demonstrate the 'inclusiveness' of Maggie's love. Donald Mull, for instance, writes that 'the inclusive love toward which Maggie works relinquishes neither father nor husband ...'[27] But maybe the scene is much more simple than that. We have to remember that this is shortly after it has come to Maggie in a flash that she must choose between her father and her husband. The word 'choice' occurs in James's comments. Maggie refuses to commit herself but the situation has now been verbalized by Fanny in this 'which one'-ambiguity and the stark brutality of it stares Maggie in the face – the scene leads up to her crying. Perhaps the referential ambiguity is yet another surface dramatization of Maggie's choice between vifehood and daughterhood.

The 'thematic' ambiguity is the question whether Maggie is ultimately motivated by love of her father or love of her husband. The passage points forward in the text by making the reader look closely for evidence of either of these, a scrutiny which demands great intensity of attention, since love of husband or love of father comes to the same thing in practice – in both cases it means keeping quiet.

In Chapter XXXI the meaning in the material of the latest stage of development is again threshed out between the Assinghams. Two cases of referential ambiguity are worthy of attention n this conversation. The first is a mix-up of Adam and the Prince.

> 'What of course will put them up, if they turn out to have less imagination than you assume, is the profit you can have found in furthering Mrs Verver's marriage. You weren't at least in love with Charlotte.'
>
> 'Oh,' Mrs Assingham, at this, always brought out, 'my hand in that is easily accounted for by my desire to be agreeable to *him*.'
>
> 'To Mr Verver?'
>
> 'To the Prince – by preventing her in that way from taking, as he was in danger of seeing her do, some husband with whom he wouldn't be able to open, to keep open, so large an account as with his father-in-law.' (429)

This referential ambiguity exists to reinforce Fanny's rueful reflections, in the preceding paragraph, over how she had procured for the Prince – being unable to have him herself, though she loved him, she arranged two beautiful women for him.

The theme reappears in the other referential ambiguity which is of general interest to our inquiry since James uses explicitly grammatical terminology in his comments.

> 'That,' said Fanny Assingham, 'will be their punishment.' And she ended, ever, when she had come so far, at the same pitch. 'It will probably also – if I get off with so little – be mine.'
>
> 'And what,' her husband liked to ask, 'will be mine?'

'Nothing – you're not worthy of any. One's punishment i
in what one feels, and what will make ours effective is that w
shall feel.' She was splendid with her "ours"; she flared u
with this prophesy. (435)

In Chapter **XXXIII** Maggie has discovered the bowl and thi
gives a jolt to her hierarchy of 'he's. We have not yet reached th
stage in the novel when she will automatically mention he
husband first in querying an ambiguous pronoun but th
discovery temporarily gives him the first place among pronomi
nal referents.

'It has everything. You'll see.' With which again, however, fo
the moment, Maggie attached to her strange wide eyes. 'H
knew her before – before I had ever seen him.'
' "He" knew – ?' But Fanny, while she cast about her for th
links she missed, could only echo it.
'Amerigo knew Charlotte – more than I ever dreamed.
(452)

After this however comes a long stretch of chaos and uncer
tainty, during which the Prince and Adam compete for the firs
place in referential confusions. Actually Mr Verver almost seem
to win for the time being and many critics[28] dislike this part o
the novel and regard Maggie's regression as a weakness in th
design of the story. Yet if James describes Maggie's and Adam'
relationship in this part of the novel in the most extrem
language, maybe the reason for Adam's presence is his defeat
not his victory. It has by now become fairly obvious that th
legitimate set of combinations is going to assert itself and Jame
wants to dramatize Maggie's loss of her father – however muc
some of us may wish that he had instead dramatized Charlotte'
loss of Amerigo.
In Maggie's and Fanny's conversation in this chapter Adam
scores two points in the pronominal referential competition.

'And it was on it all that father married *her*.'
Her visitor took it as might be. 'They both married – ah
that you must believe! – with the highest intentions.'
'Father did certainly!' And then, at the renewal of thi
consciousness, it all rolled over her. 'Ah, to thrust such thing

on *us*, to do them here between us and with us, day after day, and in return, in return – ! To do it to *him* – to him, to him!' (459)

Also:

'Then it's a good deal my fault – if everything really began so well?'

Fanny Assingham met it as she could. 'You've been only too perfect. You've thought only too much – '

But the Princess had already caught at the words. 'Yes – I've thought only too much!' Yet she appeared to continue, for the minute, full of that fault. She had it in fact, by this prompted thought, all before her. 'Of him, dear man, of *him*!'

Her friend, able to take in thus directly her vision of her father, watched her with a new suspense. *That* way might safety lie – it was like a wider chink of light. 'He believed – with a beauty! – in Charlotte.'

'Yes, and it was I who had made him believe. I didn't mean to, at the time, so much; for I had no idea then of what was coming. But I did it!' the Princess declared.

'With a beauty – ah, with a beauty, you too!' Mrs Assingham insisted.

Maggie, however, was seeing for herself – it was another matter. 'The thing was that he made her think it would be so possible.'

Fanny again hesitated. 'The Prince made her think – ?'

Maggie stared – she had meant her father. (461–2)

The merit of Maggie's torture under these confusions, is that every 'us' she uses, meaning herself and her father, accuses herself as much as Charlotte. Two individuals within the quartet (herself and her father) cannot form a couple without the implication that the remaining two form another. Therefore it is also natural that Fanny should suggest the coupling Charlotte–Adam at this point which immediately couples Maggie and Amerigo and gives him the first place in a referential confusion.

'If he doesn't then, so much the better. Leave him alone!'

'Do you mean give him up?'

'Leave *her*,' Fanny Assingham went on. 'Leave her *to* him.'

Maggie looked at her darkly. 'Do you mean leave him to

her? After this?'

'After everything. Aren't they, for that matter, intimately together now?'

' "Intimately" – ? How do I know?'

But Fanny kept it up. 'Aren't you and your husband – in spite of everything?'

Maggie's eyes still further, if possible, dilated. 'It remains to be seen!'

'If you're not then, where's your faith?'

'In my husband – ?'

Mrs Assingham but for an instant hesitated. 'In your father.' (464)

From this point through the whole of Part Fifth Adam's importance cannot really be measured in simple terms of whether he occurs first or second in a referential ambiguity, because Part Fifth is the crucial stage of the novel during which the legitimate set is established, and the ambiguities are so difficult that they not merely reflect the action but practically *constitute* the action. Many of them are rather difficult to explicate. Also their contribution to intensity is now greater than ever. This can be seen in the fact that referential ambiguities for euphemistic purposes are now more frequent than before. The characters use ambiguities to communicate incommunicable things to each other. This happens partly by deliberate mis-understandings, and partly by superfluous queries to draw attention to ambiguous pronouns but also by euphemisms. In the following example Amerigo cannot bring himself to name Adam:

> He had another hesitation, but at last this odd quantity showed. 'Then does anyone else know?'
>
> It was as near as he could come to naming her father, and she kept him at that distance. 'Anyone – ?'
>
> 'Anyone, I mean, but Fanny Assingham.'
>
> 'I should have supposed you had had by this time particular means of learning. I don't see,' she said, 'why you ask me.' (483)

The linguistic taboo naturally does not affect meaning; both Amerigo and Maggie know whom they are talking about – that is whom they are *not* talking about – exactly as in the following conversation between Fanny and Maggie:

'We alone know what's between us – we and you; and haven't you precisely been struck, since you've been here,' Maggie asked, 'with our making so good a show?'
    Her friend hesitated. 'To your father?'
    But it made her hesitate too; she wouldn't speak of her father directly. 'To everyone. To *her* – now that you understand.' (492)

These examples are clear because of authorial comment. They both make use of indefinite pronouns for the euphemistic ambiguity which is a favourite Jamesian technique. 'Anyone' is repeated immediately afterwards:

Fanny Assingham braved it. 'For the truth as from him to *her*?'
    'From him to anyone.' (493)

Part Fifth of the novel shows us Maggie growing up. But things have to be at their worst before they can get better, as night is darkest before dawn. Part Fifth is therefore also the section in which her delusion is at its most extreme; when her love for her father is described as most intense. Maggie seems not to have an existence of her own at all; she is not a person; merely a relationship; either her husband's wife or her father's daughter.

She might fairly, as she watched them, have missed it as a lost thing; have yearned for it, for the straight vindictive view, the rights of resentment, the rages of jealousy, the protests of passion, as for something she had been cheated of not least: a range of feelings which for many women would have meant so much, but which for *her* husband's wife, for *her* father's daughter, figured nothing nearer to experience than a wild eastern caravan, looming into view with crude colours in the sun, fierce pipes in the air, high spears against the sky, all a thrill, a natural joy to mingle with, but turning off short before it reached her and plunging into other defiles. (506–7)

'*Her* husband's wife' and '*her* father's daughter' are circumlocutions for 'Maggie' or the pronoun 'herself'. This type of circumlocution occurs often in *The Golden Bowl*. In Chapter XXXVII when Maggie and Adam are together for their last 'asexual fling'[29] we find this passage:

> Sharp and sudden, moreover, this afternoon, had been their well-nigh confessed desire just to rest together, a little, as from some strain long felt but never named; to rest, as who should say, shoulder to shoulder and hand in hand, each pair of eyes so yearningly – and indeed what could it be but so wearily? – closed as to render the collapse safe from detection by the other pair. It was positively as if, in short, the inward felicity of their being once more, perhaps only for half an hour, simply daughter and father had glimmered out for them, and they had picked up the pretext that would make it easiest. They were husband and wife – oh, so immensely! – as regards other persons; but after they had dropped again on their old bench, conscious that the party on the terrace, augmented, as in the past, by neighbours, would do beautifully without them, it was wonderfully like their having got together into some boat and paddled off from the shore where husbands and wives, luxuriant complications, made the air too tropical. (519–20)

The phrase 'they were husband and wife' is not placed in its syntactical and textual position by chance. James wants to trip the reader up and make him momentarily regard 'they were husband and wife' in isolation; not textually – this is why he introduces the parenthesis 'oh, so immensely'. Logically the meaning of the passage is that they are a husband and wife, one of them being married to Charlotte, and the other to Amerigo, but James also wanted to confuse us to suggest another meaning, namely that in the eyes of other persons ('as regards other persons'), i.e. Charlotte and the Prince, they (Maggie and Adam) had looked like 'husband and wife', because their union had seemed as real as that between Charlotte and Amerigo. This 'marriage' should now be at an end. One sense of the passage seems to be the opposite:

> They *had*, after all, whatever happened, always and ever each other; each other – that was the hidden treasure and the saving truth – to do exactly what they would with: a provision

full of possibilities. (520)

This may seem to suggest that the illegitimate set is in fact growing stronger, but the phrase 'they needed only *know* each other, henceforth, in the unmarried relation' (ibid.) is ambiguous. The first layer of sense is that they can now be as they were before Maggie married Amerigo and Adam married Charlotte. But the secondary meaning of the phrase 'husband and wife' suggests an alternative. They can henceforth be as 'father and daughter' and 'know each other in the unmarried relation' because they can forget about being husband and wife, one to Charlotte and the other to Amerigo (Sense 1). But they can also be father and daughter and know each other henceforth in the unmarried relation because they can forget the other relationship, i.e. being husband and wife *to each other* (Sense 2). James has played so much with the word 'married' in connection with Maggie and Adam that one cannot help feeling that he is here also playing with the word 'know' which is italicized.[30] In the conversation between Maggie and her father in Chapter XXXVII Maggie sets up a combinational model that creates a vast number of possibilities.

> 'Oh, how can I talk,' she asked, 'of "otherwise"? It *isn't*, luckily for me, otherwise. If everything were different' – she further presented her thought – 'of course everything *would* be.' And then again, as if that were but half: 'My idea is this, that when you only love a little you're naturally not jealous – or are only jealous also a little, so that it doesn't matter. But when you love in a deeper and intenser way, then you are, in the same proportion, jealous; your jealousy has intensity and, no doubt, ferocity. When, however, you love in the most abysmal and unutterable way of all – why then you're beyond everything, and nothing can pull you down.' (525–6)

To begin with, there is uncertainty as to whom this refers to. To Maggie? To Adam? Is it Maggie or Adam who loves in one of these three ways? Then, when the reader has sorted that out, he has to make a binary observation; is the person who loves jealous or not? If he or she is jealous then it means that they love in the 'middle' way. If again they are not jealous there is again a binary ambiguity; they either love very little or hopelessly much.

Finally, if the reader manages to sort even this one out, there is the binary ambiguity of the referent of love; in Maggie's case love of Amerigo or love of Adam? and in Adam's case love of Maggie or love of Charlotte?

Well, let us take a plunge and try to sort out some of these ambiguities. Immediately after Maggie has set up her model Adam suggests that the 'hopeless' state is the way *Maggie* loves.

> Mr Verver listened as if he had nothing, on these high lines, to oppose. 'And that's the way *you* love?' (526)

Moreover we may guess that Mr Verver means that that is the way Maggie loves *the Prince*. Then Mr Verver states: 'I guess I've never been jealous'. This could mean that he loves very little, which could be a possibility if the referent were Charlotte, but it could also mean that he loves her very much (Charlotte) and above all that he loves very much if the referent is Maggie. (I think we can exclude the theoretical possibility of Adam loving Maggie very little.) The likeliest interpretation is probably Adam loving Maggie very much and Charlotte very much or loving Maggie very much and Charlotte very little.[31]

Maggie insists that the subject is Adam, not herself.

> But she at last tried for one of them. 'Oh, it's you, father, who are what I call beyond everything. Nothing can pull *you* down.' (527)

But Adam stubbornly returns the ball. He wants Maggie to be the subject.

> He returned the look as with the sociability of their easy communication, though inevitably throwing in this time a shade of solemnity. He might have been seeing things to say, and others, whether of a type presumptuous or not, doubtless better kept back. So he settled on the merely obvious. 'Well then, we make a pair. We're all right.' (ibid.)

Shortly afterwards Adam insists not only that Maggie is the subject but moreover that Maggie's love for Amerigo is the proper subject.

> 'When a person's of the nature you speak of there are always

other persons to suffer. But you've just been describing to me
what you'd take, if you had once a good chance, from your
husband.'
   'Oh, I'm not talking about my husband.'
   'Then whom *are* you talking about?'
   Both the retort and the rejoinder had come quicker than
anything previously exchanged, and they were followed, on
Maggie's part, by a momentary drop. But she was not to fall
away, and while her companion kept his eyes on her, while she
wondered if he weren't expecting her to name his wife then,
with high hypocrisy, as paying for his daughter's bliss, she
produced something that she felt to be much better. 'I'm
talking about *you*.'
   'Do you mean I've been your victim?' (528)

The referential confusion here has to be studied very carefully by
the reader because a hurried reading might give him the wrong
idea. When Maggie says 'I'm not talking about my husband' one
possible sense is that the object of her love is not Amerigo but
Adam. This is how Mr Verver understands her. But Maggie is
not talking about objects, she is talking about subjects; she is
talking about Adam ('I'm talking about *you*') not as an object
but as a subject. Her idea is that Adam loves in the third, the
hopeless way, and that he loves *her* (Maggie). In the process of
the breaking up of the illegitimate set Maggie has now reached
the state when she has realized that something has happened to
her feelings for Adam. But her selfishness comes out in her
inability to face the idea that something might have happened in
Adam's feelings for her (Maggie).[32] At this stage the set that
Maggie wants is this: a destroyed combination Charlotte–
Amerigo; an established bond Amerigo–Maggie; a destroyed
relation Charlotte–Adam; and a relation Maggie–Adam which is
secretly destroyed one way (Maggie to Adam), but the integrity
and absoluteness of which she desperately clutches at in panic
the other way (Adam to Maggie). Maggie still has a long way to
go before she can face a relationship Adam–Charlotte, and when
it begins to appear she softens the impact of the shock by her
theory that Adam pretends to be interested in Charlotte for her
(Maggie's) sake which, again, is ambiguous; either a true
estimate or a self-delusion on Maggie's part.
   The subject of the conversation is now so hot for Adam that he

veers off into trivialities about American City, which creates a
pause so that Maggie can cut in again by ambiguating a phrase
about people making jokes at his expense.

> 'Then there, exactly, you are!' she triumphed. 'Everything
> that touches you, everything that surrounds you, goes on – by
> your splendid indifference and your incredible permission – at
> your expense.'
> Just as he had been sitting he looked at her an instant
> longer; then he slowly rose, while his hands stole into his
> pockets, and stood there before her. 'Of course, my dear, you
> go on at my expense: it has never been my idea,' he smiled,
> 'that you should work for your living. I wouldn't have liked to
> see it.' With which, for a little again, they remained face to
> face. 'Say therefore I *have* had the feelings of a father. How
> have they made me a victim?'
> 'Because I sacrifice you.'
> 'But to what in the world?' (529)

Here it is at last, the distinguished thing; the exact point at
which Adam finally loses and Amerigo wins the first place in
Maggie's affections. The referential ambiguity is not difficult for
either of them but the solution must not be put into words:

> At this it hung before her that she should have had as never
> yet her opportunity to say, and it held her for a minute as in a
> vice, her impression of his now, with his strained smile, which
> touched her to deepest depths, sounding her in his secret
> unrest. This was the moment, in the whole process of their
> mutual vigilance, in which it decidedly *most* hung by a hair
> that their thin wall might be pierced by the lightest wrong
> touch. It shook between them, this transparency, with their
> very breath; it was an exquisite tissue, but stretched on a
> frame, and would give way the next instant if either so much
> as breathed too hard. She held her breath, for she knew by his
> eyes, the light at the heart of which he couldn't blind, that he
> was, by his intention, making sure – sure whether or no her
> certainty was like his. The intensity of his dependence on it at
> that moment – this itself was what absolutely convinced her so
> that, as if perched up before him on her vertiginous point and
> in the very glare of his observation, she balanced for thirty

seconds, she almost rocked: she might have been for the time, in all her conscious person, the very form of the equilibrium they were, in their different ways, equally trying to save. And they were saving it – yes, they were, or at least she was: that was still the workable issue, she could say, as she felt her dizziness drop. She held herself hard; the thing was to be done, once for all, by her acting, now, where she stood. So much was crowded into so short a space that she knew already she was keeping her head. She had kept it by the warning of his eyes; she shouldn't lose it again; she knew how and why, and if she had turned cold this was precisely what helped her. He had said to himself, 'She'll break down and name Amerigo; she'll say it's to him she's sacrificing me; and it's by what that will give me – with so many other things too – that my suspicion will be clinched.' He was watching her lips, spying for the symptoms of the sound; whereby these symptoms had only to fail and he would have got nothing that she didn't measure out to him as she gave it. She had presently in fact so recovered herself that she seemed to know she could more easily have made him name his wife than he have made her name her husband. It was there before her that if she should so much as force him just *not* consciously to avoid saying, 'Charlotte, Charlotte,' he would have given himself away. But to be sure of this was enough for her, and she saw more clearly with each lapsing instant what they were both doing. He was doing what he had steadily been coming to; he was practically *offering* himself, pressing himself upon her, as a sacrifice – he had read his way so into her best possibility; and where had she already, for weeks and days past, planted her feet if not on her acceptance of the offer? Cold indeed, colder and colder she turned, as she felt herself suffer this close personal vision of his attitude still not to make her weaken. That was her very certitude, the intensity of his pressure; for if something dreadful hadn't happened there wouldn't, for either of them, be these dreadful things to do. She had meanwhile, as well, the immense advantage that *she* could have named Charlotte without exposing herself – as, for that matter, she was the next minute showing him.

'Why, I sacrifice you, simply, to everything and to everyone. I take the consequences of your marriage as perfectly natural.' (529–30)

They sacrifice each other to their spouses; the legitimate set is being formed. The sense must not be spoken aloud, but after it has been referred to by the typically euphemistic indefinite pronouns 'everything' and 'everyone',[33] the real meaning is nevertheless hinted at in the contracting hyponymic movement of the sense from indefiniteness to specificity (everything – your marriage; everyone – Charlotte [by analogy]). The specificity Charlotte of course in turn suggests the symmetrical specificity Amerigo, but it also suggests an ambiguity in the word 'sacrifice'. When Maggie 'sacrifices' Adam to Amerigo she sacrifices him *for* Amerigo; she prefers Amerigo to him. The use of the word 'sacrifice' in connection with Adam in relation to Charlotte suggests Maggie's view of the Adam–Charlotte relationship at this moment; Adam thrown on Charlotte is sacrificed in the sense of a lamb being led to the block. When Maggie and Adam are coupled in a 'we' in the continuation of the dialogue Maggie tries to discriminate but Adam wants to take his share of responsibility:

> He threw back his head a little, settling with one hand his eyeglass. 'What do you call, my dear, the consequences?'
> 'Your life as your marriage has made it.'
> 'Well, hasn't it made it exactly what we wanted?'
> She just hesitated, then felt herself steady – oh, beyond what she had dreamed. 'Exactly what *I* wanted – yes.'
> His eyes, through his straightened glasses, were still on hers, and he might, with his intenser fixed smile, have been knowing she was, for herself, rightly inspired. 'What do you make then of what I wanted?' (531)

And when Maggie does not give in he grows violent, hinting that he will return to America with Charlotte. Finally he crowns his idea in an 'us' meaning Charlotte and himself.

> 'Do you know, Mag, what you make me wish when you talk that way?' And he waited again, while she further got from him the sense of something that had been behind, deeply in the shade, coming cautiously to the front and just feeling its way before presenting itself. 'You regularly make me wish that I had shipped back to American City. When you go on as you do – .' But he really had to hold himself to say it.

'Well, when I go on –?'

'Why, you make me quite want to ship back myself. You make me quite feel as if American City would be the best place for us.'

It made all too finely vibrate. 'For "us" – ?'

'For me and Charlotte. Do you know that if we *should* ship, it would serve you quite right?' With which he smiled – oh he smiled! 'And if you say much more we *will* ship.' (532)

The relationship between Maggie and Adam could be broken up only by active contribution from Adam. In Chapter XXXVI when Maggie and Charlotte looked at the card-players from outside Maggie intensely wanted Adam to give a sign that he preferred her to Charlotte. If she had only had such a sign she could have sent them off to America with the triumph of knowing that she was really number one not only to Amerigo but to Adam. But she has to learn the full lesson; that her combination with Amerigo is possible only with a corresponding combination Adam–Charlotte.

It throbbed for these seconds as a yearning appeal to him – she would chance it, that is, if he would but just raise his eyes and catch them, across the larger space, standing in the outer dark together. Then he might be affected by the sight, taking them as they were; he might make some sign – she scarce knew what – that would save *her*, save her from being the one, this way, to pay all. He might somehow show a preference – distinguishing between them; might, out of pity for her, signal to her that this extremity of her effort for him was more than he asked. That represented Maggie's one little lapse from consistency – the sole small deflection in the whole course of her scheme. It had come to nothing the next minute, for the dear man's eyes had never moved, ... (513)

The whole thing was a test for Maggie and it showed Adam suspended in hesitation between his daughter and his wife.

His wife and his daughter were both closely watching him, and to which of them, could he have been notified of this, would his raised eyes first, all impulsively, have responded; in which of them would he have felt it most important to destroy – for *his* clutch at the equilibrium – any germ of uneasiness? Not yet, since his marriage, had Maggie so sharply and so formidably known her old possession of him as a thing divided and contested. (512)

But the test gives no result, the mystery remains. When Maggie began to reserve Amerigo for herself it did not immediately occur to her that insisting on this monopoly would make Charlotte symmetrically insist on her monopoly of Adam, and that making Amerigo abandon his illicit love (Charlotte) would result in Adam symmetrically abandoning his illicit love (Maggie). The scene where she feels the sharp pang of jealousy (over her father) had to be followed by the long conversation that we studied in which Maggie and Adam sort out whom they sacrifice each other to. They can now believe in each other more than in 'anyone' (535) in a new sense, and the scene closes without tears.

Since the decisive steps of separation have now been taken by herself and her father, Maggie's emotional life is open for a feeling of pity for Charlotte. In Chapter XXXVIII she thinks that Charlotte's voice, when she guides neighbours around Fawns, sounds like the 'shriek of a soul in pain' (548). She now feels that Charlotte could be let out of her torture and she mutely appeals to her father for agreement.

The same way as she begins to feel pity for Charlotte she also begins to feel curious about the relation Adam–Amerigo.

> Something grave had happened, somehow and somewhere, and she had, God knew, her choice of suppositions: her heart stood still when she wondered above all if the cord mightn't at last have snapped between her husband and her father. She shut her eyes for dismay at the possibility of such a passage – there moved before them the procession of ugly forms it might have taken. (552)

Also:

> These shadows rose and fell for her while Father Mitchell prattled; with other shadows as well, those that hung over Charlotte herself, those that marked her as a prey to equal suspicions – to the idea, in particular, of a change, such a

change as she didn't dare to face, in the relations of the two men. Or there were yet other possibilities, as it seemed to Maggie; there were always too many, and all of them things of evil when one's nerves had at last done for one all that nerves could do; had left one in a darkness of prowling dangers that was like the predicament of the night-watcher in a beast-haunted land who has no more means for a fire. (553)

The whole thing works in an inevitable rotary way as James wrote. The sets are being dealt with one by one. After Maggie had sorted out and shed the problems of the illegitimate set she sorts out the problems of the compromise set (herself and Charlotte; Adam+Amerigo). She 'is all but through' as Fanny says in her dialogue with Maggie in Chapter XXXIX.

> 'Splendid. Also, you know, you *are* all but "through". You've done it,' said Mrs Assingham.
> But Maggie only half took it from her. 'What does it strike you that I've done?'
> 'What you wanted. They're going.'
> Maggie continued to look at her. 'Is that what I wanted?'
> 'Oh, it wasn't for you to say. That was *his* business.'
> 'My father's?' Maggie asked after a hesitation.
> 'Your father's. He has chosen – and now she knows.' (556)

We are now back to a more simple state of affairs with the referential ambiguities. Maggie is past the turmoil of giving up her father, and Amerigo is so important to her that she hesitates even in front of Fanny's rather obvious 'his'. On the next page Maggie thinks of Amerigo first.

> For a little, after this, their eyes met on it; at the end of which Fanny said: 'She'll be – yes – what she'll have to be. And it will be – won't it? – for ever and ever.' She spoke as abounding in her friend's sense, but it made Maggie still only look at her. These were large words and large visions – all the more that now, really, they spread and spread. In the midst of them, however, Mrs Assingham had soon enough continued. 'When I talk of "knowing", indeed, I don't mean it as you would have a right to do. You know because you see – and I don't see *him*. I don't make him out,' she almost crudely

confessed. Maggie again hesitated. 'You mean you don'
make out Amerigo?'

But Fanny shook her head, and it was quite as if, as ar
appeal to one's intelligence, the making out of Amerigo had
in spite of everything, long been superseded. Then Maggie
measured the reach of her allusion, and how what she nex
said gave her meaning a richness. No other name was to be
spoken, and Mrs Assingham had taken that, without delay
from her eyes – with a discretion, still, that fell short but by ar
inch. (557)

When Maggie goes to make peace with Charlotte she pointedly
does it under the pretext of bringing Charlotte the right volume
of a three-decker novel that Charlotte has been reading
Charlotte has got hold of the wrong volume (Amerigo instead o
Adam) and Maggie brings her the right one (Adam). To many
readers it seems cheeky that Maggie, who until about a chapter
ago had got hold of the wrong volume herself (Adam), or wa:
trying to read two volumes simultaneously, should set herself up
as an instructress.

She herself could but tentatively hover, place in view the book
she carried, look as little dangerous, look as abjectly mild, as
possible; remind herself really of people she had read about ir
stories of the wild west, people who threw up their hands, or
certain occasions, as a sign they weren't carrying revolvers
She could almost have smiled at last, troubled as she yet knew
herself, to show how richly she was harmless; she held up her
volume, which was so weak a weapon, and while she
continued, for consideration, to keep her distance, she ex
plained with as quenched a quaver as possible: 'I saw you
come out – saw you from my window, and couldn't bear to
think you should find yourself here without the beginning o
your book. *This* is the beginning; you've got the wrong
volume, and I've brought you out the right.' (561–2)

Charlotte does not let Maggie run the show alone. She I
Maggie take back the second volume (Amerigo), but as to
accepting Adam from her she apparently does not think tha
Adam is Maggie's to offer to her so she leaves that volume
untouched:

She presently got up – which seemed to mean 'Oh, stay if you like!' – and when she had moved about awhile at random, looking away, looking at anything, at everything but her visitor; when she had spoken of the temperature and declared that she revelled in it; when she had uttered her thanks for the book, which, a little incoherently, with her second volume, she perhaps found less clever than she expected; when she had let Maggie approach sufficiently closer to lay, untouched, the tribute in question on a bench and take up obligingly its superfluous mate: when she had done these things she sat down in another place, more or less visibly in possession of her part. (563)

At the end of the chapter these volumes are mentioned again in this passage:

Charlotte had looked about her, picked up the parasol she had laid on a bench, possessed herself mechanically of one of the volumes of the relegated novel and then, more consciously, flung it down again: she was in presence, visibly, of her last word. (566)

This might suggest that Charlotte does not care for Adam and that Maggie is finally victoriously in possession of both of the two men.

Maggie waited; she looked, as her companion had done a moment before, at the two books on the seat; she put them together and laid them down; then she made up her mind. (567)

If this is so then not only Maggie but Charlotte too is lying in the conversation because in it she vigorously takes the pronominal initiative and couples herself and Adam in a 'we'.

'I've an idea that greatly appeals to me – I've had it for a long time. It has come over me that we're wrong. Our real life isn't here.'
Maggie held her breath.'"Ours" – ?'
'My husband's and mine. I'm not speaking of you.'
'Oh!' said Maggie, only praying not to be, not even to

appear, stupid.

'I'm speaking for ourselves. I'm speaking,' Charlotte brought out, 'for *him*.'

'I see. For my father.'

'For your father. For whom else?' They looked at each other hard now, but Maggie's face took refuge in the intensity of her interest. She was not at all events so stupid as to treat her companion's question as requiring an answer; a discretion that her controlled stillness had after an instant justified. (564)

Charlotte's 'our' could hardly be Maggie's and Charlotte's or even Amerigo's and Charlotte's (at this stage) so Maggie's query is merely a testimony of her shock at hearing the first person plural refer to Charlotte and Adam in such a brutally obvious way. Of course she is lying and acting in this scene, pretending to be more attached to her father than she really is but this behaviour coincides conveniently with what her reaction would have been anyway if the scene had come a little earlier. Charlotte's 'you' (I'm not speaking of you'.) is a beautiful ambiguity since it could be either singular (Maggie) or plural; in which latter case it is either Maggie+Adam or Maggie+Amerigo. Maggie has to admit that *him* is now unambiguously Adam but tries to combat (or pretends to try to combat) Charlotte's possession of him by referring egocentrically to him in his relation to her ('My father') rather than in his relation to Charlotte ('Your husband'). Charlotte dares her (Maggie) to name Amerigo (the illegitimate set) but Maggie keeps quiet. Charlotte is defeated over Amerigo. She can only use past triumphs for a final malicious stab at Maggie.

> 'I mean immediately. And – I may as well tell you now – I mean for my own time. I want,' Charlotte said, 'to have him at last a little to myself; I want, strange as it may seem to you' – and she gave it all its weight – 'to *keep* the man I've married. And to do so, I see, I must act.' (565)

Whether Charlotte is acting or not she has now completed the phase of sorting out the relations of the compromise set. Part Sixth, the final section of the novel, which begins immediately after this, is concerned with the remaining loose ends, i.e. the partners of the illegitimate set taking farewell of each other in a positive spirit (Maggie+her father; 'It's all right, eh?' 'Oh, my dear – rather!' [596]; the Prince+Charlotte – Maggie insists on it); the partners in the compromise set thinking well of each other; Maggie suggesting to her father his own mate (Charlotte) in the combinations of the legitimate set ('Father, father – Charlotte's great'; [599] and finally Maggie being left with her husband. Universal reconciliation is not only hinted at, it is even suggested that this reconciliation is more or less reciprocal in nearly all possible combinations.

When Fanny and Maggie discuss the situation in Chapter XL Maggie feels the legitimate set to be by now so safe that she can not only suggest that Amerigo and Charlotte could meet privately but even use the pronoun *their* italicized and the ambiguous word 'affair'.

> Mrs Assingham deferentially mused. 'But for what purpose is it your idea that they should again so intimately meet?'
> 'For any purpose they like. That's *their* affair.'
> Fanny Assingham sharply laughed, then irrepressibly fell back to her constant position. 'You're splendid – perfectly splendid.' (576)

The reader feels at first tempted to laugh with Fanny over Maggie's use of 'affair' but then perhaps to agree with Fanny that Maggie feels safe now.

> To which, as the Princess, shaking an impatient head, wouldn't have it again at all, she subjoined: 'Or if you're not it's because you're so sure. I mean sure of *him*.' (ibid.)

This *him* is no longer ambiguous – it is Amerigo. There is no insecurity about it and therefore no labile referential ambiguity. The pronominal terms of the illegitimate set can here be used coolly and detachedly. Accordingly Maggie can now use a *them* for Amerigo & Charlotte and a 'we' for herself and Adam and she needs no euphemistic replacing of one name with another or any indefinite pronouns; she can mention Amerigo and Charlotte with cold objectivity by name.

> 'Oh,' Maggie returned, 'it's what – from the moment they

discovered we could think at all – will have saved *them*. For they're the ones who are saved,' she went on. 'We're the ones who are lost.'

'Lost – ?'

'Lost to each other – father and I.' And then as her friend appeared to demur, 'Oh yes,' Maggie quite lucidly declared, 'lost to each other much more, really than Amerigo and Charlotte are; since for them it's just, it's right, it's deserved, while for us it's only sad and strange and not caused by our fault.' (557)

Nevertheless there is a mix-up soon afterwards to suggest Maggie's recently acquired lack of skill in referring to Adam as 'he'. Adam is 'he' as long as Amerigo has not been mentioned.

'He has made it a success for *them* – !'

'Ah, there you are!' Maggie responsively mused. 'Yes,' she said the next moment, 'that's why Amerigo stays.'

'Let alone that it's why Charlotte goes.' And Mrs Assingham emboldened, smiled. 'So he knows – ?'

But Maggie hung back. 'Amerigo – ?' After which, however, she blushed – to her companion's recognition.

'Your father.' (578)

In Chapter XLI, the penultimate chapter, Maggie begins to fall in love with the Prince in a physical sense. She begins to realize that her loss of her father may be well compensated for by her acquisition of her husband.

She stood there with her eyes on him, doubling the telegram together as if it had been a precious thing and yet all the while holding her breath. Of a sudden, somehow, and quite as by the action of their merely having between them these few written words, an extraordinary fact came up. He was with her as if he were hers, hers in a degree and on a scale, with an intensity and an intimacy, that were a new and a strange quantity, that were like the interruption of a tide loosening them where they had stuck and making them feel they floated. What was it that, with the rush of this, just kept her from putting out her hands to him, from catching at him as, in the other time, with the superficial impetus he and Charlotte had privately conspired to impart, she had so often, her breath failing her, known the impulse to catch at her father? (581–2)

But before Maggie lets herself go she wants to make arrangements for a decent parting of the partners in the combinations of the illegitimate set. She discusses this with the Prince. The Prince still has a need for euphemisms so he refers to 'they', on second thoughts, as 'Your father'.

> 'If they do everything that's proper,' the Prince presently asked, 'why don't they at least come to dine?'
> She hesitated, yet she lightly enough provided her answer. 'That we must certainly ask them. It will be easy for you. But of course they're immensely taken – !'
> He wondered. 'So immensely taken that they can't – that your father can't – give you his last evening in England?'
> This, for Maggie, was more difficult to meet; yet she was still not without her stop-gap. 'That may be what they'll propose – that we shall go somewhere together, the four of us, for a celebration – except that, to round it thoroughly off, we ought also to have Fanny and the Colonel. They don't *want* them at tea, she quite sufficiently expresses; they polish them off, poor dears, they get rid of them, beforehand. They want only *us* together; and if they cut us down to tea,' she continued, 'as they cut Fanny and the Colonel down to luncheon, perhaps it's the fancy, after all, of their keeping their last night in London for each other.' (582)

For Maggie to use the pronoun 'each other' about Adam and Charlotte; to suggest reciprocity in that relationship, is indeed to have come a long way. It is only after the Prince protests against the reciprocal pronoun that she agrees to use the pronouns of the illegitimate set.

> 'But it isn't – is it?' he asked – 'as if they were leaving each other?'
> 'Oh no; it isn't as if they were leaving each other. They're only bringing to a close – without knowing when it may open again – a time that has been, naturally, awfully interesting to them.' Yes, she could talk so of their 'time' – she was somehow sustained; she was sustained even to affirm more intensely her

present possession of her ground. 'They have their reasons – many things to think of; how can one tell? But there's always, also, the chance of his proposing to me that *we* shall have our last hours together; I mean that he and I shall. He may wish to take me off to dine with him somewhere alone – and to do it in memory of old days. I mean,' the Princess went on, 'the *real* old days; before my grand husband was invented and, much more, before his grand wife was: ...' (584)

The end of this ('his grand wife') intentionally confuses Adam and Amerigo. 'His grand wife' means either Charlotte or it means Maggie (Maggie in her married state).

Although Maggie was able to talk coolly about the combinations of the illegitimate set, and use clear pronouns, with Fanny, to do so with the Prince is a more ticklish business and she therefore temporarily relapses into euphemism when she suggests to the Prince that he ought to see Charlotte before they part.

'But shan't you then so much as miss her a little? She's wonderful and beautiful, and I feel somehow as if she were dying. Not really, not physically,' Maggie went on – 'she's so far, naturally, splendid as she is, from having done with life. But dying for us – for you and me; and making us feel it by the very fact of there being so much of her left.' (586)

'You and me' here means you. This is the simplest case of pronominal euphemism: redundance. There is also a latent secondary meaning: 'dying for (the sake of) us'.

In the next interchange Maggie realizes that Charlotte's unhappiness had really started the true relationship between her and the Prince – a suggestion of the 'fortunate fall' motif. The Prince agrees but challenges Maggie's ideas about Charlotte's unhappiness.

The Prince smoked hard a minute. 'As you say, she's splendid, but there is – there always will be – much of her left. Only, as you also say, for others.'

'And yet I think,' the Princess returned, 'that it isn't as if we had wholly done with her. How can we not always think of her? It's as if her unhappiness had been necessary to us – as if

we had needed her, at her own cost, to build us up and start
us.'

He took it in with consideration, but he met it with a lucid
inquiry. 'Why do you speak of the unhappiness of your
father's wife?'

They exchanged a long look – the time that it took her to
find her reply. 'Because not to – !'

'Well, not to – ?'

'Would make me have to speak of *him*.' (586–7)

By symmetrical implication Adam's unhappiness (in losing
Maggie) was necessary, and actually this sense is much more to
the point.

Maggie's die-hard self-centredness still makes her picture
Adam's loss (of Maggie) as enormous. Since James never gave
us a third volume from Adam's point of view it is difficult to
judge how far she is right. If we still expect the symmetry to
work, then the conjugal relations between Adam and Charlotte
may not be that bad because the relations between Amerigo and
Maggie have never been better. They have never been so
physically exciting as now. Maggie is at last discovering her
husband.

That consciousness in fact had a pang, and she balanced,
intensely, for the lingering moment, almost with a terror of her
endless power of surrender. He had only to press, really, for
her to yield inch by inch, and she fairly knew at present, while
she looked at him through her cloud, that the confession of
this precious secret sat there for him to pluck. The sensation,
for the few seconds, was extraordinary; her weakness, her
desire, so long as she was yet not saving herself, flowered in
her face like a light or a darkness. She sought for some word
that would cover this up; she reverted to the question of tea,
speaking as if they shouldn't meet sooner. 'Then about five. I
count on you.'

On him too, however, something had descended; as to
which this exactly gave him his chance. 'Ah, but I shall see
you – !' No?' he said, coming nearer.

She had with her hand still on the knob, her back against
the door, so that her retreat, under his approach, must be less
than a step, and yet she couldn't for her life, with the other

hand, have pushed him away. He was so near now that she could touch him, smell him, kiss him, hold him; he almost pressed upon her, and the warmth of his face – frowning, smiling, she mightn't know which; only beautiful and strange – was bent upon her with the largeness with which objects loom in dreams. She closed her eyes to it, and so, the next instant, against her purpose, she had put out her hand, which had met his own and which he held. Then it was that, from behind her closed eyes, the right word came. 'Wait!' (591)

The pairs take farewell of each other. Adam asks for the Principino.

> She glanced at the clock. 'I "ordered" him for half-past five
> – which hasn't yet struck. Trust him, my dear, not to fail you!'
> 'Oh, I don't want *him* to fail me!' was Mr Verver's reply; . . .
> (597–8)

The referential ambiguity created by Mr Verver's contrastive accent reminds us of the question 'who else has failed him,' (Maggie? Charlotte?) but perhaps also 'whom *does* he want to fail him?' if he does not want the Principino to fail him (answer: Maggie). This makes Maggie suggest, as a final tribute to the illegitimate set, that she will miss him (Adam). Fawns with its best things (Adam and Charlotte) removed would not be much fun.

> 'Fawns with half its contents and half its best things removed,
> won't seem to you, I'm afraid, particularly lively.'
> 'No,' Maggie answered, 'we should miss its best things. Its
> best things, my dear, have certainly been removed. To be
> back there,' she went on, 'to be back there – !' And she paused
> for the force of her idea.
> 'Oh, to be back there without anything good – !'
> But she didn't hesitate now; she brought her idea forth. 'To
> be back there without Charlotte is more than I think would
> do.' And as she smiled at him with it, so she saw him the next
> instant take it – take it in a way that helped her smile to pass
> all for an allusion to what she didn't and couldn't say. This
> quantity was too clear – that she couldn't at such an hour be
> pretending to name to him what it was, as he would have said,

'going to be', at Fawns or anywhere else, to want for *him*. (598–9)

Just as Maggie found it impossible to talk to the Prince in the same clear terms about the illegitimate set as she had used with Fanny so she now too, in her conversation with her father, has to use a euphemism for Adam, calling him 'Charlotte'.

Adam and Charlotte leave, the Prince takes the Principino to Miss Bogle in order to leave Maggie and him (Amerigo) alone, and while Maggie waits for him with a beating heart and a dizzy head she suddenly realizes that this was the result she wanted.

Here, at first, her husband had not rejoined her; he had come up with the boy, who, clutching his hand, abounded, as usual, in remarks worthy of the family archives; but the two appeared then to have proceeded to report to Miss Bogle. It meant something for the Princess that her husband had thus got their son out of the way, not bringing him back to his mother; but everything now, as she vaguely moved about, struck her as meaning so much that the unheard chorus swelled. Yet *this* above all – her just being there as she was and waiting for him to come in, their freedom to be together there always – was the meaning most disengaged: she stood in the cool twilight and took it in, all about her, where it lurked, her reason for what she had done. She knew at last really why – and how she had been inspired and guided, how she had been persistently able, how, to her soul, all the while, it had been for the sake of this end. (601–2)

He means everything to her now. She does not care about Charlotte, she wants no confession. She suggests to him that Charlotte is 'splendid' in order to free his mind of any necessity to talk about Charlotte. But Maggie's effort is unnecessary.

' "See"? I see nothing but *you*.' And the truth of it had, with this force, after a moment, so strangely lighted his eyes that, as for pity and dread of them, she buried her own in his breast. (603)

Amerigo cares for no other 'she'. He embraces his wife and uses the only pronoun he needs now: the second person singular.

2 End-Linking

Although James put the device of referential ambiguity in pronouns to very sophisticated artistic use the fact remains that in the end the device also reflects a deep-seated uncertainty – uncertainty about identities. On the microlevel of style the device reveals the thematic anxieties of James's fictional world where characters grope around not knowing who is who, who is the proper partner for whom, who is linking up with whom or who is being referred to by whom.

In this chapter I wish to explore briefly another characteristic feature of James's prose which also ultimately reflects uncertainty and insecurity.

The device is 'end-linking', i.e. the linking of two linguistic elements such as phrases, sentences, periods or paragraphs end-to-beginning, usually through the repetition, at the beginning of the following element, of something at the end of the preceding.

The character of the links between sentences is very idiosyncratic in James's late works, and there is an extraordinary density of links. Every sentence and period is tied to the preceding and the following in a tightly-knit pattern of relationships manifested in links of various kinds, such as repetition, reference, synonymy, antonymy, hyponymy etc.[1]

One reason for the effect of intensity can be found in the make-up of this interlacement of textual links. It upsets the balance between 'form' and 'content' and makes the former more important. Cohesion, in any text, is achieved both through a rational ordering of linguistic units in relation to each other and through a rational ordering of whatever they refer to. In James the former takes precedence over the latter. The previous utterance of one's partner in a dialogue is always there to be pondered, doubted, queried, enlarged upon etc., whereas direct reference to a new phase in the discussion of the subject is comparative rare – so rare in fact that when it occasionally occurs it has a considerable dramatic effect. Sentences in James usually grow out of preceding sentences both in dialogue and elsewhere. This creates a feeling of intensity because the prose becomes self-contained and self-sufficient. In conversations where the participants need to scrutinize each utterance or conversational move so studiously the subject should be intensely important.

Each unit in James's text is very much propped up against its linguistic neighbours rather than merely resting on its referent. This is the case with words, phrases, sentences, periods, paragraphs and also for instance, images. As Philip Grover writes: 'Images tend to refer to other, previously suggested, images, or to be taken from the same area of discourse. Therefore one gets the continuous effect of each item referring to another in the same world'.[2]

James's aim was to make content important by presenting it through a medium made important. If the participants in a dialogue find it important to make out the surface-meaning of their partners' utterances this should also give stature to the reality behind that intensely elaborated surface.

Hostile comments on James have not usually denied his technical skill. Instead the standard objection has been that there is too much technique in James and too little substance. This imbalance has been pointed out by critics again and again. Doubtless these critics have a point. But it is interesting that even as they attack James for his lack of substance they indirectly pay homage to his technical skill. H.G. Wells did not think that the felicities of technique make up for a lack of content, but even Wells uses the word 'intense'.

It is like a church lit but without a congregation to distract you, with every light and line focused on the high altar. And on the altar, very reverently placed, intensely there, is a dead kitten, an egg-shell, a bit of string ...[3]

Edmund Wilson commented on James's 'superficiality'.[4] The term is certainly factually correct whether we take it as a negative comment on James or not.[5]

Of the links between phrases, sentences, periods and paragraphs in *The Golden Bowl* repetition is a very frequent type. This is relevant to our inquiry. Repetition as a device in *The Golden Bowl* occurs on all levels and the intensity-creating effects of repetition are prominent.

Repetition can be used for intensification and emphasis in a variety of ways ranging from the simple iteration of words (epizeuxis) as in the sentence 'he is very, very old' to the highly sophisticated regular occurrence of some thematic key-words at nodal points in a narrative.[6]

Another prominent aspect of repetition is its ambiguity-creating function, and ambiguity often contributes to intensity as intensity often contributes to ambiguity. It has often been pointed out that repetition is one way of making an ambiguity explicit.[7] Repetition is thus an important intensity- and ambiguity-creating device in James, and repetition, in assorted forms, is very characteristic of James's prose in *The Golden Bowl*, including the dialogues.

James's textual strategy varies and in the movements of his thematic focus in relation to repetitional inter-sentence links all types can be found. But if we restrict our model to a bipartition of the sentence and the resulting four possible combinations which are theme to theme, rheme to theme, rheme to rheme and theme to rheme, I submit that one type is especially interesting here, namely rheme to theme:

> ... Mr Verver whose easy way with his millions had taxed to such small purpose, in the arrangements, the principle of *reciprocity*. The *reciprocity* with which ... (*The Golden Bowl*, p. 40, my italics)

This is a typical sentence transition in *The Golden Bowl* with rheme to theme repetitional link. Through repetition the material of the end of the sentence – left of the full stop – is taken up, focalizing the word 'reciprocity' through the addition of the definite article, to make it serve as the theme of the next sentence.[8]

This sentence-to-sentence link is typical of late James. It is my impression that it is more frequent in James than in other authors of the period both in absolute terms and in terms of the proportion between types of links and their positional importance.

In his article on the sentence structure of Henry James R.W. Short wrote that 'the meaning expands in a process of accretion'.[9] What Short claims about the growth of sentences essentially also holds true of the growth of texts. This is not so much in the sense that James's textual grammar differs very much in its arsenal of devices from that of other writers but rather in the total frequency of occurrence of the devices, in their profile of distribution and above all in their use. James's sentences, according to Short, grow 'organically'. This is true of his periods, paragraphs and texts too, and the device of rheme to theme repetitional sentence transition is the tell-tale sign.

The figure anadiplosis occurs very frequently in James's late style. The amount of repetition is sometimes extraordinary as in the following not too untypical paragraph from *The Wings of the Dove*:

> He *thought* of the two women, in their silence, at last – he at all events *thought* of Milly – as probably, for *her reasons*, now intensely *wishing* him to go. The cold breath of *her reasons* was, with everything else, in the air; but he didn't care for them any more than for her *wish* itself, and he would *stay in spite* of her, *stay in spite* of *odium*, *stay in spite* perhaps of some final experience that *would be*, for the pain in it, all but unbearable. That *would be* his one way, purified though he was, to mark his virtue beyond any mistake. It *would be* accepting the *disagreeable*, and the *disagreeable* would be *a proof*, *a proof* of his not having stayed for the *thing* – the *agreeable*, as it were – that *Kate had named*. *The thing that Kate had named* was not to have been the *odium* of *staying in spite* of hints. It was part of the *odium* as actual too that Kate was, for her comfort, just now well aloof.[10]

Carlo Izzo, quoting this paragraph in his article 'Henry James Scrittore Sintattico' and italicizing the phrases that I have also italicized comments:

> Snaturare se stessi completamente è tuttavia impresa difficile, forse impossibile. Nonostante le trafilature via via più sottili, rimane infatti a testimoniare della struttura prevalentemente logica di Henry James la ferrea concatenazione sintattica dello stile, chiaramente riconoscibile nella tendenza a ripetere di periodo in periodo, e anche di proposizione in proposizione – quasi anelli d'una catena – una o più parole del periodo o della proposizione che precedono.[11]

It can be argued whether a chain of linguistic units held together by repetition is a lifelike imitation of real conversation or not. Clara McIntyre in 1912 argued that James's sentences (i.e. his graphic sentences) are not lifelike because they are 'closed' sentences.

> Not merely adverbial phrases are treated in this way, but we find sentences made up of a string of loose words and phrases. 'They didn't, indeed, poor dears, know what, in that line – the line of futility – the real thing meant'. There seems to be some intention here of reproducing the natural rambling of conversation, the tacking on of thoughts as they develop, but it seems to me that Mr. James's parenthetical structure does not really reproduce conversation. We do string our thoughts together in a more or less rambling fashion, but most of us talk in loose sentences instead of periodic.[12]

It is true that James's sentences are 'closed' rather than open-ended. He moves his parenthetical material as far left in the sentence as he can and he prefers to end his periods with some word that definitely closes the sentence. As Mark Twain said about the Germans, he plunges into a sea of words and comes up at the other end with a verb in his mouth. It is as if he tried to present all his qualifications simultaneously rather than consecutively. This might suggest that there is a check in the 'organic' growth of the text at the break marked by a full stop.

But anadiplosis, which bridges commas in inter-phrasal transition, has its sister device rheme to theme repetitional sentence transition across the full stop (and very much across the indentation which marks a new paragraph). Thus there are actually no barriers for the 'organic' growth of James's text.[13]

James writes down a sentence, long-winded and tortuous, branching out in many directions, finally reaching some stage where, for rhythmic reasons at least, James finds it convenient to put down a full stop. But nothing is ever finished in James's world.[14] There is always some word, some idea at the end of the period to take up, repeat, make the theme of the next sentence and the stepping stone for an endless escalation of textual growth where rhemes reappear as themes in a regular alternation.

James's life was a perpetual tinkering with the past. He nursed the memory of his childhood and wrote several volumes of autobiography. He revised his works again and again; after serial publication for book publication, for American or English issues, for new editions. There were revisions of the revisions of the revisions of his books. He wrote long and elaborate prefaces for them in the New York Edition and it has been suggested that had he lived long enough he would have written prefaces to the prefaces.

There is always something in the past to improve upon or take up again; and thus in the creative process where what you have just written is the past, James advances through his text crabwise, with his eyes on the preceding word, phrase, sentence, period and paragraph (and even chapter – James frequently has end-linking across chapter borders). James's interest in revisions works not only in the usual sense of revisions of works. In the middle of a work he is revising the beginning by continuing the text, revising himself forwards in the text.[15]

This feature in James's style reflects an insecure world in which everything remains tentative. James is never certain that what he has put down will do after all. James does not merely hand his readers a *product*; he hands them a *process*.

What is the effect of a frequent use of rheme to theme repetitional end-linking?

Our first observation should concern the generic domicile of anadiplosis and rheme to theme repetitional sentence transition. Anadiplosis is a rather flashy, or 'purple' figure, and it easily becomes a mannerism. It is reserved by good rhetoricians for passages with a degree of sublimity. It is thus used for instance by religious speakers at prayer-meetings. The intensity-creating repetition is appropriate to the elevated subject; the sonorosity of repetition allows the speaker to include it as a device in an art which utilizes the resources of the human voice (chanting); if the preacher wishes to speak rhythmically anadiplosis very naturally becomes a unit-marker (the span between two instances of anadiplosis the span of a breath unit) and this often affects the textual grammar of the exposition; finally, as with set phrases in oral formulaic poetry (and speeches at prayer-meetings are often *ex tempore* improvisations) it gives the speaker a break of a second during which he can invent what to say next.

The last point is only one reason why James, pacing to and fro, dictating *The Wings of the Dove* in his sonorous voice, must have felt tempted to resort to anadiplosis and rheme to theme repetitional inter-sentence end-linking.[16] His personal sentiment was also involved to a great extent with the Minnylike Milly and her tragic fate. The intensity of interest in the subject sought an appropriately intensity-creating form of expression.[17]

This is intensity in relation to emotion but intensity in relation to ratiocination must also be taken into account. It has been tentatively suggested that a high proportion of rheme to theme linking is characteristic of rational exposition, of texts such as scholarly articles, textbooks, instructions, leading articles in newspapers etc. One would expect this since such texts are supposed to sort out relations and inter-connections rather than, for instance, narrate an event – in which case e.g. theme to theme repetition could be expected to be frequent. Thus rheme to theme repetitional end-linking brings with it some of the intense air of heavy ratiocination.

It 'sidetracks' in the progression of one's understanding of the text. This puts certain limits on the use of the device and makes certain demands on the reader. The reader has to follow the text in a fashion that is somehow 'linear' even if the line is a zig-zag one or resembles the figure of a series of steps because of constant side-branching. In a text with frequent theme to theme repetition (Hemingway) you can skip a sentence or paragraph and still be able to grasp the general meaning; in a text with frequent rheme to theme linking (James) you can not. An early reviewer of *The Golden Bowl* commented on this:

> This is why the success of his method depends on the significance and variety and, one might add, the humanity of the dramatic moments arising naturally from his theme, and why, too, being such a perilous and impossible author to 'skip', he is represented so often by professional skippers as an extremely involved and difficult writer. Yet, with the exception of an occasional sentence which has been asked to carry more than it conveniently can, Mr. James is, considering all he has to say, very easily followed by those who read him.
>
> But he is so exact, so continuous in his presentation of ideas, that often the omission of a single sentence may confuse the purpose of a page, and the omission of a page render unintelligible the dramatic moment – even if that be not missed too – on which an interpretative interest in the tale depends.[18]

This reviewer then goes on to use phrases such as 'the

atmosphere often so oppressively intense'[19] and 'intensity of dramatic action'[20] to describe the novel.

End-linking simply demands, on a prosaic technical level, great intensity of attention in reading and this is one reason why James is so often given epithets like 'enigmatic' and why his genius is so often called 'labyrinthine'.[21]

If the proportion of rheme to theme linking rises above a certain level the organic growth of the text becomes a cancerous growth. There are restrictions on the reduplication of the device as people know who have taken part in parlour games where you take turns, sentence by sentence, at telling a story. Otherwise the textual progression becomes stalled in perpetual side-branching as the sense is catapulted further towards the periphery by the centrifugal force of the iteration.

An example of absurdification through reiterated rheme to theme referential transition can be seen in the story 'The Head-Cold' in Eugène Ionesco's *The Bald Soprano*. A beautiful example of a story absurdified through iterated rheme to theme transition is Mark Twain's 'The Story of the Old Ram' from *Roughing It*. This is the way Jim Blaine begins his story:

'I don't reckon them times will ever come again. There never was a more bullier old ram than what he was. Grandfather fetched him from Illinois – got him of a man by the name of Yates – Bill Yates – maybe you might have heard of him; his father was a deacon – Baptist – and he was a rustler, too; a man had to get up ruther early to get the start of old Thankful Yates; it was him that put the Greens up to jining teams with my grandfather when he moved West. Seth Green was prob'ly the pick of the flock; he married a Wilkerson – Sarah Wilkerson – good cretur, she was – one of the likeliest heifers that was ever raised in old Stoddard, everybody said that knowed her. She could heft a bar'l of flour as easy as I can flirt a flapjack. And spin? Don't mention it! Independent? Humph! When Sile Hawkins come a-browsing around her, she let him know that for all his tin he couldn't trot in harness alongside of *her*. You see, Sile Hawkins was – no, it warn't Sile Hawkins, after all – it was a galoot by the name of Filkins – I disremember his first name; but he *was* a stump – come into pra'r meeting drunk, one night, hooraying for Nixon, becuz he thought it was a primary; and old deacon

Ferguson up and scooted him through the window and he lit
on old Miss Jefferson's head, poor old filly. She was a good
soul – had a glass eye and used to lend it to old Miss Wagner
that hadn't any, to receive company in; it warn't big enough,
and when Miss Wagner warn't noticing, it would get twisted
around in the socket, . . .'[22]

Maybe rheme to theme transition is not startlingly frequent here
but its role when it occurs is important. The repetitions (Sile
Hawkins – Sile Hawkins), reference (Miss Jefferson['s head] –
she), contracting hyponymy (Yates – Bill Yates; Greens – Seth
Green; Wilkerson – Sarah Wilkerson) are all thematizations (in
the case of the hyponymy, for instance, achieved through a
contrastive or clarifying addition) of a unit from the end of the
previous sentence. Thus these transitions serve as 'switch-
words'[23] that sidetrack Jim Blaine so that he never gets to the
point – his grandfather's old ram. This is a sick textual grammar
made use of by Twain who said that one trick of the American
humorous art is to string absurdities together.

Since the ridiculous, in this case too, lies so close to the
sublime, it was predictable that Max Beerbohm should pick on
rheme to theme transition in his parodies and exaggerate and
absurdify the device. In his book *The Later Style of Henry James*
Seymour Chatman used two parodies of James as a touchstone
to test the success of his analysis of James's style.[24] The two
parodies were 'The Guerdon' by Max Beerbohm and 'The
Enchanted Copse' by W.H.D. Rouse. The impression of any
James reader is that Beerbohm's is the more successful parody
and Chatman explains why with the aid of the occurrence or
non-appearance of the stylistic features he analyses in his book.
Chatman stays within sentence grammar in the main. Perhaps
we may note here, as an extension of Chatman's argument, that
his observations hold true on the textual level as well. This is the
beginning of 'The Guerdon':

That it hardly was, that it all bleakly and unbeguilingly *wasn't*
for 'the likes' of *him* – poor decent Stamfordham – to rap out
queries about the owner of the to him unknown and unsugges-
tive name that had, in these days, been thrust on him with
such a wealth of commendatory gesture, was precisely what
now, as he took, with his prepared list of New Year *colifichets*

and whatever, his way to the great gaudy palace, fairly flicked his cheek with the sense of his having never before so let himself in, as he ruefully phrased it, without letting *anything*, by the same token, out.

'*Anything*' was, after all, only another name for *the* thing. But he was to ask himself . . . (Chatman, p. 114; italics of *anything–anything* mine)

Both in 'The Guerdon' and in another brilliant parody, 'The Mote in the Middle Distance', Beerbohm caricatures James's textual strategy by overdoing rheme to theme linking. He takes particular care to provide links across paragraph boundaries. Hardly anything could evoke the Jamesian atmosphere better.

There are stylistic restraints on the iteration of rheme to theme links. It seems a reasonable hypothesis that of the different types of links the severest restraints should be on repetition (– since this is so frequent anyway). If James wanted to avoid becoming ridiculous; wanted to cut down on repetition but nevertheless keep rheme to theme linkage, he must choose some other type of link; some method for cheating and circumventing the stylistic constraints. Reference is one obvious alternative to choose, but I think it is particularly rewarding to look at James's use of synonymy and hyponymy in this light.[25]

James uses synonymy extensively. 'Elegant variation' plays an important part textually. Beerbohm realized this, and the word cat from the phrase 'letting the cat out of the bag' is reincarnated in several avatars as 'the imagined captive', 'the thing' and 'the bristling and now all but audibly scratching domestic pet'.

Even more important than synonymy is hyponymy. To proceed by some modification of contraction or expansion, still letting the continuation of the text grow out of the preceding part, affords James endless possibilities of rheme to theme linkage. In the conversations in *The Golden Bowl* the characters can always hyponymically take up the last words of the previous utterance and make exploration of yet another facet of the subject. This contributes greatly to intensity.

The enormously full-blown images and metaphors that mushroom in James's prose like some outlandish pagoda should also be considered in terms of text strategy. What is the most common variety of James's 'heightened cliché'[26] if not yet another trick to allow the organic growth of the text, and rheme

to theme transition? A dead cliché is taken up, stirred into life
and then blossoms and flowers through conversational exchange
after exchange; is returned to by means of synonymy (elegant
variation), hyponymy and antonymy. This contributes to intensity in several ways. Sometimes the image or metaphor exists in
order for some character to visualize feelings or ideas that cannot
be formulated verbally without the aid of metaphor. Different
aspects or ramifications of such a subject (it can for instance be a
taboo subject) can then be analyzed through a continuous
growth of the image or simile. The anarchic images are a
compositional device.

But intensity need not come only from seriousness. To take up
and improve on such images is typical of the sort of bantering
dialogue in which intensity comes from playfulness as between
two lovers. You then link your remark linguistically to the
previous remark of your partner, rather than going on to a new
phase in the conversation by introducing an utterance that is
more related to its referent than to its neighbour, because to do
this is an act of courtship. The importance of your partner is
implied in your act of rooting your remark in her (or his)
utterance (and usually in the rheme of it), rather than basing it
merely on its referent.

In his article, 'The Sentence Structure of Henry James' Short
said that conventional prose resembles a chain with its links and
that James's prose is different. However, even though one senses
that Short is right, the links are obviously there in James and
actually quite numerous. Carlo Izzo argues that the links are
what remains from normal prose after James's style has developed in a direction of its own.[27]

Maybe, paradoxically, a digression here is a short-cut to an
explanation of this apparent contradiction. James's style has
often been described as 'baroque'[28] and the more one looks into
it the more appropriate one finds this epithet. It is strange, for
instance, how many of Morris Croll's observations in his article
'The Baroque Style in Prose' could have been made about James
rather than about writers of the late sixteenth and seventeenth
centuries. There must somehow be a deep affinity of tempera-
ment between these writers and James.[29] Would not James have
felt some *Wahlverwandtschaft* with writers whose aim Croll
pictures as follows:

Expressiveness rather than formal beauty was the pretension of the new movement, as it is of every movement that calls itself modern. It disdained complacency, suavity, copiousness, emptiness, ease, and in avoiding these qualities sometimes obtained effects of contortion or obscurity, which it was not always willing to regard as faults. It preferred the forms that express the energy and labor of minds seeking the truth, not without dust and heat, to the forms that express a contented sense of the enjoyment and possession of it. In a single word, the motions of souls, not their states of rest, had become the themes of art.[30]

James chose to use fictional techniques that are often more concerned with *process* than *product* – many of his characteristic devices, such as misunderstandings in dialogues, testify to his preference for depicting unordered, immediate experience rather than the ordered and clear memory of that experience. In this respect James is perfectly 'baroque'.

Their purpose was to portray, not a thought, but a mind thinking, or, in Pascal's words, *la peinture de la pensée*. They knew that an idea separated from the act of experiencing it is not the idea that was experienced.[31]

Croll discusses two stylistic modes of the baroque period, the *période coupé* and the loose period. He states that one characteristic feature of the *période coupé* is the lack of connectives between its members.[32] It must be remembered here that Croll is discussing syntactic connectives in a narrow sense ('argument markers'). Because if we look at the examples quoted, we find a wealth of links between members, e.g:

The world that I regard is myself; it is the microcosm of my own frame that I cast mine eye on: for the other, I use it but like my globe, and turn it round sometimes for my recreation. (Browne, *Religio Medici*, II, 11)

There are numerous links here: 'The world that I regard is myself', and 'it is the microcosm of my own frame that I cast mine eye on' could be said to be linked in iconic repetition of the whole of the sentence-pattern, despite chiastic reversal between the last two analogous elements in the second instance (1. world

(a) – regard (b) – myself (c); 2. microcosm (a) – my own frame (c) – cast mine eye on (b)), the second member being a variation of the first. There is surface linking of many kinds: repetition *I*, *I*; *my*self, *my*; *the*, *the*; *is*, *is*; synonymy: world, *microcosm*; *regard*, *cast mine eye on*; *myself*, *own*. The rest of the period is linked to the first two members by a hidden link of repetition of *world*, invisible because of ellipsis ('for the other [world]'); repetition *I – I*; *my – my*; reference *world – it*; sameness of vocabulary: *world – microcosm – globe – turn round* etc.

The character of this prose is therefore a matter of the nature of the links and the use of the links rather than a question of absence or presence of links.[33] This fits very well with Croll's findings in connection with the second type, the 'loose period'. End-linking is present but used in a loose manner. Croll's description of the 'organic growth' of baroque curt periods echoes many comments on James's style with its growth of images and similes:

> Second, there is a characteristic order, a mode of progression, in a curt period that may be regarded either as a necessary consequence of its omission of connectives or as the causes and explanation of this. We may describe it best by observing that the first member is likely to be a self-contained and complete statement of the whole idea of the period. It is so because writers in this style like to avoid prearrangements and preparations; they begin, as Montaigne puts it, at *le dernier point*, the point aimed at. The first member therefore exhausts the mere fact of the idea; logically there is nothing more to say. But it does not exhaust its imaginative truth or the energy of its conception. It is followed, therefore, by other members, each with a new tone or emphasis, each expressing a new apprehension of the truth expressed in the first. We may describe the progress of a curt period, therefore, as a series of imaginative moments occurring in a logical pause or suspension. Or – to be less obscure – we may compare it with successive flashes of a jewel or prism as it is turned about on its axis and takes the light in different ways.[34]

Henry James's prose shows a consderable resemblance to the prose of these writers in its reliance on iconic links; links of repetition, synonymy, hyponymy; or cohesion achieved by staying within the same word-field, and in its occasional lack of more normal connectives ('argument markers').

The difficulty of the apparent contradiction between Short's comment and the frequency of end-linking in James can be resolved with the aid of Croll's study of the loose periods of the baroque style. Links exist (particularly end-linking) but the links are used in a loose way.

> The figure of a circle, therefore, is not a possible description of the form of loose period; it requires rather the metaphor of a chain, whose links join end to end. The 'linked' or 'trailing' period is, in fact, as we have observed, an appropriate name for it. But there is a special case for which this term might better be reserved, unless we should choose to invent a more specific one, such as 'end-linking', or 'terminal linking', to describe it. It is when a member depends, not upon the general idea, or the main word, of the preceding member, but upon its final word or phrase alone. And this is, in fact, a frequent, even a characteristic, kind of linking in certain authors, notably Sir Thomas Browne and his imitators.[35]

It is a characteristic of James's baroque style as well, and explains why Short's statement, which we feel intuitively to be correct, may at first seem false. The links are there but they are different and their use is different. James was attracted to this method because each unit in his prose is created in relation to those already in existence and particularly the last element of the last one. James resembles Montaigne who said: 'J'ecris volontiers sans project; le premier trait produit le second'.[36]

That rheme to theme linkage in James is not 'logical', i.e. that links are often between some element (often the last one) of the rheme of the first sentence and the beginning of the next rather than between their main word (or words) contributes even more to intensity than a more ordinary kind of rheme to theme linkage would have done. It slows down the reader further and if James discovered his whole fictional truth as he went along, the reader obviously has to follow exactly in his footsteps without being allowed any shortcuts, no matter how meandering a course James has actually followed.

I have refrained from quantification because it would explode the format of this chapter and I have also refrained from quoting, mainly because of hesitation in front of the *embarras de richesse* one is faced with – the whole text ought to be quoted. Just as a sample, though, let us look at a few lines of dialogue from Fanny's and the Colonel's conversation in Chapter XXXI:

'So it is, therefore, that I shall probably, by the closest possible shave, escape the penalty of my crimes.'
'You mean being held responsible.'
'I mean being held responsible. My advantage will be
5 that Maggie's such a trump.'
'Such a trump that, as you say, she'll stick to you.'
'Stick to me, on our understanding – stick to me. For our understanding's signed and sealed.' And to brood over it again was ever, for Mrs Assingham, to break out again
10 with exaltation. 'It's a grand, high compact. She has solemnly promised.'
'But in words – ?'
'Oh, yes, in words enough – since it's a matter of words. To keep up *her* lie so long as I keep up mine.'
15 'And what do you call "her" lie?'
'Why, the pretence that she believes me. Believes they're innocent.'
'She positively believes then they're guilty? She has arrived at that, she's really content with it, in the absence
20 of proof?'
It was here, each time, that Fanny Assingham most faltered; but always at last to get the matter, for her own sense, and with a long sigh, sufficiently straight. 'It isn't a question of belief or of proof, absent or present; it's in-
25 evitably, with her, a question of natural perception, of insurmountable feeling.' (431)

In line 3 Bob takes up Fanny's utterance in his question which begins with the disambiguation-request 'you mean'. This implies that what follows after 'you mean' will be a synonymic or hyponymic variant of the rheme of Fanny's utterance. The disambiguation-request links Bob's utterance not only to Fanny's preceding utterance but also to her next since Bob's guess should be confirmed or denied. The link 'penalty'–'being held responsible' should probably be regarded as expanding hyponymy. The alternation between pronouns such as 'you' and

'I' is also a link in dialogue, the pronouns having the same referent if they alternate in a certain way.

Fanny confirms his guess by a word-for-word repetition which is the most emphatic form of affirmation. 'Escape' has been stored up until now and the sense of that word is now enlarged upon in Fanny's bringing in 'My advantage ...'. 'Advantage' in the theme of Fanny's sentence is a faint link to the rheme of her first statement. There is a synonymic pronominal link 'I'–'my' with the first sentence in Fanny's utterance.

Fanny's rheme in line 5 '... Maggie's such a trump' is probably an outgrowth of 'advantage' in the theme. 'Advantage' sounds like a term from some game, and 'trump' certainly is.[37]

In lines 5–7 we find two typical cases of repetitional end-linking: '... Maggie's *such a trump*'. '*Such a trump* that ...' and '... she'll *stick to* you'. '*Stick to* me on ...'. 'Stick to me' is repeated again but the real rheme of line 7 is 'our understanding' and therefore when Fanny goes on: 'For our understanding's' there is again rheme to theme repetitional linking. The 'it' in James's intrusion is textually vague; it could be a case of theme to theme referential linking but then James may have meant Mrs Assingham brooding over the fact of its being signed and sealed; or both of these.

'It's a grand, high compact' in line 10 could be regarded as being iconically linked with 'our understanding's signed and sealed' apart from being linked referentially theme to theme (*'our understanding*'s–'*it*'s) and rheme to rheme (in a growth of the image).

In line 13 Fanny's 'words' repeats 'words' in Bob's question, and 'words' is in turn repeated by Fanny (rheme to rheme). The sentence ending 'promised' in line 11 was elliptical and Fanny now goes on to fill it in. In line 15 Bob again asks a disambiguation-question which again, by definition, is linked to the preceding and the following sentence. 'The pretence that she believes me' is therefore expanding hyponymy of ' "her" lie'.

Lines 15 and 16 are linked through rheme to theme synonymy *lie–pretence* and rheme to theme synonymy '*her*'–*she* and theme to rheme synonymy *you–me*. Fanny's two sentences in lines 16–17 again have end-linking rheme to theme repetitional sentence transition ('believes me' – '*Believes* they're ...').

In line 18 there is repetition of 'she' from line 16, and repetition of *believes* and *they're*, and antonymy (innocent–guilty).

Bob's second sentence has theme to theme pronominal repetition *she–she* and rheme to rheme reference *they're guilty–that*. His third sentence again has theme to theme pronominal repetition (*she–she's*), rheme to rheme reference (*that–it* – or should this be regarded as synonymy?). There is some mild iconic linkage between Bob's sentences in relation to each other and to Fanny's preceding sentence. Bob's final word 'proof' again ends his utterance with a sense of ellipsis.

James's intrusion in line 21 is linked referentially to Bob's last rheme, 'here'. Fanny's analysis beginning in line 23 (and going on far beyond our quotation) is linked to Bob's remark with an abundance of links of repetition and hyponymy, and when she continues her speculative flights of imagination the textual links become such an intricate interlacement that to sort them out here would demand too much space. Let us instead look at the beginning of the passage again with all the clear cases of end-linking italicized.

> 'So it is, therefore, that I shall probably, by the closest possible shave, escape the penalty of my crimes.'
> 'You *mean being held responsible*.'
> 'I *mean being held responsible*. My advantage will be that
> 5 Maggie's *such a trump*.'
> '*Such a trump* that, as you say, she'll *stick to* you.'
> '*Stick to* me, on *our understanding* – stick to me. For *our* understanding's signed and sealed.' And to brood over it again was ever, for Mrs Assingham, to break out again
> 10 with exaltation. 'It's a grand, high compact. She has solemnly promised.'
> 'But *in words* – ?'
> 'Oh, yes, *in words* enough – since it's a matter of words. To keep up *her lie* so long as I keep up mine.'
> 15 'And what do you call *"her" lie?*'
> 'Why, the pretence that she *believes* me. *Believes* they're innocent.'

Actually the exaggerated use of the end-linking device does not look quite as strange in a dialogue as one might have thought. A real conversation, with a degree of intensity, might conceivably sound like this.

Part of the effect of intensity is undoubtedly created by the end-linking device. It testifies to the intense attention that the participants in the dialogue pay to the utterances of their partners. Ultimately it also testifies to the insecurity of James's fictional world – a world in which the inability to regard anything as finished or certain is reflected in the textual grammar in the device of end-linking.

3 Emphatic Affirmation

'The word "yes" is not in their vocabulary' wrote an angry critic, complaining about the peculiar answers to yes/no questions that the characters in *The Golden Bowl* are in the habit of giving each other in their dialogues. Although, literally speaking, the word 'yes' does occur, it is nevertheless quite correct that the form of affirmative answers in the dialogue is unusual.[1] The type of affirmation that the participants in the dialogues of *The Golden Bowl* prefer is actually yet another intensity-creating device.

There are several ways of expressing affirmation in English, ranging from the simple 'yes' to a word for word repetition of most elements in the preceding question – all of them if it is made interrogative by intonation alone and has, in fact, the same surface form as if it were affirmative. It is generally accepted that the latter type of affirmation is more emphatic. It is therefore used in ritual affirmation, as for instance when the American president is sworn in. He takes his oath not merely answering the master of ceremonies with an affirmative 'yes' or 'I do' but by actually repeating word for word the sentences spoken by the master of ceremonies (with certain necessary changes of pronouns etc.). The form of the oath implies that the new president undertakes his promise not only in the abstract or as a vague whole, but fully conscious of each single part ot it. That the details make up a list of items is symbolized in the rite by a rising intonation at the end of each unit (except the last).

In James too we may imagine that the word-for-word repetitions are meant to be thought of as having a strong emphasis on each word. Often the word-for-word repetition goes to prodigious lengths:

> Fanny Assingham weighed it. 'Under her direct appeal for the truth?'
> 'Under her direct appeal for the truth.'
> 'Her appeal to his honour?'
> 'Her appeal to his honour. That's my point.'

84

Fanny Assingham braved it. 'For the truth as from him to *her*?'

'From him to anyone.'

Mrs Assingham's face lighted. 'He'll simply, he'll insistently have lied?'

Maggie brought it out roundly. 'He'll simply, he'll insistently have lied.' (493)

When James creates intensity through repetition in emphatic affirmation his scenes often become similar to various types of ritual affirmation. It is not surprising then that he uses some of the formulae of such occasions, as in the reference to 'honour' in the quotation above. The 'upon-my-honour'-formula is used also in Maggie's and Charlotte's scene on the terrace in Chapter XXXVI when Maggie realizes what an enormous power lying and dissembling give her.

It was only a question of not, by a hair's breadth, deflecting into the truth. So, supremely, was she braced. 'You must take it from me that your anxiety rests quite on a misconception. You must take it from me that I've never at any moment fancied I could suffer by you.' And, marvellously, she kept it up – not only kept it up, but improved on it. 'You must take it from me that I've never thought of you but as beautiful, wonderful and good. Which is all, I think, that you can possibly ask.'

Charlotte held her a moment longer: she needed – not then to have appeared only tactless – the last word. 'It's much more, my dear, than I dreamed of asking. I only wanted your denial.'

'Well then, you have it.'

'Upon your honour?'

'Upon my honour.'

And she made a point even, our young woman, of not turning away. Her grip of her shawl had loosened – she had let it fall behind her; but she stood there for anything more and till the weight should be lifted. With which she saw soon enough what more was to come. She saw it in Charlotte's face, and felt it make between them, in the air, a chill that completed the coldness of their conscious perjury. 'Will you kiss me on it then?' (517–8)

Our sense of the deception is made intense because the formula 'upon my honour' is used and because of the ceremonial kiss. It is the supreme test of a lie whether it can stand up under an appeal to one's honour. And if you can use a kiss to seal a falsehood (James uses the word 'perjury') you are already competing in the same league as Judas, one of the greatest liars and traitors of literary history, who betrayed Jesus with a kiss.

James refers to ritual affirmation in a scene between the Assinghams too. The dialogue between Fanny and Bob is sometimes so formalized that James feels slightly embarrassed and uses some self-parody to hide his embarrassment. Often the role of Bob is merely to draw Fanny out, to grunt during the proper pauses, to ask 'echo questions' and essentially to say things that allow what is in fact her monologue to continue. The usual division of roles is for Fanny to boss her husband about, and for the Colonel to defer to his wife, though often under protest or with resigned derision. It is during a passage in which Fanny decides on a policy of wilful self-deception and pretended ignorance that James likens Bob's affirmative answer to the signing of a deed or to the giving of a watchword.

> 'Nothing – in spite of everything – *will* happen. Nothing *has* happened. Nothing *is* happening.'
> He looked a trifle disappointed. 'I see. For *us*.'
> 'For us. For whom else?' And he was to feel indeed how she wished him to understand it. 'We know nothing on earth –!' It was an undertaking he must sign.
> So he wrote, as it were, his name. 'We know nothing on earth.' It was like the soldiers' watchword at night.
> 'We're as innocent,' she went on in the same way, 'as babes.' (330)

The type of emphatic affirmation which consists of a word-for-word repetition of the previous utterance in the dialogue in *The Golden Bowl* has something of the same intensity as affirmation in certain rituals and James's use of formulae like 'upon my honour' and his reference to ceremonies such as signing an undertaking or giving a watcword reflect the nature of these affirmative answers.

Before we go on to study in detail some passages from *The*

Golden Bowl that are particularly rich in emphatic affirmation it may be appropriate to explain why it is more rewarding to study the language of scenes rather than, for instance, the linguistic idiosyncrasies of each character.

Style exists in relation to a number of things. We talk about the style of a person, the style of a period, a sex, an age-group, a social class etc., but also of a genre or a situation. Several of these normally overlap, but sometimes certain demands of a specific case can make one of them dominate. If an author's art is caricature or any form of literature that traditionally uses 'flat' characters, then style in relation to the individual will be an important aspect. The author will use style for characterization.

But there are cases where the situation determines the style and individual differences are completely overshadowed. In certain situations certain 'utteremes' are appropriate and entirely predictable. When the American president is sworn in, for instance, the verbal form of his oath is completely determined by the situation; and his age, sex, social class etc. are totally irrelevant. In other words, on certain occasions, under certain circumstances, everyone talks alike.

A persistent theme in the criticism of James's late works is that all his characters talk alike. 'One very noticeable thing in the later books of Mr James is that all his people talk alike', wrote Clara McIntyre in 1912.[2] This is true, but one should observe that the reason for it is not only James's inability to vary his style – though that certainly comes into it – but also the demands of the fiction he is trying to write.[3] In his early and middle period James is still quite interested in characterization and it is therefore possible to study his dialogues in the works of this period with an eye to style in relation to individuals. One critic, for example, comments on the frequency of 'repeater questions' as a contribution to the characterization of Ralph Touchett in *The Portrait of a Lady*.[4] In the late works such things are pushed into the background because now it is no longer individuals but situations that determine the style. Thus intensity-creating emphatic affirmation is typical not of persons but of scenes in *The Golden Bowl* and whoever takes part in a scene which demands emphatic affirmation will also use it.

Between *The Portrait of a Lady* and *The Golden Bowl* came James's attempts to write for the stage in the early nineties. Though James produced only second-rate plays, these years nevertheless

nevertheless had a considerable influence on his later art. His narrative became scenic and a result of this is the shift from using style mainly in relation to people to using style mainly in relation to occasions. In *The Golden Bowl* the use of emphatic affirmation is therefore a context-bound rather than a character-bound phenomenon.

Whenever a scene becomes charged with dramatic intensity in *The Golden Bowl* emphatic affirmation irresistibly creeps into the verbal behaviour of whoever takes part in the conversations. And, as we know, such scenes recur at very regular intervals throughout the novel.

The first comes very early, at the end of Chapter II when the Prince, visiting Fanny Assingham, learns that Charlotte Stant is in London. Fanny is scared; the Prince tries to hide his excitement and the air is heavy with portent. Earlier in the chapter there have already been some conversational interchanges with emphatic affirmation in embryonic form, e.g. in the form of expanding hyponymy, i.e. with an affirmative repetition of the key-word of the preceding utterance, plus a qualification usually adverbial:

> 'Do you mean you're afraid?' his hostess had amusedly asked.
> 'Terribly afraid.' (56)

Also:

> 'Don't you really after all feel,' she added while nothing came from him – aren't you conscious every minute of the perfection of the creature of whom I've put you into possession?'
> 'Every minute – gratefully conscious. But that's exactly ...
> (58)

In these cases it is the Prince who gives the affirmative answers. The inflationary shift in methods of affirmation that occurs during conversational scenes of intensity in *The Golden Bowl* means that special emphatic insistence is demanded for strong affirmation. The Prince's answers are too weak and therefore actually come over as evasion, which is demonstrated in the second quotation by the fact that when the Prince goes on he uses the word 'but', which is an adversative marker suitable for bringing the drift of one's remark back on the right course after a momentary concession.

In this scene as elsewhere, however, the person who really engages in evasion is Fanny. One of her methods is to use what I have called the 'two-person sentence',[5] i.e. the typically Jamesian device of one person interrupting and completing another's remark – completing it in a way which is not necessarily that intended by the speaker who started it. The Prince has complained that there is something he lacks – the moral sense:

> 'I should be interested,' she presently remarked, 'to see some sense *you* don't possess.'
> Well, he produced one on the spot. 'The moral, dear Mrs Assingham. I mean, always, as you others consider it. I've of course something that in our poor dear backward old Rome sufficiently passes for it. But it's no more like yours than the tortuous stone staircase – half-ruined into the bargain! – in some castle of our *quattrocento* is like the "lightning elevator" in one of Mr Verver's fifteen-storey buildings. Your moral sense works by steam – it sends you up like a rocket. Ours is slow and steep and unlighted, with so many of the steps missing that – well, that it's as short, in almost any case, to turn round and come down again.'
> 'Trusting,' Mrs Assingham smiled, 'to get up some other way?'
> 'Yes – or not to have to get up at all. However,' he added, 'I told you that at the beginning.'
> 'Machiavelli!' she simply exclaimed. (60)

This exchange is a good demonstration of how the inflationary shift in methods of affirmation in *The Golden Bowl* has reduced the word 'yes' to a very insignificant role. The word 'yes' is almost invariably only the lead-in to an evasion or else a soft, seemingly affirmative beginning to what is in fact a negation. The Prince's 'Yes', coming after Fanny's addition to his utterance, is in fact a 'no'.

At the end of the chapter we get into the first of those scenes, so typical throughout the novel, in which the participants in a dialogue fall into the ritual of emphatic affirmation.

> 'One admires her if one doesn't happen not to. So, as well,

one criticises her.'
   'Ah, that's not fair!' said the Prince.
   'To criticise her? Then there you are! You're answered.'
   'I'm answered.' (67)

The Prince, however, immediately adds that there may be better things to be done with Miss Stant than to criticize her. Fanny admonishes him to keep out of it.

> Mrs Assingham, however, made no more of this, having before anything else, apparently, a scruple about the tone she had just used. 'I quite understand, of course, that, given her great friendship with Maggie, she should have wanted to be present. She has acted impulsively – but she has acted generously.'
>   'She has acted beautifully,' said the Prince. (ibid.)

This affirmative exchange, involving repetition ('She has acted . . .' – 'she has acted') and synonymy or hyponymy ('generously' – 'beautifully') is typical of a very large portion of Jamesian conversational exchanges in that it exemplifies the close inter-connection of intensity and ambiguity. Such vague words as 'beautifully' have hardly any stable meaning at all in James. Instead they function in his prose as blanks which the readers as well as the characters have to give a specific meaning in each specific occurrence. The words have lost their paradigmatic stability; they exist only in the syntagmatic relation and it is the context which in each case determines their meaning. In order to find the meaning of these words we are forced to scrutinize the context in each case and thus these words contribute greatly to intensity by enhancing the importance of their context.
   What is the context in this case? Charlotte has ominously returned on the eve of the Prince's marriage and Fanny is scared. The whole chapter bristles with 'foretelling' and one of James's methods of giving dramatic intensity to the vague forebodings is the device of emphatic affirmation. This is how the conversation continues:

> 'I say "generously" because I mean she hasn't in any way, counted the cost. She'll have it to count, in a manner, now,' his hostess continued. 'But that doesn't matter.'

He could see how little. 'You'll look after her.'
'I'll look after her.'
'So it's all right.'
'It's all right,' said Mrs Assingham.
'Then why are you troubled?'
I pulled her up – but only for a minute. 'I'm not – any more than you.' (67–8)

On the surface of it the purpose of emphatic affirmation is to remove any doubts that one's interlocutor or interlocutress may have. It is, however, in the nature of things that the contexts in which the strongest stylistic measures are used are also at the same time those where they are most needed, and a study of this quotation shows how little the two cases of emphatic affirmative sentence repetition contribute to certainty and how much, on the contrary, they help to create uncertainty.

To begin with we may note that the characteristic form of this type of conversational exchange is for person A (in this case the Prince) to make a guess as to what person B (Fanny) thinks ('You'll look after her'), and for person B then to affirm that the guess was correct by giving a word-for-word affirmative repetition.[6]

Now despite the affirmation it is to be observed that guessing is not one of the cognitive methods that best contribute to epistemological certainty. It is also to be observed that person A's guess is interrogative (though this is not typographically signalled by a question-mark in this case), i.e. it is an *invitation* to person B to affirm something, and there may be many other reasons for acting on an invitation than a desire to impartially state whether the guess was correct or not – in fact throughout *The Golden Bowl* these invitations are mostly issued when there is a need to have pretended or real belief in a falsehood confirmed.

The quotation ends with a case of Jamesian equivocation. Fanny says she is no more troubled than the Prince, which of course makes little sense until we arrive at an estimate of how troubled *he* may be. The context suggests that he may be very troubled indeed, and actually the passage itself, and the very device of emphatic affirmation, suggest it as well.

It is inevitable that intensity and ambiguity should be linked. In a sense intensity and ambiguity are merely different sides of the same coin. In an uncertain world, where ambiguity reigns supreme, if anything is to be affirmed at all it has to be affirmed with special intensity and insistence. Thus James's use of the device of emphatic affirmation is merely complementary to his use of ambiguity. The more ambiguity there is, the bigger will be the need for intensity and insistence in those cases in which ambiguity is denied.

This, however, is not the end of the matter. It is precisely in those situations in life where there is most uncertainty that stylistic devices of affirmative insistence are used. They are used to allay doubts and uncertainties. But insofar as they fail in their task these devices themselves become signals of unreliability for the suspicious. It is a well-known development in language that words expressing emphatic insistence tend to degenerate. Words that originally meant 'at once' come to mean 'soon' or 'later'. Words that originally meant 'with absolute certainty' come to mean 'maybe' etc. Similarly over-indulgence in emphatic affirmation becomes an unreliability-signal to the suspicious eye and ear; a case of over-much protesting. Whatever needs such insistent, intense, emphatic affirmation must be suspect for that very reason, and thus what should have been the device *par excellence* to counteract uncertainty or ambiguity may actually in the end aid it. Emphatic affirmation is basically meant to induce stability but excessive use of it defeats its own purpose and reintroduces lability; a lability moreover which is worse than before. And in *The Golden Bowl* the device of emphatic affirmation is frequently not only used but prodigiously over-used, which ultimately contributes further to ambiguity.

It is not only in Chapter II that emphatic affirmative repetition is used for foretelling. At the end of Chapter III the Prince and Charlotte, in Fanny's presence, arrange for their Bloomsbury ramble, under the pretext of finding Maggie a wedding present, and the ominousness of the plan is enhanced by a double repetition (by the Prince and by Fanny) of Charlotte's phrase that the Prince must find the hour, and by an extravagant amount of reported laughter in the delivery of these remarks – which is, again, yet another Jamesian ambiguity-signal.

A case of emphatic affirmation in the conversation in Chapter IV between Fanny and the Colonel establishes ambiguity as to how intimate the Prince and Charlotte have been in the past. Has Charlotte been Amerigo's mistress?

'She might have been anything she liked – except his wife.'
'But she wasn't,' said the Colonel very smokingly.
'She wasn't,' Mrs Assingham echoed.
The echo, not loud but deep, filled for a little the room. (90)

Whatever this is meant to tell (or not tell) the reader about Charlotte's and Amerigo's relationship in the past it is obvious what it suggests about their relationship in the future. If the existence of a liaison in the past is possible enough to be an ambiguous point it is obvious that a liaison in the future will need very little help to come into existence.

The grand finale of Part One is the intensely dramatic scene in Chapter VI in which the Prince and Charlotte, at the antiquario's shop, discuss their relationship and its future in terms that ostensibly refer to the real, material golden bowl, but in reality to something else. Since Maggie and her present is only a pretext the conversation quickly finds its real subject: themselves. Charlotte can see nothing that would do for a present to Maggie.

'There's nothing here she could wear.'
It was only after a moment that her companion rejoined. 'Is there anything – do you think – that you could?'
It made her just start. She didn't, at all events, look at the objects; she but looked for an instant very directly at him. 'No.' (117)

Since the case with negation in *The Golden Bowl* is to a large extent similar to that of affirmation this brutal, simple, short 'No' has considerable dramatic force. It is with the 'no's as it is with the 'yes'es, that, being in general so rare, when they *do* occur they are all the more expressive.

The Prince wanted to give Charlotte a present as a small *ricordo*, which gives Charlotte the chance to make her refusal a pretext to get closer still to the real subject; their relationship with each other. It would be a *ricordo* of nothing, since they have not as yet shared any experience worth commemorating. Charlotte's refusal, expressed in a 'No' is paralleled soon after by the Prince's refusal of Charlotte's gift.

He had lifted the lid of his box and he looked into it hard.

'Do you mean by that then that you would be free – ?'
' "Free" – ?'
'To offer me something?'
This gave her a longer pause, and when she spoke again she
might have seemed, oddly, to be addressing the dealer.
'Would you allow me – ?'
'No,' said the Prince into his little box.
'You wouldn't accept it from me?'
'No,' he repeated in the same way. (118)

Immediately afterwards comes an exchange where the context of
an ambiguous pronominal reference is made dramatic by
emphatic affirmation:

> 'Well, that's, at any rate,' she returned, 'my own affair. But
> it won't do?'
> 'It won't do, *cara mia.*'
> 'It's impossible?'
> 'It's impossible.' (ibid.)

Superficially the 'it' here refers to his accepting a present from
her or her accepting a present from him, but the real referent is
of course their relationship. The present they would like to give
each other, were it not impossible, would be, precisely, each
other.
   Charlotte makes the event of their excursion important by
insisting that it is to be kept secret, that Maggie is not to know.
This is important, and, as usual, some repetitional affirmation
helps in creating the sense of importance:

> 'If I should pin one of these things on for you would it be, to
> your mind, that I might go home and show it to Maggie as
> your present?'
> . . .
>   Why in the world not?'
> 'Because – on our basis – it would be impossible to give her
> an account of the pretext.'
> 'The pretext – ?' He wondered.
> 'The occasion. This ramble that we shall have had together
> and that we're not to speak of.'
> 'Oh yes,' he said after a moment – 'I remember we're not to

speak of it.'

'That of course you're pledged to. And the thing, you see, goes with the other. So you don't insist.'

He had again, at random, laid back his trinket; with which he quite turned to her, a little wearily at last – even a little impatiently. 'I don't insist.' (119)

One function of affirmative repetition is to draw the reader's attention to important ambiguities in the text. There is one very typical exchange of this kind later on in the chapter when Charlotte reports the price of the golden bowl to the Prince.

'Is he a rascal?' Charlotte asked. 'His price is so moderate.' She waited but a moment. 'Five pounds. Really so little.'

He continued to look at her. 'Five pounds?'

'Five pounds.'

He might have been doubting her word, but he was only, it appeared, gathering emphasis. (125)

We know that Charlotte is lying here since we have just witnessed her dialogue with the shopkeeper in which the price was given as fifteen pounds. The intensity-creating repetition, aided by one of James's innumerable stares ('He continued to look at her' – these ubiquitous stares are also intensity and ambiguity signals), invites us to consider the significance of Charlotte's lie. Is she cheapening herself? Is she acting on the shopman's advice that 'one can sometimes afford for a present more than one can afford for one's self'. (122) and showing her willingness to pay more than she can afford in order to be able to give Amerigo a present?

Such questions make the bowl and the characters' relation to it important, which was James's purpose, since the bowl is the central symbol of the novel. The bowl is supposed to have a crack and this crack is supposed to be symbolic of an imperfection in the relationship between some of the characters. But which characters? Charlotte and Amerigo? Amerigo and Maggie? Charlotte and Maggie? All three? (Later on in the novel when Maggie buys the golden bowl for her father, it becomes obvious that we can also add the remaining pair, Maggie and Adam, to the list – maybe even Charlotte–Maggie and Adam-Amerigo as well).

The importance of the role of the golden bowl, in symbolizing a personal relationship with a flaw, is celebrated with a veritable orgy of emphatic affirmation:

> 'The danger – I see – is because you're superstitious.'
> '*Per Dio*, I'm superstitious! A crack is a crack – and an omen's an omen.'
> 'You'd be afraid – ?'
> '*Per Bacco!*'
> 'For your happiness?'
> 'For my happiness.'
> 'For your safety?'
> 'For my safety.'
> She just paused. 'For your marriage?'
> 'For my marriage. For everything.' (125–6)

The Prince will do nothing that could endanger his marriage. Charlotte's designs upon him at the moment have a flaw, a crack, and that is not to the Prince's liking:

> 'Anything you consent to accept from me –' But he paused.
> 'Well?'
> 'Well, shall be perfect.' (126)

The Prince then urges Charlotte to marry and the whole scenario is revealed – they are to carry on and consummate their relationship after she has married:

> Before she did so, however, she said what had been gathering while she waited. 'Well, I would marry, I think, to have something from you in all freedom.' (127)

The beginning of Part Second is devoted to James's remaining task in peopling the stage, mainly getting Charlotte married to Adam. Charlotte's final promise to marry him features an exchange involving emphatic affirmation:

> 'Will you promise me then to be at peace?'
> She looked, while she debated, at his admirable present. 'I promise you.'
> 'Quite for ever?'

'Quite for ever.'

'Remember,' he went on, to justify his demand, 'remember that in wiring you she'll naturally speak even more for her husband than she has done in wiring me.' (211)

The interest of this exchange lies in the fact that it is only on condition that their marriage is sanctioned by Maggie (i.e. in reality by the Prince) that Charlotte will accept Adam. The crucial point in Adam's courtship, Charlotte's ritual promise, therefore comes in a context where not only Adam but above all Amerigo (through Maggie; and later, by his telegram, directly) is involved.

The use of emphatic affirmation in connection with a promise reveals a significant aspect of the nature of the device. It links emphatic affirmation to a very important type of utterance; to the so-called performatives.[7] In a promise the linguistic act, speaking or writing, is very important, because it is precisely that act which constitutes the promise. In this kind of use of language it could be said that language is supposed to govern the world directly and this makes such use of language outstandingly important.

It is a matter of 'how to do things with words' which takes us right to the centre of everything that is important and essential, as well as strange and problematical, in James's psychology and philosophy. In the universe of James's fiction the range and the limitations of the power of language over reality is one of the most central questions of all. It is worthwhile to look a little more closely into the question of the way 'things are done with words' in James, and a study of the device of emphatic affirmation provides as good a starting point as any. We shall do so in Chapter 4.

First let us complete our survey of the scenes in *The Golden Bowl* in which emphatic affirmation plays an important role.

The drama of the scene which in Chapter XVIII leads up to Amerigo's and Charlotte's kiss is heightened by some emphatic affirmation though not very extensively. It is symptomatic that emphatic affirmation abounds above all in those scenes where the drama is epistemological in nature: where a discovery has been made; where a betrayal is being perpetrated; where a shared lie is collectively upheld; where a character is desperately trying to make out reality etc. In the scene in Chapter XVIII excitement is emotional rather than intellectual which does not call for such extensive use of emphatic affirmation.

Nevertheless the key-line in the dialogue, the line which really determined things for Charlotte and Amerigo, *is* emphatically repeated.

> 'They feel a confidence,' the Prince observed.
> He had indeed said it for her. 'They feel a confidence.' (259)

Maggie and Adam are ripe to be betrayed, and this is the precise point at which the Prince and Charlotte decide to act.

Before acting, however, a beautiful name, or a pleasant formula, has to be found for the act and the Prince and Charlotte agree on a splendid description of their future behaviour as their 'conscious care' (264) which is expanded to the typical Jamesian ambiguous word 'wonderful' (ibid.), which is reincarnated synonymically in the Prince's affirmation as 'beautiful' (ibid.) and finally, immediately before the kiss, in the emphatically repeated, blasphemous 'sacred'.

> 'It's sacred,' he said at last.
> 'It's sacred,' she breathed back to him. They vowed it, gave it out and took it in, drawn, by their intensity, more closely together. Then of a sudden, through this tightened circle, as at the issue of a narrow strait into the sea beyond, everything broke up, broke down, gave way, melted and mingled. Their lips sought their lips, their pressure their response and their response their pressure; with a violence that had sighed itself the next moment to the longest and deepest of stillnesses they passionately sealed their pledge. (ibid.)

A nice name for something that without the cosmetic power of language might appear less nice is essential to characters in James's world. This device, which could be called the 'finding a formula'-syndrome, is also an aspect of the problem of how far it is possible to 'do things with words' and we shall return to the question in the next chapter.

By the fire-place in the dining-room at Matcham, in Chapter XXI, Amerigo and Charlotte renew their pledge, this time only verbally, but with some use of emphatic repetition:

> 'We hang, essentially, together.'

Well, the Prince candidly allowed she did bring it home to
him. Every way it worked out. 'Yes, I see. We hang,
essentially, together.'

His friend had a shrug – a shrug that had a grace, '*Cosa
volete?*' The effect, beautifully, nobly, was more than Roman,
'Ah, beyond doubt, it's a case.'

He stood looking at her. 'It's a case. There can't,' he said,
'have been many.'

'Perhaps never, never, never any other. That,' she smiled, 'I
confess I should like to think. Only ours.'

'Only ours – most probably. *Speriamo.*' To which, as after
hushed connections, he presently added: 'Poor Fanny!' (287–
8)

There is also some verbal fencing involving repetition when the
pair, at the end of the chapter, dismiss Mrs Assingham who has
desperately tried to dissuade them from 'staying to luncheon'
and tried to make them take the same train as she back to
London. Fanny threatens to go to Maggie and Adam:

'I'll go to our friends then – I'll ask for luncheon. I'll tell
them when to expect you.'

'That will be charming. Say we're all right.'

'All right – precisely. I can't say more,' Mrs Assingham
smiled.

'No doubt.' But he considered, as for the possible importance of it. 'Neither can you, by what I seem to feel, say less.'

'Oh, I *won't* say less!' (292)

A little later:

'I think I'll send home my maid from Euston,' she was then
prepared to amend, 'and go to Eaton Square straight. So you
can be easy.'

'Oh, I think we're easy,' the Prince returned. 'Be sure to *say*,
at any rate, that we're bearing up.'

'You're bearing up – good. And Charlotte returns to
dinner?'

'To dinner. We're not likely, I think, to make another night
away.'

'Well then, I wish you at least a pleasant day.'

'Oh,' he laughed as they separated, 'we shall do our best for it!' (ibid.)

Fanny's and the Colonel's conversation in Chapter XXIV displays a fair number of instances of emphatic repetition, usually in rather short conversational units, e.g:

'And then both of them together to Maggie.'
'To Maggie?' he wonderingly echoed.
'To Maggie.' (324)

The Colonel took it in. 'Then she's a little heroine.'
'Rather – she's a little heroine.' (327)

'It's awfully quaint.'
'Of course it's awfully quaint!' (ibid.)

'Like a Prince?'
'Like a Prince.' (329)

He looked a trifle disappointed. 'I see. For *us*.'
'For us. For whom else?' And he was to feel indeed how she wished him to understand it. 'We know nothing on earth – !' It was an undertaking he must sign.
So he wrote, as it were, his name. 'We know nothing on earth.' It was like the soldiers' watchword at night. (330)

'Absolute idiots then?'
'Absolute idiots.' (ibid.)

Such cases of emphatic affirmation as these may seem slight, but their role in Fanny's exposition is not quite devoid of significance. The dialogues between Fanny and the Colonel are essentially Fanny's monologues, and the Colonel often confines his affirmation to echoes or derisive remarks, when he is not actually providing a running commentary on an alternative – a cruder and more realistic – possibility of interpretation. Fanny is never bothered by such contradictions, but there are stages in her exposition when she feels her own doubts rise and these are precisely the occasions when the Colonel's assent is needed so that her doubts can be dismissed. Her fears are allayed with the aid of emphatic affirmation, the ritual that soothes and half-convinces.

In Book Second, 'The Princess', James carries on the habit of the first book of giving special weight to critical points in the narrative by using emphatic affirmation. There is some use of the device in Chapter XXVII when Maggie tries to separate the lovers by proposing the 'compromise set' (Amerigo–Adam; Maggie–Charlotte), e.g:

> 'That you think it would be so charming?'
> 'That I think it would be so charming.' (382–3)

and in Chapter XXIX when Maggie and Adam have their long and serious talk:

> 'Well, I don't know. We get nothing but the fun, do we?'
> 'No,' she had hastened to declare; 'we certainly get nothing but the fun.'
> 'We do it all,' he had remarked, 'so beautifully.'
> 'We do it all so beautifully.' (401)

The reader should by now be so tuned into the function of emphatic affirmation as to realize not only what it means when it does occur, but also realize what the significance is if it fails to occur in a context where it should have occurred. One such context is Chapter XXX and Fanny's lying denial of a knowledge of Amerigo's and Charlotte's intrigue:

> 'What your idea imputes is a criminal intrigue carried on, from day to day, amid perfect trust and sympathy, not only under your eyes, but under your father's. That's an idea it's impossible for me for a moment to entertain.'
> 'Ah, there you are then! It's exactly what I wanted from you.'
> 'You're welcome to it!' Mrs Assingham breathed.
> 'You never *have* entertained it?' Maggie pursued.
> 'Never for an instant,' said Fanny with her head very high.
> Maggie took it again, yet again as wanting more. 'Pardon my being so horrid. But by all you hold sacred?'
> Mrs Assingham faced her. 'Ah, my dear, upon my positive word as an honest woman.' (422–3)

Familiar as we are with Jamesese we realize that this is deviant language. The proper 'uttereme' for Fanny after Maggie's 'by all you hold sacred' should have been an emphatically affirmative word-for-word repetition: 'By all I hold sacred'. Since the inflationary shift in affirmative methods in James has made even the strongest device (word-for-word emphatic repetition) rather weak, it is obvious that a failure to produce even this in a situation where it is very much demanded, is very, very weak indeed.

This is noticed not only by the reader but by Maggie and Fanny as well. The dialogue continues:

> 'Thank you, then,' said the Princess.
> So they remained a little; after which, 'But do you believe it, love?' Fanny inquired.
> 'I believe *you*.'
> 'Well, as I've faith in *them*, it comes to the same thing.'
> Maggie, at this last, appeared for a moment to think again; but she embraced the proposition. 'The same thing.'
> 'Then you're no longer unhappy?' her guest urged, coming more gaily toward her.
> 'I doubtless shan't be a great while.' (423)

Fanny's deviance is matched by Maggie's when Maggie instead of producing the required 'I believe it' in answer to Fanny's 'do you believe it' makes a distinction and restricts her belief to 'I believe *you*'. Maggie manages a partial repetition which is 'grammatical' according to the rules of Jamesese in her repetition 'The same thing' but when Fanny goes on, inviting her to a final repetition of 'Then you're no longer unhappy', Maggie again fails to perform and produces only the weak 'I doubtless shan't be a great while' instead of the grammatical 'I'm no longer unhappy'. This forces Fanny to go on and issue yet another invitation to an assent in the proper ritual form of a word-for-word emphatic repetition:

> But it was now Mrs Assingham's turn to want more. 'I've convinced you it's impossible?'
> She had held out her arms, and Maggie, after a moment, meeting her, threw herself into them with a sound that had its oddity as a sign of relief. 'Impossible, impossible,' she

emphatically, more than emphatically, replied; yet the next minute she had burst into tears over the impossibility, and a few seconds later, pressing, clinging, sobbing, had even caused them to flow, audibly, sympathetically and perversely, from her friend. (ibid.)

After much postponement the emphatic affirmation comes: 'Impossible, impossible', but it forces the epistemological crisis and the two women break down and cry and Fanny communicates through tears that the sense of everything they have said is to be reversed.

Fanny now has to brush up her scenario for future events and she proceeds to this task with her husband in Chapter XXXI in a conversation in which there is a regular riot of affirmative repetition:

'Kept her, on that sweet construction, to be his mistress?'
'Kept her, on that sweet construction, to be his mistress.' (430)

'I see. It's the way the Ververs have you.'
'It's the way the Ververs "have" me.' (ibid.)

'She lets you off?' He never failed to insist on all this to the very end; which was how he had become so versed in what she finally thought.
'She lets me off.' (ibid.)

'You mean being held responsible.'
'I mean being held responsible.' (431)

Mrs Assingham's need of emphatic reassurance is great at this stage of the action, because in the chapter following Maggie discovers the bowl which clinches the matter for her: she knows that her suspicions were well-founded.

The bowl is symbolically important and is therefore honoured with a case of emphatic affirmation in Chapter XXXII in the conversation between Fanny and Maggie:

'Do you mean the gilt cup?'
'I mean the gilt cup.' (451)

In this chapter Maggie gains the initiative, by winning the Prince over on her side, so that she and the Prince can now in turn keep Charlotte in the dark the same way as Charlotte and the Prince had earlier kept Maggie in the dark. This successful turning of the tables is celebrated with some modest indulgence in emphatic affirmation in a conversation between Maggie and Fanny in Chapter XXXV, when Maggie realizes that she has succeeeded.

> 'He has made up his mind; he'll say nothing about it Therefore, as she's quite unable to arrive at the knowledge by herself, she has no idea how much I'm really in possession. She believes,' said Maggie, 'and, so far as her own conviction goes, she *knows*, that I'm not in possession of anything. And that, somehow, for my own help seems to me immense.'
>
> 'Immense, my dear!' Mrs Assingham applausively murmured, though not quite, even as yet, seeing all the way. 'He's keeping quiet then on purpose?'
>
> 'On purpose.' Maggie's eyes lighted, at least, looked further than they had ever looked. 'He'll *never* tell her now.' (490)

Later on in the scene this modest celebratory beginning swells to the full emphatic crescendo of the extraordinary passage I already quoted at the beginning of this chapter and which was such an eyesore to some critics:

> 'Why, exactly what I mean,' said Maggie, 'is that he will have done nothing of the sort; will, as I say, have maintained the contrary.'
>
> Fanny Assingham weighed it. 'Under her direct appeal for the truth?'
>
> 'Under her direct appeal for the truth.'
>
> 'Her appeal to his honour?'
>
> 'Her appeal to his honour. That's my point.'
>
> Fanny Assingham braved it. 'For the truth as from him to *her*?'
>
> 'From him to anyone.'
>
> Mrs Assingham's face lighted. 'He'll simply, he'll insistently have lied?'

Maggie brought it out roundly. 'He'll simply, he'll insistently have lied.' (493)

At the end of Chapter XXXVI Maggie completes her victory by lying to Charlotte in the most consummate way possible with an emphatic repetition of the 'upon my honour'-formula and a ceremonial kiss:

'I only wanted your denial.'
'Well then, you have it.'
'Upon your honour?'
'Upon my honour.' (517–8)

It remains for Maggie to sort out her father's position, which she does in Chapter XXXVII, in a dialogue which is intense and ambiguous enough to warrant some use of the standard devices, including emphatic affirmation:

She kept her eyes on him a moment. 'That I was so happy as I was?'
'That you were so happy as you were.' (524)

At this she helped him out with it. 'You won't take it from me?'
'I won't take it from you.' (528)

Worthy of the heavy artillery of devices is of course above all the conclusion of the chapter:

This was all in the answer she finally made him.
'I believe in you more than anyone.'
'Than anyone at all?'
She hesitated, for all it might mean; but there was – oh a thousand times! – no doubt of it. 'Than anyone at all.' (535)

Things are settled and the final repetition of the confirmative 'well then' is strengthened by the non-occurrence of tears, meaning that the sense of the preceding utterances is *not* to be inverted:

'Well then – ?' She spoke as for the end and for other

matters – for anything, everything, else there might be. They would never return to it.

'Well then – !' His hands came out, and while her own took them he drew her to his breast and held her. He held her hard and kept her long, and she let herself go; but it was an embrace that august and almost stern, produced, for its intimacy, no revulsion and broke into no inconsequence of tears. (ibid.)

Maggie still has to lie one more time to Charlotte and after her training in the last few chapters she finds it easy to do it in the most effective way, i.e. through the use of emphatic affirmation, thus contributing yet another instance to the numerous cases in this novel in which emphatic affirmation is used to uphold a falsehood:

'What does it matter – if I've failed?'

'You recognise then that you've failed?' asked Charlotte from the threshold.

Maggie waited; she looked, as her companion had done a moment before, at the two books on the seat; she put them together and laid them down; then she made up her mind. 'I've failed!' she sounded out before Charlotte, having given her time, walked away. She watched her, splendid and erect, float down the long vista; then she sank upon a seat. Yes, she had done all. (567)

The rest of the novel is devoted to Maggie's tidying up; reassuring the Prince, reconciling Adam to Charlotte (from Maggie's point of view – it is of course a moot point just how much reconciliation is needed), and making Charlotte and Amerigo part in a civilized manner. Some of these operations are honoured with a sprinkling of emphatic affirmations:

'But at least here he doesn't funk.'

Our young woman accepted the expression. 'He doesn't funk.' (572)

'Father, father – Charlotte's great!'

It was not till after he had begun to smoke that he looked at her. 'Charlotte's great.' (599)

The end of Chapter XL sums up the situation:

> 'What I should rather say is does he know how much?' She found it still awkward. 'How much, I mean, they did. How far' – she touched it up – 'they went.'
>
> Maggie had waited, but only with a question. 'Do you think he does?'
>
> 'Know at least something? Oh, about him I can't think. He's beyond me,' said Fanny Assingham.
>
> 'Then do you yourself know?'
>
> 'How much – ?'
>
> 'How much.'
>
> 'How far –?'
>
> 'How far.' (578)
>
> . . .
>
> On which Mrs Assingham reflected. 'Then how is Charlotte so held?'
>
> 'Just *by* that.'
>
> 'By her ignorance?'
>
> 'By her ignorance.'
>
> Fanny wondered. 'A torment – ?'
>
> 'A torment,' said Maggie with tears in her eyes.
>
> Her companion a moment watched them. 'But the Prince then – ?'
>
> 'How is *he* held?' Maggie asked.
>
> 'How is *he* held?'
>
> 'Oh, I can't tell you that!' And the Princess again broke off. (579)

An answer to the question of how the Prince is held is given in the final paragraph of the novel when the Prince takes up and repeats Maggie's 'see', and, with the aid of the repetition and the typographic intensity-signal of italicization, places his affirmative emphasis where it now belongs – with Maggie.

> ' "See"? I see nothing but *you*.' (603)

4 The 'Finding a Formula'-Formula

In William Dean Howells's short story 'Editha' the main structuring device of the plot is the conflict between the militaristic idealism of the relatives and friends of the heroine, whose name (Editha) reveals that she delights in battle-slaughter, and the relatives and friends of the hero, whose name (George) reveals a pacifist, agrarian disposition.

Editha will accept George for her husband but she longs for something that would effect 'the completion of her ideal of him' (211).[1] What this something finally comes round to being is enlisting for the war which has just broken out. 'She had always supposed that the man who won her would have done something to win her; she did not know what, but something' (ibid.).

She sends him off to war, and he is killed. Before he leaves for the war he makes her promise to help his mother through if anything should happen to him, and although Editha on hearing the news of his death has 'the fever that she expected of herself' (221), she rapidly recovers in the 'exaltation of the duty laid upon her' (ibid.).

George's mother, however, is a pacifist, and her view of Editha's behaviour is an all-out condemnation:

> 'No, you didn't expect him to get killed,' Mrs Gearson repeated, in a voice which was startlingly like George's again. 'You just expected him to kill some one else, some of those foreigners, that weren't there because they had any say about it, but because they had to be there, poor wretches – conscripts, or whatever they call 'em. You thought it would be all right for my George, *your* George, to kill the sons of those miserable mothers and the husbands of those girls that you would never see the faces of.' The woman lifted her powerful voice in a psalmlike note. 'I thank my God he didn't live to do it! I thank my God they killed him first, and that he ain't livin'

108

with their blood on his hands!' She dropped her eyes, which
she had raised with her voice, and glared at Editha. 'What
you got that black on for?' She lifted herself by her powerful
arms so high that her helpless body seemed to hang limp its
full length. 'Take it off, take it off, before I tear it from your
back!' (223)

The story ends with Editha sitting for her portrait. Since it
would take as much space to paraphrase the final scene as to
quote it, we may as well look at Howells's concluding paragraphs in full:

> The lady who was passing the summer near Balcom's
> Works was sketching Editha's beauty, which lent itself
> wonderfully to the effects of a colorist. It had come to that
> confidence which is rather apt to grow between artist and
> sitter, and Editha had told her everything.
> 'To think of your having such a tragedy in your life!' the
> lady said. She added: 'I suppose there are people who feel that
> way about war. But when you consider the good this war has
> done – how much it has done for the country! I can't
> understand such people, for my part. And when you had come
> all the way out there to console her – got up out of a sick-bed!
> Well!'
> 'I think,' Editha said, magnanimously, 'she wasn't quite in
> her right mind; and so did papa.'
> 'Yes,' the lady said, looking at Editha's lips in nature and
> then at her lips in art, and giving an empirical touch to them
> in the picture. 'But how dreadful of her! How perfectly –
> excuse me – how *vulgar*!'
> A light broke upon Editha in the darkness which she felt
> had been without a gleam of brightness for weeks and months.
> The mystery that had bewildered her was solved by the word;
> and from that moment she rose from grovelling in shame and
> self-pity, and began to live again in the ideal. (223–4)

I have started this chapter with Howells's short story because
that final scene gives such a marvellous illustration of one of the
questions involved in the relationship of language and reality,
and above all of the power of language over reality. The word
'vulgar' has a magic power; it washes away Editha's misgivings
and regrets, and she can again begin to live in the ideal.

What happens is that *calling* the behaviour of George's mother 'vulgar', *makes it* vulgar in Editha's consciousness. Things are *made* something by being *called* something, and this, which Howells here makes use of momentarily in one of his short stories, is in James a nagging problem that lies at the centre of his curious epistemology. The present chapter will be devoted to what one might call the 'saying-so-will-make-it-so'-syndrome in James.

In 'Editha' Howells foreshadows the ultimate punchline of *'vulgar'* in several passages in which Editha's tendency to rely on the magic power of language is explicitly prefigured:

> 'That ignoble peace! It was no peace at all, with that crime and shame at our very gates.' She was conscious of parroting the current phrases of the newspapers, but it was no time to pick and choose her words. (211)

Also:

> 'I am yours, for time and eternity – time and eternity.' She liked the words; they satisfied her famine for phrases. (218)

The 'famine for phrases' is half the picture. The other half is the fact that whatever the contents of these phrases may be in each case, it need never be too closely checked against reality. Howells's narrator attributes this to a thought about a sexual difference:

> She had noticed that strange thing in men: they seemed to feel bound to do what they believed, and not think a thing was finished when they said it, as girls did. (212)

George feels bound to keep his actions consistent with his words:

> 'There's only one way of proving one's faith in a thing like this.' (ibid.)

The one way of proving one's faith is, of course, to enlist, i.e. to make reality fit language. (The other alternative, for George, would have been to make sure that language fits reality, i.e. to abstain from purple patriotic rhetoric, if he did not intend to enlist.)

Editha lives in the ideal; George in the real. If the ideal could be left to its own consistency maybe everything would be all right, but when it comes into contact with the real the mixture is poisonous; it kills George. This implies that in a confrontation between the ideal and the real it is the real that suffers.

Howells's attitude to his heroine is fairly clear. She may not be quite as culpable as George's mother thinks – there are moments when she wavers, and there is a subplot with a letter that George's mother does not know the whole truth about, i.e. that George had decided to enlist before he saw it. But she still comes over as sufficiently ridiculous and dislikeable for the story to be classifiable as satire. She is a day-dreamer and Howells makes the reader share his own negative view of her techniques of furthering her own delusions, techniques which include making use of the magic power of language.

The division of attitudes towards the magic power of language is clear in 'Editha'. Whereas the heroine believes in it the author does not, and he invites the reader to share his disbelief. The role of verbal magic in James is much more complex. Verbal magic is used by reliable narrators as well as unreliable and above all there is always a vast no-man's-land of uncertainty and insecurity.

Editha has many parallels in James's fiction. A very close one is Lyon, the narrator in the short story 'The Liar'. Lyon also arrives at the formula of 'vulgar' in order to be able to think what he wishes to think.

The plot of 'The Liar' involves two men, the narrator Lyon and a Colonel Capadose who is married to a woman whom Lyon has been in love with and unsuccessfully courted. Discovering, at a country-house party where all three are guests, that the Colonel tells tall tales, Lyon seizes on this as an excuse to try to make out that the wife, Everina, is ashamed of her husband and regrets her choice. Lyon does not have much to go upon and has to interpret even the slightest signs in his own favour. He wishes that Everina would give some indication of secretly preferring him to her husband. When Everina visits Lyon's studio while he is painting a portrait of her daughter Lyon presses even this fact into service. In Lyon's thoughts Everina's liking him comes to the same as her disliking her husband, and Lyon therefore eagerly waits for signs of the latter.

What he wanted her to do for him was very little; it wasn't

even to allow that she was unhappy. She would satisfy him by letting him know even by some quite silent sign that she could imagine her happiness with him – well, more unqualified. Perhaps indeed – his presumption went so far – that was what she did mean by contentedly sitting there.[2]

Lyon tries to make out that Everina is unhappy with her husband and finds a reason in the fact that Everina sometimes stays at home while her husband goes visiting. But Everina gives another reason for staying at home – she likes to be with her child. Lyon takes this to be a lie and, arriving at the formula of 'vulgar' in the same way as Editha in Howells's story, is able to think what he wishes to think:

> It wasn't perhaps criminal to deal in such 'whoppers,' but it was damned vulgar: poor Lyon was delighted when he arrived at that formula. (319)

'Arrive at a formula' is something that James's characters do again and again. Language helps them to believe whatever they wish to believe. They put language to quite extraordinary private uses. As the heroine of *In the Cage* expresses it: 'Everything, so far as they chose to consider it so, might mean almost anything'.[3] The result of this use of language is that the characters tax the paradigmatic stability of language beyond all endurance. After a word such as 'vulgar' has been used a dozen times in a James work the perceptive reader realizes that the dictionary is no longer of any use whatsoever as a guide to the meaning of that word in James. The only guide is the word's own context in each separate case. Thus James increases enormously the importance of the syntagmatic dimension of language. Words such as 'vulgar' are total blanks and in order to fill in such blanks with a meaning in each case we have to study the context in great detail. This contributes greatly to intensity.

Naturally it also contributes to ambiguity. Clear cases of ambiguity are those instances in which James's characters make the 'finding a formula'-process a tool in wilful self-deception. Then there are at least two alternative ways of interpreting the word. To the character the word has some sort of 'straightforward' meaning. But since we know that the formula-word is being used for the cosmetic purpose of giving a nice name to a nasty reality we also know that this 'straightforward' meaning is suspect. We do not know how far to trust the private semantics of the characters.

In the example from Howells the problem is fairly easy. Howells more or less winks at the reader behind the back of the character and we know that the word is not to be trusted at all. But in James things are far more complicated. James's capacity for entering the point of view of the most diverse characters is very great. He can sympathetically speak from two mutually exclusive points of view in the same work and at the same time. He enters the point of view of the most unlikely characters not only in their reported speech or reported thoughts but also in comments which on the face of it would seem to be the author's.

Formula-finding for cosmetic purposes is prominent in Chapter XVIII of *The Golden Bowl*, since this on the one hand is the chapter in which the Prince and Charlotte decide to act – and begin by sealing their understanding with a kiss – but also on the other the chapter in which there is a culmination of the hypocrisy into which they have almost been forced.

Cosmetic formulae abound in the chapter. Charlotte's and Amerigo's task is described as their 'conscious care' (264). Going on from this phrase, while, at the same time, 'their hands instinctively found their hands' (ibid.) the Prince resorts to the number one Jamesian formula of 'wonderful' ('It's all too wonderful', ibid.). This is synonymically improved upon in Charlotte's 'beautiful' ('It's too beautiful') and given its final, perfect form in the likewise typically Jamesian 'sacred' (ibid.), which is emphatically repeated.

No matter how much Maggie and Adam may have driven their spouses into this situation, and no matter how seemingly noble the sentiments of the Prince and Charlotte may be, the reader nevertheless feels that in all this formula-finding there is a good portion of sophistry.

The interesting thing is that the author seems to take part in the formula-finding. A little earlier in the chapter when Amerigo and Charlotte decide that Fanny no longer matters there is an interesting use of the words 'privilege' and 'duty'.

> 'And really, my dear,' Charlotte added, 'Fanny Assingham doesn't matter.'
> He wondered again. 'Unless as taking care of *them*.'

'Ah,' Charlotte instantly said, 'isn't it for us, only, to do that?' She spoke as with a flare of pride for their privilege and their duty. 'I think we want no one's aid.'

She spoke indeed with a nobleness not the less effective for coming in so oddly; with a sincerity visible even through the complicated twist by which any effort to protect the father and the daughter seemed necessarily conditioned for them. It moved him, in any case, as if some spring of his own, a weaker one, had suddenly been broken by it. These things, all the while, the privilege, the duty, the opportunity, had been the substance of his own vision; they formed the note he had been keeping back to show her that he was not, in their so special situation, without a responsible view. A conception that he could name, and could act on, was something that now, at last, not to be too eminent a fool, he was required by all the graces to produce, and the luminous idea she had herself uttered would have been his expression of it. She had anticipated him, but, as her expression left, for positive beauty, nothing to be desired, he felt rather righted than wronged. A large response, as he looked at her, came into his face, a light of excited perception all his own, in the glory of which – as it almost might be called – what he gave her back had the value of what she had given him. 'They're extraordinarily happy.'

Oh, Charlotte's measure of it was only too full. 'Beatifically.' (262–3)

This is a clearcut case of cosmetic formula-finding. The Prince hesitates but the magic power of the words 'privilege' and 'duty' washes away his misgivings. When things have been given a nice name in this way he is ready to act.

As to the words 'privilege' and 'duty' it is not quite clear to whom they beautifully belong. Charlotte is speaking 'as with a flare for their privilege and their duty', and in a sense the words are therefore hers. But this half of the novel is supposed to be narrated from the Prince's point of view and thus in a sense they are also his. But, finally, they also seem to some extent to be the author's, although he borrows the attitude of Charlotte, or maybe of Charlotte as seen by the Prince.

James frequently contributes to the formula-finding in his direct authorial voice. This can seem rather disconcerting and somewhat misleading when he sympathetically helps both sides with formulae on an occasion when the views of the two sides are absolutely irreconcilable and mutually exclusive. James does not arbitrate, he is not the referee of his fictional soccer-matches. Rather he is a strange schizophrenic fan supporting both sides and cheering them both on at the same time.

It is not always easy to know when a formula is so suspect as to be primarily ironic. One type of formula, however, is usually so glaringly suspect in James that any reader who is familiar with James's fictional idiolect even to a moderate extent knows to be on his guard. Whenever formula-finding involves some theory of common morality this is usually a sign that whitewashing or covering up is in progress.

Typical examples of this in *The Golden Bowl* are Charlotte's 'commonest tact' in Chapter XVII and the Prince's 'common prudence' in Chapter XIX. Charlotte's 'commonest tact' occurs in a context where it is suggested that much more formula-finding is going on than what is being reported.

> It appeared thus that they might enjoy together extraordinary freedom, the two friends, from the moment they should understand their position aright. With the Prince himself, from an early stage, not unnaturally, Charlotte had made a great point of their so understanding it; she had found frequent occasion to describe to him this necessity, and, her resignation tempered, or her intelligence at least quickened, by irrepressible irony, she applied at different times different names to the propriety of their case. The wonderful thing was that her sense of propriety had been, from the first, especially alive about it. There were hours when she spoke of their taking refuge in what she called the commonest tact – as if this principle alone would suffice to light their way; (246–7)

The Prince's 'common prudence' comes in the midst of his rationalizations of the reasons for a behaviour – staying at home – which will give him and Charlotte the best opportunity.

> This error would be his not availing himself to the utmost of the convenience of any artless theory of his constitution, or of Charlotte's, that might prevail there. That artless theories could and did prevail was a fact he had ended by accepting,

under copious evidence, as definite and ultimate; and it consorted with common prudence, with the simplest economy of life, not to be wasteful of any odd gleaning. To haunt Eaton Square, in fine, would be to show that he had not, like his brilliant associate, a sufficiency of work in the world. (270)

A similar case is the use of 'ungracious' (282) at the end of Chapter XX.

Frequently the formula-finding is combined with Jamesian puns. One humorous word occurring in such contexts is 'decent', which James loved to use ambiguously throughout his career. In *The Golden Bowl* 'decent' is used in this way on a number of occasions. In Chapter XXI, for instance, when the Prince has to find a pretext for staying on at Matcham, he tells ˙Fanny Assingham that he has to stay in order to see Charlotte 'decently home' (291). Similar cases abound.

There are two particularly interesting aspects of Jamesian formula-finding that I want to deal with in this chapter. One concerns the relationship between language and reality, particularly the question of the power of language over reality. The other is the habit of verbal formulation itself and the curious shift in James which makes verbal formulation an activity of the characters as much as of the author.

Let us begin with the latter. What I mean by the 'finding a formula'-formula is not only that the characters find euphemistic language for questionable realities. By the 'finding a formula'-formula I also mean simply James's habit of constantly attributing epithets and phrases to his characters, rather than acknowledging these epithets and phrases as his own. There need not always be a specific meaning in this shift of responsibility nor any discernible reason why it should take place. But it happens again and again. Examples can be found by opening any late novel, e.g. *The Golden Bowl*, almost at random.

> Amerigo always being, as the Princess was well aware, conveniently amenable to this friend's explanations, beguilements, reassurances, and perhaps in fact rather more than less dependent on them as his new life – *since that was his own name for it* – opened out. (154–5, my italics)

A little later:

She was there to keep him quiet – *it was Amerigo's own description of her influence*; (155, my italics)

and so on.

Formulating the literary work might have been thought to be the author's job, but in James it seems as if a great deal of the task has been shifted to the characters. James's characters are inordinately verbal; they think *in words*:

Maggie watched her husband – if it now could be called watching – offer this refreshment; she noted the consummate way – *for 'consummate' was the term she privately applied* – ... (595, my italics)

Another author might have been bold enough to lay the responsibility for the word 'consummate' on his own shoulders, but James preferred to withdraw and to minimize his authorial presence. But despite his withdrawal he does not sacrifice any of the rights of an old-fashioned author, e.g. the right to bring in descriptive epithets, such as 'consummate'. He does put them in, but attributes them to the characters instead of taking the responsibility himself. The result is that most characters in his late fiction suffer from an extraordinary hypertrophy of verbality – their world is one of words, words, words.

James's late works are like a set of Chinese boxes. We remove the verbalizing author and find another little author – the narrator or centre of consciousness who is engaged in the same activity of verbalizing. We remove the narrator and try to get a picture of some other character and find yet another little author, forever verbalizing and formulating.

Of course all human beings sometimes think verbally and formulate phrases that reflect their non-verbal thoughts and feelings. A certain amount of formula-finding is no more than natural and we easily accept, for example, Adam Verver's formula of the Prince's lack of 'angularity':

It all came then, the great clearance, from the one prime fact that the Prince, by good fortune, hadn't proved angular. He [Adam Verver] clung to that description of his daughter's husband as he often did to terms and phrases, in the human, the social connection, that he had found for himself: it was his way to have times of using these constantly, as if they just then lighted the world, or his own path in it, for him – even when for some of his interlocutors they covered less ground. (136)

Similarly it is easy to accept Maggie's and Adam's 'sequestered' in the following quotation. But even in such formulae as these there are some curious features.

They knew the bench; it was 'sequestered' – they had praised it for that together, before, and liked the word; ... (154)

What they like is 'the word'; not the bench, nor the fact that the bench is sequestered. Experience has to be verbal before it counts. Things have to be formulated. And formulating them sometimes seems to be the only method of experience.

In his essay 'The Ambiguity of Henry James' Edmund Wilson very perceptibly wrote that James was an 'extrovert' who preferred to dramatize rather than contemplate or reflect.

One comes to the conclusion that Henry James, in a special and unusual way, was what is nowadays called an 'extrovert' – that is, he did not brood on himself and analyze his own reactions, as Stendhal, for example, did, but always dramatized his experience immediately in terms of imaginary people. One gets the impression here that James was not introspective. Nor are his characters really so. They register, as James himself registered, a certain order of perceptions and sensations; but they justify to some degree the objection of critics like Wells that his psychology is superficial – though it would be more correct to put it that, while his insight is not necessarily superficial, his 'psychologizing' tends to be so. What we are told is going on in the characters' heads is a sensitive reaction to surface which itself seems to take place on the surface.[4]

This habit is perhaps nowhere more evident than in the Jamesian mannerism of the 'unuttered utterance'. Let us look at some examples of James's use of this device in the second half of *The Golden Bowl*.

The second half of the novel is basically told from Maggie's point of view. But when Maggie speculates about the Prince's thoughts, or the remarks that the Prince *may be on the brink of uttering*, these speculations are reported in a particular form, namely that of a direct dramatization. They are presented to the reader as utterances, enclosed within quotation-marks, and having every other characteristic feature of an utterance. These utterances differ from real utterances only in the fact that they are never spoken.

> Three words of impatience the least bit loud, some outbreak of 'What in the world are you "up to", and what do you mean?' any note of that sort would instantly have brought her low – and this all the more that heaven knew she hadn't in any manner designed to be high. (345)

The point about these three words is that they never come which in this case is easily explained by the fact of the situation. It is also easy to accept these words as Maggie's speculations about what sort of question 'would have brought her low' even though the question is hypothetically attributed to the Prince. Similarly in the following example, though the verbalization is complete it is easy to accept it as Maggie's 'interior monologue'. Since Maggie is the centre of narration James's method is not too far removed from conventional narrative technique.

> It would have been most beautifully, therefore, in the name of the equilibrium, and in that of her joy at their feeling so exactly the same about it, that she might have spoken if she had permitted the truth on the subject of her behaviour to ring out – on the subject of that poor little behaviour which was for the moment so very limited a case of eccentricity.
>   ' "Why, why" have I made this evening such a point of our not all dining together? Well, because I've all day been so wanting you alone that I finally couldn't bear it, and that there didn't seem any great reason why I should try to. *That* came to me – funny as it may at first sound, with all the things we've so wonderfully got into the way of bearing for each other. You've seemed these last days – I don't know what: more absent than ever before, too absent for us merely to go on so. It's all very well, and I perfectly see how beautiful it is, all round; but there comes a day when something snaps, when

the full cup, filled to the very brim, begins to flow over. That's
what has happened to my need of you – the cup, all day, has
been too full to carry. So here I am with it, spilling it over you
– and just for the reason that is the reason of my life. After all,
I've scarcely to explain that I'm as much in love with you now
as the first hour; except that there are some hours – which I
know when they come, because they frighten me – that show
me I'm even more so. They come of themselves – and, ah,
they've been coming! After all, after all – !' Some such words
as those were what *didn't* ring out, yet it was as if even the
unuttered sound had been quenched here in its own quaver
(346–7)

But these examples are so numerous that it almost seems normal
for characters *not to speak*. Yet their 'utterances' are explicitly
reported, though always in the form of what someone 'might
have' said and of words that '*didn't* ring out'. Again and again we
get these phrases.

It was *as if he might for a moment be going to say*: 'You needn't
pretend, dearest, quite so hard, needn't think it necessary to
care quite so much! – it was *as if* he stood there before her with
some such easy intelligence, some such intimate reassurance,
on his lips. Her answer *would have been* all ready – that she
wasn't in the least pretending; and she looked up at him, while
he took her hand, with the maintenance, the real persistence,
of her lucid little plan in her eyes. (353, my italics)

'But my poor child,' Charlotte *might under this pressure have
been on the point of replying*, 'that's the way nice people are, all
round –'
. . .
'you've allowed me now, between you, to make so blessedly
my own.' Mrs Verver *might in fact have but just failed to make
another point*, a point charmingly natural to her as a grateful
and irreproachable wife. 'It isn't a bit wonderful, I may also
remind you,' . . . 'his acquaintance should be cultivated and
his company enjoyed.'
   Some such happily-provoked remarks as these, from Charlotte, at the other house, *had been in the air*, . . . (363–4, my
italics)

She might have been made to give it by pressure of her stomach; she *might have been expected to articulate*, with a rare imitation of nature, 'Oh yes, I'm *here* all the while; ...' (371, my italics)

Maggie is able to carry on quite lengthy conversations with her father without a word being spoken:

She was powerless, however, was only more utterly hushed, when the interrupting flash came, when she would have been all ready to say to him, 'Yes, this is by every appearance the best time we've had yet; but don't you see, all the same, how they must be working together for it, and how my very success, my success in shifting our beautiful harmony to a new basis, comes round to being *their* amiability, their power to hold out, their complete possession, in short, of our life?' For how could she say as much as that without saying a great deal more? without saying 'They'll do everything in the world that suits us, save only one thing – prescribe a line for us that will make them separate.' How could she so much as imagine herself even faintly murmuring that without putting into his mouth the very words that would have made her quail? 'Separate, my dear? Do you want them to separate? Then you want *us* to – you and me? For how can the one separation take place without the other?' That was the question that, in spirit, she had heard him ask – ... (388)

Moreover she is able to carry on lengthy conversations between two other characters as in the following case between Charlotte and Adam:

The Princess took it in, on the spot, firmly grasping it; she heard them together, her father and his wife, dealing with the queer case. 'The Prince tells me that Maggie has a plan for your taking some foreign journey with him, and, as he likes to do everything she wants, he has suggested my speaking to you for it as the thing most likely to make you consent. So I speak – see? – being always so eager myself, as you know, to meet Maggie's wishes. I speak, but without quite understanding, this time, what she has in her head. Why *should* she, of a sudden, at this particular moment, desire to ship you off together and to remain here alone with me? The compliment's all to me, I admit, and you must decide quite as you like. The Prince is quite ready, evidently, to do his part – but you'll have it out with him. That is you'll have it out with *her*.' Something of that kind was what, in her mind's ear, Maggie heard ... (398, see also 413)

These unuttered utterances are often connected with a *fear of speaking*. When Maggie in the following example 'potentially' hears Amerigo utter an unuttered utterance his *potential* decision to speak is likened to a decision to jump.

From hour to hour she fairly expected some sign of his having decided on a jump. 'Ah yes, it *has* been as you think; I've strayed away, I've fancied myself free, given myself in other quantities, with larger generosities, because I thought you were different – different from what I now see. But it was only, only, because I didn't know – and you must admit that you gave me scarce reason enough. Reason enough, I mean to keep clear of my mistake; to which I confess, for which I'll do exquisite penance, which you can help me now, I too beautifully feel, to get completely over.'
    That was what, while she watched herself, she potentially heard him bring out; and while she carried to an end another day, another sequence and yet another of their hours together, without his pronouncing it, she felt herself occupied with him beyond even the intensity of surrender. (438–9, see also 401)

The unuttered utterances may also be what somebody *cannot* say.

She couldn't – and he knew it – say what was true: 'Oh, you "use" her, and I use her, if you will, yes; but we use her ever so differently and separately – not at all in the same way or degree. There's nobody we really use together but ourselves, don't you see? – by which I mean that where our interests are the same I can so beautifully, so exquisitely serve you for everything, and you can so beautifully, so exquisitely serve me. The only person either of us needs is the other of us; so why, as a matter of course, in such a case as this, drag in Charlotte?' (390, see also 486)

Or, alternatively, what someone *wants to* say:

> She wanted to say to him. 'Take it, take it, take all you need of
> it; arrange yourself so as to suffer least, or to be, at any rate,
> least distorted and disfigured. Only *see*, see that *I* see, and
> make up your mind, on this new basis, at your convenience.
> Wait – it won't be long – till you can confer again with
> Charlotte, for you'll do it much better then – more easily to
> both of us. Above all don't show me, till you've got it well
> under, the dreadful blur, the ravage of suspense and embar-
> rassment, produced, and produced by my doing, in your
> personal serenity, your incomparable superiority.' After she
> had squared again her little objects on the chimney, she
> was within an ace, in fact, of turning on him with that
> appeal; ... (470)

Sometimes the characters almost have to prevent themselves
from speaking: 'those were the words he had to hold himself from
speaking' (476). The characters come 'within an ace' of speaking. They are 'almost moved to saying' (542). Remarks are
'brought to [a character's] lips', but not uttered since the
character 'succeed[s] in repressing' such inquiries:

> The high pitch of her cheer, accordingly, the tentative,
> adventurous expressions, of the would-be smiling order, that
> preceded her approach even like a squad of skirmishers, or
> whatever they were called, moving ahead of the baggage train
> – these things had at the end of a fortnight brought a dozen
> times to our young woman's lips a challenge that had the
> cunning to await its right occasion, but of the relief of which,
> as demonstration, she meanwhile felt no little need. 'You've
> such a dread of my possibly complaining to you that you keep
> pealing all the bells to drown my voice; but don't cry out, my
> dear, till you're hurt – and above all ask yourself how I can be
> so wicked as to complain. What in the name of all that's
> fantastic can you dream that I have to complain *of?*'
> Such inquiries the Princess temporarily succeeded in repress-
> ing, ... (411)

The implications of this type of extraordinary communication –
if that be the right word – are far-reaching. What sort of

communication, or pseudo-communication, is it? The unuttered utterances are given *as if they had been* spoken, and often, as in the following quotation, the reader has to be on the alert to remember that it is all merely *Maggie's* verbalizing after all:

> He had said to himself, 'She'll break down and name Amerigo; she'll say it's to him she's sacrificing me; and it's by what that will give me – with so many other things too – that my suspicion will be clinched.' (530)

In the end it all comes back to Maggie. When a feeling comes to her she dramatizes it by putting it into verbal form and attributing it, in an unuttered utterance, to some other person, as in the following example to Father Mitchell:

> She met the good priest's eyes before they separated, and priests were really, at the worst, so to speak such wonderful people that she believed him for an instant on the verge of saying to her, in abysmal softness: 'Go to Mrs Verver, my child – *you* go: you'll find that you can help her.' This didn't come, however; nothing came but the renewed twiddle of thumbs over the satisfied stomach and the full flush, the comical candour, of reference to the hand employed at Fawns for mayonnaise of salmon. (554)

Or in the following to Charlotte:

> Yes, it was positive that during one of these minutes the Princess had the vision of her particular alarm. 'It's her lie, it's her lie that has mortally disagreed with her; she can keep down no longer her rebellion at it, and she has come to retract it, to disown it and denounce it – to give me full in my face the truth instead.' This, for a concentrated instant, Maggie felt her helplessly gasp – but only to let it bring home the indignity, the pity of her state. (561)

The reader's choice in such passages as these is to regard the utterance either as Charlotte's or Maggie's. It ought to be Charlotte's since it is 'spoken' in her voice, with quotation marks and all, but in the end, of course, it is only what '*Maggie felt her helplessly gasp*'.

The communication, or pseudo-communication, seems to take place mainly through the method of verbal gazes. In the next example it is 'something in the depths of the eyes he finally fixed upon her'. Interpreting the verbal gaze Maggie *hears* these 'unspoken words'.

> It had been but the matter of something in the depths of the eyes he finally fixed upon her, and she had found in it, the more she kept it before her, the tacitly offered sketch of a working arrangement. 'Leave me my reserve; don't question it – it's all I have, just now, don't you see? so that, if you'll make me the concession of letting me alone with it for as long a time as I require, I promise you something or other, grown under cover of it, even though I don't yet quite make out what, as a return for your patience.' She had turned away from him with some such unspoken words as that in her ear, and indeed she *had* to represent to herself that she had spiritually heard them, had to listen to them still again, to explain her particular patience in face of his particular failure. (495)

The number of these gazes is astronomical. Practically every Jamesian page features an 'extasy' with 'eye-beams twisted', but twisted not from the intensity of feeling between two lovers as in Donne but intertwined because gazes and stares have taken the place of uttered words:

> She affected him as speaking more or less for her father as well, and his eyes might have been trying to hypnotise her into giving him the answer without his asking the question. 'Had *he* his idea, and has he now, with you, anything more?' – those were the words he had to hold himself from not speaking and that she would as yet, certainly, do nothing to make easy. (476)

Sometimes two conversations are carried on, one with uttered utterances and the other with unuttered:

> 'Yes, look, look,' she seemed to see him hear her say even while her sounded words were other – 'look, look, both at the truth that still survives in that smashed evidence and at the

even more remarkable appearance that I'm not such a fool as you supposed me. Look at the possibility that, since I *am* different, there may still be something in it for you – if you're capable of working with me to get that out. Consider of course, as you must, the question of what you may have to surrender, on your side, what price you may have to pay, whom you may have to pay with, to set this advantage free; but take in, at any rate, that here *is* something for you if you don't blindly spoil your chance for it.' He went no nearer the damnatory pieces, but he eyed them, from where he stood, with a degree of recognition just visibly less to be dissimulated; all of which represented for her a certain traceable process. And her uttered words, meanwhile, were different enough from those he might have inserted between the lines of her already-spoken. 'It's the golden bowl, you know, that you saw at the little antiquario's in Bloomsbury, ...' (472–3)

Consider the extraordinary nature of the phrase 'she seemed to see him hear her say'. An even stranger variant is used in the following example – 'some such question as that she let herself ask him to suppose in her'.

The high voice went on; its quaver was doubtless for conscious ears only, but there were verily thirty seconds during which it sounded, for our young woman, like the shriek of a soul in pain. Kept up a minute longer it would break and collapse – so that Maggie felt herself, the next thing, turn with a start to her father. 'Can't she be stopped? Hasn't she done it *enough*?' – some such question as that she let herself ask him to suppose in her. Then it was that, across half the gallery – he struck her as confessing, with strange tears in his own eyes, to sharp identity of emotion. 'Poor thing, poor thing' – it reached straight – '*isn't* she, for one's credit, on the swagger?' After which, as held thus together they had still another strained minute, the shame, the pity, the better knowledge, the smothered protest, the divined anguish even, so overcame him that, blushing to his eyes, he turned short away. The affair but of a few muffled moments, this snatched communion yet lifted Maggie as on air – so much, for deep guesses on her own side too, it gave her to think of. (548)

Maggie here thinks of a two-way communication through a

verbal gaze. But can the reader accept these 'communications' at face value? Can he accept them moreover when James himself does not seem quite ready to do so? Adam's 'remark' in the mute 'conversation' in our example is not quite unambiguous. In addition, there is James's comment on the voice that 'its quaver was doubtless for conscious ears only' – in other words that it need not sound the same to everyone.

In the end it all comes back to Maggie, and in the following example though Adam 'addresses' his daughter 'two or three mute facial intimations' in a 'wordless, wordless smile' their verbalization is nevertheless presented as 'Maggie's translation'.

> Charlotte hung behind, with emphasised attention; she stop-ped when her husband stopped, but at the distance of a case or two, or of whatever other succession of objects; and the likeness of their connection would not have been wrongly figured if he had been thought of as holding in one of his pocketed hands the end of a long silken halter looped round her beautiful neck. He didn't twitch it, yet it was there; he didn't drag her, but she came; and those indications that I have described the Princess as finding extraordinary in him were two or three mute facial intimations which his wife's presence didn't prevent his addressing his daughter – nor prevent his daughter, as she passed, it was doubtless to be added, from flushing a little at the receipt of. They amounted perhaps only to a wordless, wordless smile, but the smile was the soft shake of the twisted silken rope, and Maggie's translation of it, held in her breast till she got well away, came out only, as if it might have been overheard, when some door was closed behind her. 'Yes, you see – I lead her now by the neck, I know what it is, though she has a fear in her heart which, if you had the chances to apply your ear there that I, as a husband, have, you would hear thump and thump and thump. She thinks it *may* be, her doom, the awful place over there – awful for *her*; but she's afraid to ask, don't you see? just as she's afraid of so many other things that she sees multiplied round her now as portents and betrayals. She'll know, however – when she does know.' (544–5)

The problem for the reader is to determine how far the translation agrees with the original. The basic choice is either to attribute unuttered utterances to the person who 'translates' them or to the person who is supposed by the translator to have been on the point of uttering them, or to have silently uttered them, etc. Some critics have opted whole-heartedly for the latter and regard these 'translations' as James's way of circumventing the rules of narration that he had himself imposed, i.e. that of telling his story from the point of view of one character.[5] On this interpretation the unuttered utterances should be taken at face value and attributed to the character who is supposed to utter (i.e. *not* utter) them.

But such a view is patently absurd. Various forms of non-communication are extensively depicted in James's works. James made misunderstandings a major artistic device – cf. Chapter 1. In an author where the characters mistake each other's *spoken* utterances it would surely be absurd to assume that there is no ambiguity in their *unspoken* ones.

James used misunderstandings not only as artistic 'pointers' in the manner described in Chapter 1. He used them also for comedy, and sometimes the humour is at the expense of solipsistic day-dreamers as in the following inconsequential exchange in *In the Cage*:

> He bade her good-morning always now; he often quite raised his hat to her. He passed a remark when there was time or room and once she went so far as to say to him that she hadn't seen him for 'ages'. 'Ages' was the word she consciously and carefully, though a trifle tremulously, used; 'ages' was exactly what she meant. To this he replied in terms doubtless less anxiously selected, but perhaps on that account not the less remarkable, 'Oh yes, hasn't it been awfully wet?' That was a specimen of their give and take; it fed her fancy that no form of intercourse so transcendent and distilled had ever been established on earth. Everything, so far as they chose to consider it so, might mean almost anything. (204–5)

But in addition to their use as pointers and their use for humour, misunderstandings in James also contribute to sheer, unmitigated epistemological chaos. Against this background I find it impossible to accept the view that verbalized unuttered utterances should be taken at face value.

On the other hand, I find it impossible to take the opposite view that they are suspect as a rule. Though it is clearly their primary function to characterize the 'interpreter' we can as little assume that the interpreter is always wrong as that she or he is always right. In other words, the unuttered utterances create ambiguity.

They reflect the insecurity of a world where communication is of a very strange nature. Utterances in James should preferably not be uttered. Wills should not be read, instead one should speculate over their contents (*The Ivory Tower*). Letters should not be opened and read; it is much better to throw them unopened into the fire (*The Wings of the Dove*) or give them unopened to a friend ('Eugene Pickering'). That way one knows their contents much better than by reading them.

Or does one? It seems that we are meant to think that Kate Croy and Merton Densher in *The Wings of the Dove* guess the contents of Milly's letter correctly. But what about the characters in 'Eugene Pickering'? In this story the hero, Eugene Pickering, gives an unopened letter to his friend (the narrator), and asks him to keep it for him. Eugene says he knows the contents anyway. At the end of the story the letter *is* opened and the contents are nothing like what Eugene had expected.

If the interpretation is shown, even by James himself, to be wrong in one case, how can we as readers be sure that it is right in another? It seems to me that we cannot. Instead the effect of this device is a feeling of insecurity and uncertainty, which highly improves those of James's works in which that element was aimed for, but fatally damages some others. Above all the device reveals a very important aspect of the question of the relation of language and reality in James.

In his parody 'The Mote in the Middle Distance' Max Beerbohm made the two children, Keith Tantalus and his sister, decide *not* to peer into their Christmas stockings. Beerbohm has indeed caught the essence of James's world. If Keith and his sister *did* peer, their speculations, fantasies etc. would be checked against reality and that is always the great risk in James. If you do *not* utter utterances you can (can you?) live on in the belief that whatever you make other people out to have understood you as silently 'saying' – or them to have been on the point of saying, etc. – is true. If you do *not* read letters you can think (can you?) that you know what their contents are. If you do *not* read wills you can yourself (can you?) create their contents verbally.

One way to ensure that language has power over reality is to see to it that whatever has been imagined verbally is never checked against reality. Therefore you must not utter utterances, must not read letters, must not break the seal of wills etc.

In James's production during the nineties there is a story in which a decision *not* to publish a document is rewarded, a real reason being given why it is better not to 'peer'. In 'Sir Dominick Ferrand' the hero Peter Baron discovers some old letters in a secret compartment of a davenport which he has bought. The heroine, Mrs Ryves, tries to dissuade Peter Baron from breaking the seals of the letters or reading them. He nevertheless does so and discovers that the letters contain some compromising material about Sir Dominick Ferrand, a leading diplomatist of the country's past. He approaches a review and is eventually offered 300 pounds for the letters. Nevertheless he hesitates and finally burns the papers.

Immediately after this the rewards magically start pouring in. A song which he and Mrs Ryves had collaborated on has been sold for fifty pounds; Mrs Ryves, whom Peter Baron had estranged by his near-decision to publish the papers, returns to tell the good news, and the two are reconciled. Finally Mrs Ryves reveals that she is Sir Dominick's illegitimate daughter! By deciding *not* to 'peer' Peter Baron has saved their relationship.

In this story a factual, though occult, reason why one should not 'peer' is given and there are similar works from James's early and middle period. In late James the conviction that it is better 'not to peer' is stronger than ever, but factualistic justifications are no longer given.

The longing is for a world in which language reigns alone without the constant threat from reality. If only there existed a world in which verbal magic worked! If only there was a world in which 'saying makes it so'!

Well, the world of literature *is* such a world. Literary verbalizing is self-sufficient; contact with reality is a distraction. When reality has helped to put the verbal literary imagination in motion reality is no longer needed. When James, listening in real life to some anecdote or story, got a 'germ' for a work he deliberately avoided hearing any more.[6] Any further role of reality would have been an unwelcome interference with the process of formulation and literary invention.

James's characters are to a large extent projections of the author's own self. They are artist-figures who would like to manipulate reality in the same way as the author manipulates them.

They might have been really charming as they showed in the beautiful room, and Charlotte certainly, as always, magnificently handsome and supremely distinguished – they might have been figures rehearsing some play of which she herself was the author; (*The Golden Bowl*, 506)

In performatives such as promises, oaths, bets, etc. reality is supposed to be governed by language. You are supposed to keep your promise, be true to your oath, stand by your bet. Nevertheless people sometimes break their promise, ignore their oath and welch on a bet. The intense attempt to fetter reality with verbal chains sometime remains only an intense attempt. Whether or not reality will let herself be governed by language is the problem that creates the feeling of uncertainty which adds ambiguity to the intensity inherent in performatives.

Even more intensely ambiguous are a few shady relatives of the performatives, such as spells, incantations and verbal magic in the literal sense. The people who try to govern reality by reading a spell are usually not quite sure whether the verbal magic will work.

In the 'verbal magic' in James one can hear this note of desperation which is a result of the marriage of intensity and ambiguity. In verbal rituals such as emphatic affirmation, formula-finding etc. the characters reveal a desperation which stems from an intense wish to believe that language *can* govern reality, coupled with an ambiguous doubt as to whether it is possible after all.

The degree of belief in verbal magic varies from one character to another. Some go very far. A few sometimes drift into the belief that the whole world is in the power of one verbally manipulative person – oneself. They can *create* (verbally) what they *find out*. The week-end guest in *The Sacred Fount* knows the 'joy of determining, almost of creating results'.[7] He regresses in day-dreams to a childhood world of enchanted castles, moving 'in a world in which the strange "came true"'. (101).

It was the coming true that was the proof of the enchantment, which, moreover, was naturally never so great as when such coming was, to such a degree and by the most romantic stroke of all, the fruit of one's own wizardry. I was positively – so had the wheel revolved – proud of my work. I had thought it all out, and to have thought it was, wonderfully, to have brought it. (ibid.)

Characters like the week-end guest carry on an advanced flirtation with the mental habits that lead to paranoia. They have a curious attitude towards the question of the balance of one's active creativity and one's passive receptivity. Many of the views they express read like perfect recipes for solipsism.

The 'wizardry' of the week-end guest is a regression into infantility. Children, like authors, enjoy the privilege of fantasizing with impunity. Adults in contrast have to strike a balance between the self and the other, between subjectivity and objectivity, creativity and receptivity, tychism and synechism, the force of variation and that of selection, the freedom factor and the controlling factor. When James makes his characters projections of himself the result inevitably is ambiguity.

It does not take much intellectual detective-work to find the philosophical counterpart of Henry James's fiction. William and Henry were, after all, brothers and there are interesting parallels and similarities between the works of the two. The old joke that William's philosophical works read like novels and Henry's novels like philosophy is true in more than one sense. To concentrate on the aspect we are concerned with now, it is obvious that the provocative every-day language into which William James put his ideas lent itself very easily to shocking misinterpretations of his theory – misinterpretations that he, in a sense, invited and deserved. In particular the one popular misconception which he had more or less asked for was the accusation that his theory is a *carte blanche* for solipsism. In other words, the philosophical problem which is so relevant in the epistemology of such Jamesian protagonists as the week-end guest in *The Sacred Fount* is also a problem in William James's philosophy.

Henry James's 'finding a formula'-formula seems to suggest that 'saying makes it so'. This was also precisely what William James's critics accused *him* of saying. William indignantly replied:

A favourite formula for describing Mr. Schiller's doctrines and mine is that we are persons who think that by saying whatever you find it pleasant to say and calling it truth you fulfil every pragmatistic requirement.

I leave it to you to judge whether this be not an impudent slander.[8]

On another occasion he also warned against solipsism:

Truth, in these cases, meaning nothing but eventual verification, is manifestly incompatible with waywardness on our part. Woe to him whose beliefs play fast and loose with the order which realities follow in his experience; they will lead him nowhere or else make false connexions. (205)

But whether the criticism was 'impudent slander' or not William James had done much to deserve it. Dealing with subjectivity and objectivity, creativity and receptivity, tychism and synechism or any related dichotomy in his books William James's emphasis was consistently in each case on the former. On the one hand this is a healthy empiricist attitude.[9] But on the other it seems to postpone the checking of subjectivist truth against objective reality to some late point of an ultimate test – relying meanwhile on a provisional, instrumental truth – whereas some other philosophies try to keep the interconnection between the two continuous and have it start as early as possible.

Many of Henry James's characters believe in a pragmatist philosophy in the worst sense of the word. They distort evidence, adopt curious methods of verification of their hypotheses and delude themselves with subjectivist 'truth' until some catastrophe occurs. William James would presumably have argued that such catastrophes show that they were mistaken. His critics would answer that there is little solace in that knowledge – that it was the stages that led up to the catastrophe which were important, if it was to be avoided.

William James's books at times sound as if they had been written as an apologia for the strange mental habits of Henry James's worst characters such as the governess in *The Turn of the Screw*. A very important thematic question in that story is whether the governess does not in fact *invent* the things she claims to *discover*. A defender of the governess might very well quote

William James:

> In our cognitive as well as in our active life we are creative.
> We *add*, both to the subject and to the predicate part of reality.
> The world stands really malleable, waiting to receive its final
> touches at our hands. Like the kingdom of heaven, it suffers
> human violence willingly. Man *engenders* truths upon it. (256–
> 7)

The week-end guest in *The Sacred Fount* also 'almost create[s]
results'. But on the other hand Henry James represents this as a
regression to childhood. It has justly been said that Henry's
works are related to William's philosophy. But what precisely is
the relation when Henry relegates William's philosophy to the
nursery?

Of course I am speaking unhistorically here – the relegation
had taken place long before it could have been known that what
was relegated was William's ideas. *The Sacred Fount* appeared in
1901 and those of William's works in which his pragmatistic
ideas were presented at length almost a decade later. Nevertheless, chronology is not all-important here since the question does
not concern a direct influence one way or the other, but rather
the relationship between the ways of thinking of the two
brothers.

Discussions of Henry's pragmatism usually start out from the
letter he wrote to his brother on October 17th, 1907, in which he
stated:

> Why the devil I didn't write to you after reading your
> *Pragmatism* – how I kept from it – I can't now explain save by
> the very fact of the spell itself (of interest and enthralment)
> that the book cast upon me; I simply sank down, under it, into
> such depths of submission and assimilation that *any* reaction,
> very nearly, even that of acknowledgement, would have had
> almost the taint of dissent or escape. Then I was lost in the
> wonder of the extent to which all my life I have (like M.
> Jourdain) unconsciously pragmatised. You are immensely
> and universally *right*, and I have been absorbing a number
> more of your followings-up ...[10]

Even this letter is not quite devoid of ambivalence. In Henry's way of admitting that he had 'all his life ... unconsciously pragmatised' it is worth noting the irony in the playful reference to M. Jourdain, who was told – to his great surprise – that for many years, without knowing it, he had been speaking prose. The wit of Henry's remark could really be very double-edged – compare the value of the two related terms in the analogy: 'pragmatism' and 'prose'.

Henry's works were certainly a flirtation with pragmatist ideas but Henry presented manifestations of the negative possibilities inherent in the philosophy as well as of the positive. If Henry James realized in fiction, when he 'unconsciously pragmatised', what his brother was doing in philosophy, it is clear that he did not only realize the possibilties that arise out of a benevolent interpretation of William's philosophy – even more he gave substance to, exemplified and tested out, the possible abuses that could result from it.[11]

The peculiar perverted 'empiricism' of the governess in *The Turn of the Screw* or the week-end guest in *The Sacred Fount* could be defended with a number of well-selected quotations from William James's *Pragmatism*, such as, for instance, the following:

> She [pragmatism] has in fact no prejudices whatever, no obstructive dogmas, no rigid canons of what shall count as proof. She is completely genial. She will entertain any hypothesis, she will consider any evidence. (*Pragmatism*, 79)

> *'The true', to put it very briefly, is only the expedient in the way of our thinking, just as 'the right' is only the expedient in the way of our behaving.* (222)

> Any idea upon which we can ride, so to speak; any idea that will carry us prosperously from any one part of our experience to any other part, linking things satisfactorily, working securely, simplifying, saving labor; is true for just so much, true in so far forth, true *instrumentally*. (58)

But at the same time as he made his characters feed their delusions with the aid of such rules as these, Henry James also made these stories end in disasters or in sterile, inconclusive ways. Thus if he believed in pragmatist philosophy in the sense of accepting the instrumentalist criterion of truth he still did not believe entirely.

Similarly he may also have been attracted to that other idea which is characteristic of pragmatism – the idea of subjective activeness which 'engenders truth' on reality. But he did not believe wholeheartedly in that either. The belief that the world is in the power of one verbally manipulative character would have been dear to him but though he yearningly half-accepted it he also retained strong doubts. These doubts are manifested in the ambiguity of such devices as 'unuttered utterances' and 'cosmetic formula-finding'.

The 'pragmatistic' element in Henry's thinking makes the uncertainty and insecurity of his world worse. It feeds a tendency towards extremist separation of the two alternatives of interpretation in ambiguous interpretanda, a tendency which will be dealt with at length in Chapter 5. 'Pragmatistic' ways of thinking help James's characters to dismiss their doubt, hesitation, vacillation and uncertainty in the face of choices as long as these choices are trifling details. The characters pragmatically decide to believe whatever it is convenient to believe. But scepticism must inevitably come. By postponing the sceptical approach to their questions and choices the characters ensure that the choices are no longer trifling details when scepticism ultimately cannot be warded off any longer. The intense wish for an unambiguous universe only makes the ambiguity worse when in the end it can no longer be ignored.

5 Chiastic Inversion, Antithesis and Oxymoron

In *The Golden Bowl*, Chapter XXIII, after we have just seen the Prince and Charlotte leave for their adulterous afternoon at Gloucester, there is a conversation in which Fanny and the Colonel try to size up the new situation. Fanny justifiably fears the worst:

> 'I think there's nothing they're not now capable of – in their so intense good faith.'
> 'Good faith?' – he echoed the words, which had in fact something of an odd ring, critically.
> 'Their false position. It comes to the same thing.' (312)

A strange semantic world this, where 'good faith' and 'false position' come to the same thing! Nevertheless, the coupling of such antonymic terms is perfectly reasonable in the context. In fact what happens again and again in James is that absolute opposites lie down peacefully together as lamb and lion might in a different world.

The purpose of this chapter is to illuminate James's use of various types of devices involving the coupling of opposites, in particular antithesis and oxymoron. But to understand the nature and function of these devices one must first botanize a little among James's mental habits so that his favourite thought patterns can be isolated and brought to light. There is in particular one pattern which dominated James's thinking to such an extent that phenomena such as antithesis and oxymoron can be regarded merely as its inevitable consequences or side-effects.

This pattern I shall here call *chiastic inversion*. It is the same phenomenon that E.M. Forster had in mind when he commented on the 'hour-glass shape' of *The Ambassadors*.[1] Chiastic inversion, however, does not only determine the structure of *The Ambassadors*; it is an abstract model whose influence permeates

James's entire fictional world and dominates his thinking.

The pattern in its basic form could be illustrated as in Figure 1. If chiastic inversion in this basic form dominates the unfolding

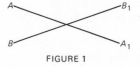

FIGURE 1

of a plot it simply means that '*A* changes and becomes what *B* has been; while *B* changes and becomes what *A* has been'.

A pure example of this, as Forster pointed out, is *The Ambassadors*. The protagonist Lambert Strether is sent to Paris to collect young Chad Newsome and save him from the influence of Paris and Mme de Vionnet who keeps him in Europe. At the beginning the antagonistic forces are clearly defined: Strether and New England, in conflict with Chad and Europe. But gradually things change. Strether's determination is eroded by the influence of Europe and he begins to procrastinate and postpone the execution of his task. He meets Mme de Vionnet and is even further diverted from his path. Finally he openly professes himself a renegade and urges Chad to stay. Meanwhile Chad's development has been the opposite. His attitude towards going back to America has changed from determined opposition to eager expectation. Thus Chad and Strether have changed places at the end of the novel. Apart from being one of the artistically most pleasing executions of a theme involving chiastic inversion in James *The Ambassadors* is also an example of the pattern in one of its simplest and purest manifestations.

The chiastic switches may also be multiple. This, in the plot-development variant of chiastic inversion, is the case in *The Golden Bowl*, though the inversions involve couples rather than individuals. In Figure 2 M stands for Maggie, C for Charlotte, A

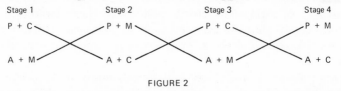

FIGURE 2

for Adam and P for the Prince. The novel opens with Maggie about to marry the Prince, and the Prince about to marry Maggie. Nevertheless, despite the impending marriage, the

Prince is shown to be very much interested in Charlotte and Maggie very much interested in her father (Stage 1 – the illegitimate set). Maggie and Amerigo then marry, and Adam marries Charlotte (Stage 2 – the legitimate set). But soon afterwards (in Stage 3) Maggie relapses into a condition which is the same as that of Stage 1 and begins to spend most of her time with her father – or maybe it is more correct to say that she never really goes in whole-heartedly for Stage 2 (the legitimate set). This presents Amerigo and Charlotte with a situation that not only allows them but almost forces them too to relapse into the illegitimate set (in Stage 3 – which is a repetition of Stage 1). Finally Maggie realizes her mistake and forces a return to the legitimate set in Stage 4 (which is the same as Stage 2). Apart from these switches there is also some tentative play with the identico-sexual compromise set, but the above four stages, with the three inversions, constitute the basic structure of the plot.

While playing with multiple inversions James sometimes ran totally amuck and his most highly patterned creations are not necessarily always his best. Even in *What Maisie Knew* the symmetrical growth of relationships sometimes begins to seem rather riotous. Some critics have felt that these combinational abstractions are a cold and bloodless element in this novel whose theme, of childish innocence corrupted or preserved, could otherwise have had more emotional appeal.

Chiastic inversion dominating the development of the plot is only one of its manifestations. It can equally well involve the 'appearance versus reality'-dichotomy, in which case the basic pattern could be read thus: 'A *seems to be* what B actually *is*; at the same time as B *seems to be* what A *is*'. There are naturally both simple and complex variants of this type too, with one or multiple switches of roles.

The 'plot-development' and 'appearance and reality' categories of chiastic inversion are not the only types but they are the most common and the most important and it is sufficient for the time being to keep these in mind while we search for the essential significance of chiastic patterning in James's fictional world.

Edmund Wilson once wrote about *The Sacred Fount* that it is 'not merely mystifying but maddening'. But he also added that 'If one got to the bottom of it, a good deal of light would be thrown on the author'.[2] Since then a number of eager divers have volunteered. Those who appear to have reached the deepest depths so far are probably Jean Blackall in *Jamesian Ambiguity and The Sacred Fount*, and Shlomith Rimmon in *The Concept of Ambiguity: The Example of James*. I am firmly convinced that anyone who wishes to get down the fount even to a moderate depth ought to prepare himself or herself with the leaden shoes provided by a realization of the importance of chiastic inversion in James's thinking.

James's mind was characterized by a strong tendency towards lability. Nothing is ever finished or definite in James's world. We already saw one manifestation of this on the level of style in 'end-linking' which was dealt with in Chapter 2. On the level of plot-development the same tendency often makes James hesitate and change his mind after beginning a work in perfectly straightforward fashion. His labile mind is attracted by the possibility of an inversion and he begins to ask 'What if everything were the other way? What if everything were upside down? What if the main characters were to change roles?' and so the rot sets in, everything is undermined, and soon chiastic inversion is a rampant fact.

One often finds Jamesian works that seem to have been planned as straightforward but which gradually fall victim to one of the subversive influences of which the foremost is the corrupting effect of chiastic inversion. In other words, chiastic inversion is often a force that irresistibly creeps in and transforms what had been begun as something else.

The Sacred Fount is special in that this novel *begins* with the element which in so many other works is the undermining force *par excellence* – chiastic inversion. In *The Sacred Fount* the pattern of chiastic inversion is itself the starting point; the narrator has a theory about vampiric personal relationships according to a see-saw model – if one wins then the other loses; if one loses then the other wins. James's donnée was, in other words, precisely a variant of the pattern of chiastic inversion.

James first mentions the idea in his *Notebook* on February 17, 1894:

> Last night, at Mrs Crackanthorpe's, Stopford Brooke suggested to me 2 little ideas.
>
> . . .
>
>   (2) The notion of the young man who marries an older

woman and who has the effect on her of making her younger and still younger, while he himself becomes her age. When he reaches the age that *she* was (on their marriage), she has gone back to the age that *he* was. – Mightn't this be altered (perhaps) to the idea of cleverness and stupidity? A clever woman marries a deadly dull man, and loses and loses her wit as he shows more and more. Or the idea of a *liaison*, suspected, but of which there is no proof but this transfusion of some idiosyncrasy of one party to the being of the other – this exchange or conversion? The fact, the two things – the two elements – beauty and 'mind,' might be correspondingly, concomitantly exhibited as in the history of two related couples – with the opposition, in each case, that would help the thing to be dramatic.[3]

Returning to the subject in February 1899 he calls his idea a 'little *concetto*':

Don't lose sight of the little *concetto* of the note in former vol. that begins with fancy of the young man who marries an old woman and becomes old while she becomes young. Keep my play on idea: the *liaison* that betrays itself by the *transfer* of qualities – qualities to be determined – from one to the other of the parties to it. They *exchange*. I see 2 couples. One is married – this is the *old–young* pair. I watch *their* process, and it gives me my light for the spectacle of the other (covert, obscure, unavowed) pair who are *not* married.[4]

In order for chiastic inversion – the prime tool of subversion – to be able to play its usual role in *The Sacred Fount* it ought to have somehow self-destructively undermined itself. In the light of such analyses as Rimmon's it is not too fanciful to suggest that this is in fact precisely what happens, and doubtless this is one possible explanation why readers and critics have found the work 'maddening' and why James himself wrote 'it isn't worth explaining, and I mortally loathe it!'[5]

James's fondness of chiastic inversion resulted from the combined effect of three of his characteristic mental habits: firstly and secondly his tendency to think in opposites and parallels, and, thirdly, the lability of his mind. He acquired all of these mental habits very early in his career. By and by they became inveterate and so did chiastic inversion.

All the constituent elements of chiastic inversion can be found in embryonic form in James's early works. His first short story 'A Tragedy of Error' (1864), in which a hired assassin kills the wrong man, already exhibits – though as yet only in a conventional form – what is to be one of the chief elements of chiastic inversion in its complete form, i.e. the interchangeability of the roles of two characters. James named his story a 'tragedy' of error, but the accuracy of the term 'tragedy' is limited in application. The event is a tragedy for the lady character who hires the assassin, but to the reader, to the gods, and above all to the author it is really more of a comedy. This type of switch of roles appealed very much to James's sense of humour.

The lability manifested in the total interchangeability of roles in James's fiction is partly a result of the author's *playfulness*. There are theories of the mode of 'the comic' in which a change of roles is cited as a standard element in one of the main types of jokes. Arthur Koestler, who argues that the mechanism of humour involves the bisociation of two matrices, gives the following story as one of his examples (originally reported by Freud in his essay on the comic):

> Chamfort tells a story of a Marquis at the court of Louis XIV who, on entering his wife's boudoir and finding her in the arms of a Bishop, walked calmly to the window and went through the motions of blessing the people in the street.
>
> 'What are you doing?' cried the anguished wife.
>
> 'Monseigneur is performing my functions,' replied the Marquis, 'so I am performing his.'[6]

A change of roles is usually an element in the plot of such plays as we traditionally call comedies. The plot of these plays often involves an opposition between two different groups, such as two social classes; then a blurring of the dividing line between these through the emergence of some anomalous individuals, and finally the reestablishment of order. The final return to order frequently makes use of the 'appearance and reality'-variant of chiastic inversion. Of the character rising in status it is then said that although he seemed lower-class he was actually upper-class (this to be discovered and proved with the aid of, for example, a birthmark in the form of a lily on his shoulder proving him to be the long-lost son of a duke). Of a character reduced in status it can be said that although he seemed upper-class he was actually an impostor and in reality therefore lower-class. Often two such characters exchange positions quite literally, the beggar becoming a duke and the duke a beggar. Thus it seems that chiastic inversion may be of fundamental importance not only as a structure in jokes but in the entire genre of comedy. Chiastic inversion certainly appealed to James's sense of humour. Let us look briefly at some examples.

One of James's hobby-horses was masculine women and feminine men. This inversion of sexual roles is in particular found in the author's treatment of minor characters, and it is characteristic of James's art that he uses minor figures in a work for purposes of comedy, caricature and satire, at the same time as he may use the main characters for quite serious purposes.

These feminine males and masculine females are not, I think, to be seen only as androgynous beings, or as evidence of a diluted femininity on part of the women and a diluted mascu-linity on part of the men. Instead I think that the main reason for their existence in James's fiction is his fascination with the inversion of roles itself and the superficial comedy to be extracted from the chiastic switch. Thus it would be wrong to read a very strong anti-feminist attitude into James's ridicule of masculinized women. James showed little interest in politics, philosophy, religion or in ideas in general. For better or worse it is true as T.S. Eliot observed that '[James] had a mind so fine that no idea could violate it'.[7]

The inversion of sexual roles is evident for instance in James's onomastic practice.[8] He sometimes amuses himself, and possibly the reader, by giving women in 'male' roles absurdly phallic names – take for instance Henrietta Stackpole in *The Portrait of a Lady*. Henrietta is definitely funny and a great deal of the comedy is generated as a byproduct of her daring excursions into traditionally male territory. Her opposite is Bob Bantling in whose name semic and phonosemic connotations combine to demasculinize it. Bob Bantling's sister is Lady Pensil.[9] James makes violent fun of Henrietta. But the satire is not really very malicious, on the contrary it often seems humorously tolerant. There is a good deal of sympathy in James's attitude towards Henrietta – maybe even some identification (Henry–Henrietta?). A great deal of James's juggling of sexual roles is explained by the amusement he found in the thought of the inversion of roles.

This is even more apparent in the short story 'The Death of the Lion'. In this story we find an author called Guy Walsingham. The name is a pseudonym, and behind it is a woman. Modesty and delicacy would conventionally be expected of a woman, but Guy, true to the demands of her inverted role, goes in for the 'larger latitude'.[10] Guy's complement, in the same story, is another author, Dora Forbes. Behind this female pseudonym is a man, and Dora is the author of a book with the appropriate title 'The Other Way Round'.

Whether we find these inversions funny or not there can be little doubt that James did. What particularly appealed to him was the lability in the attribution of roles – which is the main element in chiastic inversion – and it appealed to him for several reasons. One of these, though doubtless a minor one, was that the obliteration of sexual distinction gave a further twist to James's device of pronominal ambiguity. In Chapter 1 we saw how James in *The Golden Bowl* exploited every theoretical possibility of referential ambiguity in pronouns. The growth of ambiguity was nevertheless to some extent checked by the fact that English, in contrast to some other languages such as Finnish, makes a sexual distinction in the singular between several third person pronouns. In *The Golden Bowl* a 'he' can often mean either the Prince or Adam, but naturally neither Maggie nor Charlotte; and a 'she' can mean either Charlotte or Maggie, but naturally neither Adam nor the Prince. The sexual inversion in 'The Death of the Lion' does away with this restriction, since the woman is also a man, and the man also a woman, thanks to the pseudonyms. This is the ultimate in James's destruction of the stability and reliability of pronominal reference. Possibilities of confusion have been maximized and James contentedly settles down in 'The Death of the Lion' to some quiet fun with obscure references to 'he', 'she' and such expressions as *ces dames* etc.

This is all *playful*, even the lability, but ultimately it reveals a relativism which has some frightening implications of insecurity and uncertainty.

Another ironic inversion in James's onomastic practice is his habit of giving names with incongruously high-sounding classical or mythological allusions to servants.[11] James was a social snob, but to explain the callousness of his practice we need not know that he was. It suffices to recognize James's fondness of ironic inversion. For the satisfaction of indulging in chiastic inversion James is ready to sacrifice even his most cherished attitudes, to undermine his own beliefs and trample on the most noble sentiments he shares with his characters. No value, belief, attitude, emotion or theme is sacred enough to be allowed to stand in the way of chiastic inversion.

In the same way as James amuses himself with masculine and feminine he sometimes also plays with American and European. Many of his ostensibly European characters are in actual fact Americans in disguise. The two arch-European villains in *The Portrait of a Lady*, Mme Merle and Gilbert Osmond, are actually both Americans, like so many other 'Europeans' in this as well as in other works, and Mme Merle was born near the Brooklyn Navy Yard, one of the few places where the American flag is always flying. Even in James's ironic variations on his favourite theme of European–American there are obvious traces of chiastic inversion.

Relevant for an understanding of the anatomy of the pattern are also those of James's works that involve a '*Stellvertreter*-figure' – such as 'The Great Good Place' – and also those stories that deal with a 'split personality' – such as 'The Private Life' – since these two types of works are closely related to the case of a pure and complete occurrence of the pattern of chiastic inversion. What are stories about 'substitutes' and 'split personalities' if not yet another testimony of uncertainty about roles?

Definitely related are those numerous Jamesian works in which the plot abounds in 'turning the tables'-inversions. In James's ghost story 'The Jolly Corner' the protagonist Spencer Brydon, on returning at the age of 56 to America and his native city New York, finds that a large and empty building, of which he is the owner, houses a ghost. The ghost is his *alter ego*, the man he would have become if he had stayed in America instead of emigrating to Europe at the age of 23. Normally, in literature, ghosts pursue the living, but in a typical 'turning of the tables'-inversion Spencer decides to pursue the ghost. James's works abound in such inversions as this. But in particular they abound in *multiple* inversions. In 'The Jolly Corner' too there is soon another inversion of roles, when the ghost becomes the hunter and Spencer Brydon the hunted.

This 'turning of the tables'-element, which is so frequently used by James, again, like the full pattern of chiastic inversion, reveals the typical uncertainty as to roles: 'Who chases whom? Who haunts whom? In general, in life and the world, who does what to whom?'

'The Jolly Corner' is also interesting in that the *alter ego*-theme epitomizes the general tendency in James of the identification, one with the other, of the two agents whose roles are mutually interchangeable. We shall find later that there is often not a whit of difference between the two forces in many instances, and in 'The Jolly Corner' this tendency found its symbolic psychological epitomization: Spencer Brydon and the ghost really are one and the same. We shall return to the symbolic identification of the two opposing forces with each other later in this chapter, in connection with 'The Liar' and *The Turn of the Screw*.

Another elementary component that went into the making of the mechanism of chiastic inversion in its complete form is the idea of 'changing sides'. In 'Owen Wingrave' the hero's supervisor, Spencer Coyle, who was supposed to coach Owen in order to get him into the military profession, gets very angry on hearing Owen raise pacifist objections, and he sets in motion a machinery of pressure from the Wingrave family and their friends which in the end crushes the young man. But having started the whole thing Spencer Coyle rapidly regrets his action and soon fairly openly changes sides and comes to regard Owen's adherence to his principles as his real show of true courage. Coyle is a foreshadowing of Strether, who also changes sides, and there are numerous parallels at all stages of James's career.

The Ambassadors is one of James's artistically most successful uses of chiastic inversion. It belongs to the type of stories in which James put the pattern to use in connection with an 'educational theme'. The gradual, inevitable awakening of insecurity as to roles in James can lead to very satisfying results when the starting point is a situation in which the two opposing forces are characterized by rigid inflexibility, prejudice and blindness. The gradual weakening of belief in their original position on the part of the characters then becomes a record of their growth in wisdom, perception and tolerance.

There are a number of highly diagrammatical but very successful James stories of this type, whose plot-development resembles the initial stages of chiastic inversion, even though these stories do not really qualify as examples of the pattern. One such story is 'Madame de Mauves'.

For an excellent work in which chiastic inversion *is* used let us turn to 'The Real Thing'. In this story the protagonist, who is an artist, is visited in his studio by Major and Mrs Monarch, an upper-class couple who have lost their money and now want to earn a trifle by working as models. They try to talk the artist into accepting them, arguing that since they are 'the real thing' he could use them as models when he draws upper-class characters.

The artist already has a model, a Miss Churm, a cockney girl who possesses neither 'h's nor refinement but does have an ability to inspire the artist and make him draw whatever is needed at the moment. Major and Mrs Monarch in contrast are 'the real thing', but the real thing only, and they have a harmful influence on his art. The artist also picks up an itinerant Italian, Oronte, giving him employment first as a servant but by and by to an increasing extent also as a model.

The artist thus has two models who are upper-class and two who are lower-class. In the work he is supposed to illustrate there are upper-class people, above all the hero and the heroine, and lower-class people, such as servants. The temptation of chiastic inversion is irresistible. Gradually the artist reaches a decision to use Miss Churm and Oronte as models for the heroine and hero. The complementary decision, which makes the chiastic pattern complete, is to use Major and Mrs. Monarch as models for the pictures of servants, which he also does.

Major and Mrs Monarch had thought they would be used for the pictures of the hero and the heroine and when they discover the truth there is a scene and they leave the studio. After three days, however, they return. They are poor and have no choice. While Oronte and Miss Churm sit for pictures of the hero and the heroine, Major and Mrs Monarch begin to tidy up and wash dishes. The servants have become masters and the masters servants.

In the final scene the chiastic situation is reflected in a sentence which itself has precisely a chiastic structure:

If my servants were my models, then my models might be my servants.[12]

'The Real Thing' is a little masterpiece of its kind, and chiastic inversion helps in its creation. The suggestiveness of the pattern enriches the theme with a number of important and interesting questions. The pathos, or even tragedy, of the action gives rise to a number of questions for the reader as well as the protagonist. What is 'the real thing'? What are the relations between life and art? No clear answers are provided and even the role of the protagonist in the early part of the story is open to several interpretations. But all of these things combine to enrich the effect. The uncertainty brought about by the chiastic inversion is thematically meaningful.

Chiastic inversion reappears in one James story after another. It did not always make his works better, and in a number of cases it quite possibly made them worse, but 'The Real Thing' shows how fruitful the pattern could be.

A number of James stories which depend on the pattern of chiastic inversion are rather shallow and artificial. In 'The Wheel of Time', for instance, the whole interest lies in the chiastic switch. In the first half of the story a Lady Greywood tries to make her son, Maurice, marry a young woman, Fanny Knocker, who is thought to be very ugly. Maurice, who is very handsome, tries hard but cannot in the end bring himself to do it. In the second part of the story the wheel of time has effected the chiastic switch. Maurice is now forty-nine and has a daughter of eighteen, Vera, who is very ugly. The symmetrical development is of course that Fanny has a boy of about the same age who is very good-looking. The situation is reversed for Maurice and Fanny in the lives they live vicariously through their children. Fanny's son cannot bring himself to like Vera. She is rejected in the same way as Maurice had earlier rejected Fanny. But a reversal has also taken place with Fanny and Maurice themselves. Fanny has become a brilliant beauty whereas Maurice is reported as rather wasted.

The working out of the chiastic pattern in 'The Wheel of Time' is rather mechanical. The story suffers from the same weakness as many of James's works, particularly during the early nineties, in which abstract patterns and symmetries take precedence over human interests and lives.[13]

In using the pattern of chiastic inversion James sometimes clearly and unambiguously spelt it out, as in *The Ambassadors* or 'The Wheel of Time'. In 'The Real Thing' the pattern is also clearly presented even though the interpretation of its precise significance is another matter. But James was very fond of ending the development of chiastic inversion half-way so as to leave it an ambiguous suggestion. This is the most important type of his various uses of chiastic inversion and the type that properly concerns us here.

In these works the new position of the agents *after* the inversion has taken place does not cancel out the meaning of their positions *before* the inversion. We get a curious 'double exposure' of two stories in one. A better understanding of these 'double-exposure'-works also brings with it a better understanding of the role of oxymoron in James's style because to a large extent oxymoron is a direct result of the type of chiastic structure in which the inversion and the new division of roles it brings with it does not cancel out the original situation.

Two examples of Jamesian 'double-exposure'-stories resulting from incompletely realized chiastic inversion are 'The Liar' and *The Turn of the Screw*. The former story initially seems to be about a liar, Colonel Capadose, and an honest artist, Lyon, who is James's 'centre' of narration. By and by the chiastic reversal of roles is suggested. Colonel Capadose, who should have been the villainous liar, is gradually revealed as a rather harmless Baron von Münchausen-type raconteur, whereas the narrator Lyon, who should have been blameless, more and more comes over as the real liar.

Nevertheless, the inverted reading does not entirely cancel out the initial 'straight' one, and in Lyon's own perception the situation remains uninverted. Accordingly Lyon talks about the situation in the language of the uninverted chart. But at the same time James has to suggest the inverted reading to the reader and the only contact that an author has with his readers is the text. Accordingly James also has to put in material that deals with the situation in the language of the inverted chart. It is precisely this double allegiance of language, on the one hand to Lyon and the uninverted state, and on the other to Capadose and the inverted state, that explains why oxymora are so characteristic of James's prose.

When Lyon has decided to make the portrait of the Colonel a malicious caricature he congratulates himself in advance with the following reflection:

He would draw him out, he would set him up in that totality

about which he had talked with Sir David, and none but the initiated would know. They, however, would rank the picture high, and it would be indeed six rows deep – a masterpiece of fine characterization, of *legitimate treachery*.[14] (my italics)

The self-contradictory nature of 'legitimate treachery' can be explained as a result of the 'double-exposure'-technique. In Figure 3 Level 1 stands for good and Level 2 for bad. The tension

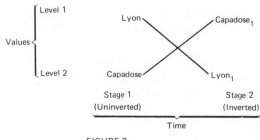

FIGURE 3

within the combination 'legitimate treachery' exists because 'legitimate' is pre-inversion vocabulary, loyal to Lyon and the 'straight' reading in which the narrator is regarded as reliable, whereas 'treachery' is post-inversion vocabulary, loyal to Capadose and the alternative reading which takes the narrator to be unreliable. Oxymoron comes into existence because the passing of plot-time does not cancel out pre-inversion values in these double-exposure works. On the contrary two complete but mutually exclusive sets of values coexist during the later stages of the story, and this, taken to its extreme, inevitably leads to oxymoron.

What gives the impression of a 'double exposure' to the reader must of course be the result of a 'double vision' on the part of the author. The lability of values which led to this was undoubtedly fed by ironic appreciation of the element that I already mentioned – humour. The role of humour in connection with oxymoron-producing chiastic inversion can be studied, for example, in the story 'The Next Time' in which there is a pure case of a chiastic situation. In this story there is one author who writes good books that do not sell, and another who writes bad books that do sell. The person writing good books that do not sell would like to write a bad book that *would* sell – he needs the money – whereas the person writing bad books that *do* sell would like to write a good book that would *not* sell – she needs the glory. The good author strives for the bad and the bad for the good. (Ironically both constantly fail). The friends of the good writer try to encourage him and exchanges like the following occur:

> 'The book has extraordinary beauty.'
> 'Poor duck – after trying so hard!'[15]

It is of course a result of the chiastic pattern that the bad is spoken about in terms of the good and the good in terms of the bad. As a consequence oxymoronic coupling, e.g. of a positive adjective with a negative noun (or *vice versa*), become common in stories with this type of chiastic situation, and in 'The Next Time' we find phrases such as 'an exquisite failure' (142); 'the hard doom of popularity' (143); 'magnificent mistake' (175); 'an unscrupulous, an unsparing, a shameless merciless masterpiece' (174) etc.

In passing I would like to remark here that the more one studies chiastic inversion the less inclined one becomes to take stories such as 'The Next Time' as serious statements on art with any extractable definite message whatsoever. Such stories as 'The Next Time' are undoubtedly related to James's own life, his lack of popular recognition etc., but I think the parallels are limited. Events of James's own life may have suggested the germ for such stories as 'The Next Time' but once pen was put to paper the lability of values inherent in the semi-obligatory pattern of chiastic inversion undermined any serious or unambiguous 'moral'. The lability, i.e. the easiness with which inversion occurs, was *funny* to James, in such cases as 'The Next Time', and this worked against the formulation of any definite moral or serious statement. The pattern also led to relativistic lability in works which are *not* funny, which is again testimony of the insecurity and uncertainty of James's world.

Oxymoron was a real mannerism with James. It is so frequent, in so many of his works, in so many contexts, that it cannot be attributed to the characters alone but must be taken to be characteristic also of the author who created them. Stories are told about celebrated oxymoronic *bons mots* delivered by James in his private life. Joseph Pennell wrote that James had described some visitors to Lamb House as 'sad wantons, one of whom was not without a pale cadaverous grace'.[16] James's 'stony twinkle of innocent malice' is also reported.[17] These reports suggest that James's private rhetoric was similar to his public.[18]

It is possible that the importance of oxymoron in James's style was inherited. Expressions such as 'flagrant morality' were household words for the James family.[19] Indeed one would imagine that the attitude of Henry James senior would very easily lead to a rise in the frequency and importance of oxymoron in his speech. Henry James senior was something of an outsider whose views were often opposed to current convention. Would he not then, in talking about things rated good by convention but judged bad in his own view, be bound to end up with an idiolect of which oxymoron was a characteristic feature? Insofar as I am able to make out, it seems that the principle of inversion – and even of the inversion of extreme opposites – plays an important role in Swedenborgianism. It is therefore quite possible that those of James's thought patterns that involve inversion were to a large extent handed over from his father.

Chiastic structuring on the thematic macrolevel in James's works is matched by chiastic structuring on the stylistic microlevel of the sentence. James made extensive use of the figure of *chiasmus*. It is particularly frequent in such works as *The Sacred Fount* where chiastic structuring on the thematic level was the starting point anyway.[20] Let us look at a few examples:

'I don't think, you know,' I made it out for her, 'it was my person, really, that gave its charm to my theory; I think it was much more my theory that gave its charm to my person.'

'Yours *was* mine, wasn't it? for a little, this morning. Or was it mine that was yours?' (147)

Poor Briss was in love with his wife – that, when driven to the wall, she had had to recognise; but she had not had to recognise that his wife was in love with poor Briss. (133)

In resisted observation that was vivid thought, in inevitable thought that was vivid observation. (75)

Gilbert Long had for her no connection, in my deeper sense, with Mrs Server, nor Mrs Server with Gilbert Long, nor the husband with the wife, nor the wife with the husband, nor I with either member of either pair, nor anyone with anything, nor anything with anyone. (132)

Chiastic structuring in the form of the figure of chiasmus on the sentence-level thus heralds its own presence in a different form on the thematic level. There are naturally examples of chiasmus in *The Golden Bowl* but there is not such a neat direct relationship between microlevel and macrolevel as in *The Sacred Fount*. Ultimately the use of chiasmus on the sentence-level in *The Golden Bowl* does provide evidence of the importance of the patterns of chiastic inversion on the thematic level too, but in a more indirect way, and it is more difficult to show such a strikingly obvious relation as in *The Sacred Fount*. It could be objected that chiasmus belongs to every author's arsenal of rhetorical figures and that their use in *The Golden Bowl* is merely decorative.

The case becomes much clearer when one realizes how closely antithesis and oxymoron are related to the pattern of chiastic inversion. In *The Golden Bowl* the presence of macrolevel chiastic inversion is signalled much more by microlevel antithesis and oxymoron than by chiasmus itself.

Maggie's 'blameless egoism' (441) in *The Golden Bowl* can be analyzed in the same way as Lyon's 'legitimate treachery' in 'The Liar'. And the strange coupling of the antithetical 'good faith' and 'false position' can be understood in the context of James's use of antitheses in general and their connection with thematic chiastic inversion.

It is worthwhile to take a closer look at James's antitheses. To begin with, one must note their sheer overwhelming frequency. It is indeed a favourite device. But not only is it very frequent; it is also very significant when it occurs.

The anatomy of James's antitheses is rather special. Of the features that make it up two are particularly important. One is the extreme separation of the opposed terms, i.e. the tendency to make any opposition an opposition of absolute extremes. The second is their labile interchangeability, which is necessary to make chiastic inversion possible.

The juxtaposition of interchangeable opposites on the sentence-level is connected with *humour* in the same way as the interchangeability on the thematic level. This is evident even from the amount of reported laughter and amusement. In the following example from *The Golden Bowl*, the Prince is 'amused' by an antithetical distinction of 'in' and 'out'.

> 'Ah, darling, goodness, I think, never brought any one out. Goodness, when it's real, precisely, rather keeps people *in*.' He had been interested in his discrimination, which amused him (42)

The governess in *The Turn of the Screw* reports that she 'laughed' while filling in the antithetical 'out':

> 'Then how did he get in?'
> 'And how did he get out?' I laughed. (23)

Miss Gostrey in *The Ambassadors* likewise 'laugh[s]':

> 'No – I think she finds she does. But that's what I mean by so describing her. It's *if* she does that she's splendid. But we'll see,' he wound up, 'where she comes out.'
> 'You seem to show me sufficiently,' Miss Gostrey laughed, 'where she goes in!' (241)

While the characters laugh the author presumably chuckled, and the characters laugh again and again in connection with 'playful' antitheses. Giving in to the lability of antithetic vacillation between one extreme and another always amuses James's characters, no matter how serious the occasion may be or what dreadful business may be in hand. Even the governess's exchange of divine for infernal is 'almost cheerful':

> 'The trick's played,' I went on; 'they've successfully worked their plan. He found the most divine little way to keep me quiet while she went off.'
> 'Divine?' Mrs Grose bewilderedly echoed.
> 'Infernal then!' I almost cheerfully rejoined. (67)

In the world of James's fiction opposites are mutually inter-changeable and the switch is funny, sometimes gruesomely funny, when it suggests the mental lability characteristic of people suffering from paranoia (– the 'turns' of the governess are strikingly similar to the drastic inversions typical of the mental processes of sick minds).

Another highly characteristic feature of the antitheses is that the antonymic structuring often appears to be obligatory. The best illustrations of this tendency are naturally to be found in *The Sacred Fount*:

> How I remember saying to myself that if she didn't get better she surely *must* get worse! (78)

Also:

> 'If she isn't now beastly unhappy –'
> 'She's beastly happy?' he broke in, getting firmer hold, if not of the real impression he had just been gathering under my eyes, then at least of something he had begun to make out that my argument required. (153)

Of course these views should primarily be attributed to the narrator rather than to James and the narrator may not be 'reliable'. But most of James's characters make use of this pattern of thinking. Even Strether, in *The Ambassadors*, is not above resorting to the lazy logic of obligatory antithetical structuring.

> Miss Gostrey gave him a look which broke the next moment into a wonderful smile: 'He is not as good as you think.'
> They remained with him, these words, promising him, in their character of warning, considerable help; but the support he tried to draw from them found itself, on each renewal of contact with Chad, defeated by something else. What could it be, this disconcerting force, he asked himself, but the sense, continually renewed, that Chad was – quite in fact insisted on being – as good as he thought? It seemed somehow as if he couldn't *but* be as good from the moment he wasn't as bad. (108)

Several critics, above all Shlomith Rimmon, have pointed out that it is a fallacy to apply such arguments as that of obligatory antithetical structuring to life. In *The Ambassadors* the development of the plot shows Strether his mistake. It is obvious that

James was aware of the doubtful nature of the pattern of obligatory antithetical structuring since he wrote many works in which such thinking leads his characters astray.

Yet the picture is far from clear. The pattern is all-pervasive in James and finally one can hardly avoid the conclusion that Strether's doubts are James's doubts, and that the narrator's frustration in *The Sacred Fount* is James's frustration, just as the insight and knowledge of those characters who discover the fallacy is also James's insight and knowledge. James doubtless, at least partly, undercuts the narrator in *The Sacred Fount* and casts doubt on his methods of reasoning. But they are methods that were, nevertheless, to a large extent James's own, and the epistemological insecurity of the characters and the readers can therefore be taken also as the author's insecurity.

The tendency is towards extremism. There is to be no middle ground or compromise, only extremist antonymic juxtaposition and then doubt and vacillation and total interchangeability. Often James juxtaposes absolutes like 'everything' and 'nothing' as in the following example from *The Golden Bowl*:

> 'Why that of having loved so intensely that she's as you say, "beyond everything"?'
> Maggie had scarcely to reflect – her answer was so prompt.
> 'Oh no. She's beyond nothing.' (175–6)

Cf. also:

> It was for Maggie to wonder, at present, if she had been sincere about their going, to ask herself whether she would have stuck to their plan even if nothing had happened.
> Her view of the impossibility of sticking to it now may give us the measure of her sense that everything had happened. (368)

and

> 'Then nothing, that evening of the Embassy dinner, passed between you?'
> 'On the contrary, everything passed.'
> 'Everything –?'
> 'Everything.' (491)

'Best' and 'worst' also often occur in the same way in many works, e.g. *The Golden Bowl*:

> 'But how – at the worst?'
> 'Oh, "the worst" – don't talk about the worst! I can keep them quiet at the best, I seem to feel, simply by our being there.' (432)

So do 'up' and 'down',

> 'Well, if they don't come down – ?'
> 'Then we'll come up.' (106)

also 'much' and 'little',

> 'Ah that's too much,' he laughed – 'or too little!' (*The Ambassadors*, 321)

and so on.

It is obvious that antithesis far from being a separating factor is on the contrary a strong *link* in James. Accordingly it has a close relationship with the type of textual progression that was dealt with in Chapter 2. When James, unable to let go of some idea within a sentence he has just written down, proceeds to let it grow over the sentence-border into the next sentence, the form that this growth takes is not only that of an addition of more material of the same tendency, but quite often the addition of a contradiction.

The feeling of 'not-quite-finished-yet' which leads to the kind of repetitional end-linking described in Chapter 2 also leads to typical Jamesian phrases such as 'he amended with a further thought'. Such further thoughts are not always, or even normally, content to remain minor modifications; on the contrary they often rush all the way to the absolute opposite and produce antitheses as in the following examples from *The Golden Bowl*:

> 'It's too soon – that is if it isn't very much too late.' (317)

Also:

> 'She has only twopence in the world – but that has nothing to

do with it. Or rather indeed' – she quicky corrected herself –
'it has everything.' (170)

And:

'You see too much – that's what may sometimes make you
difficulties. When you don't, at least,' he had amended with a
further thought, 'see too little.' (45)

Only the funny thing, he had respectfully submitted, was that
her father, though older and wiser, and a man into the
bargain, was as bad – that is as good – as herself.
   'Oh, he's better!' the girl had freely declared – 'that is he's
worse.' (ibid.)

These enthusiastic rushes to the other extreme on a continuum
are primarily typical of late James, but in fact he acquired the
habit early. Even in the early story of 'The Sweetheart of M.
Briseux' (1873), for instance, we find the following typical
example:

I was satisfied, and I left the Musée.
   It would perhaps be more correct to say that I was wholly
unsatisfied. I strolled . . .[22]

A natural inevitable effect of the interchangeability of antithetical opposites is ambiguity. One of the ways in which such
ambiguity arises is of course the problem of deciding what is
much, or little, when it is all relative to one's point of view. How
much, or how little, does Vanderbank, in *The Awkward Age*,
hesitate?

'I see,' Mitchy dropped. 'Such an inquiry might suggest to
him moreover that you're hesitating more than you perhaps
really are.'
   'Oh, as to *that*,' said Vanderbank, 'I think he practically
knows how much.'
   'And how little?'[23]

Naturally the ambiguity could here be seen as the problem of
deciding where precisely Vanderbank is on a scale of hesitation.

But what the example really illustrates is that *much and little mean the same* in James's world and in this phenomenon lies the real relevance of antitheses for ambiguity.

The belief that antithetical opposites are really the same is illustrated in James's love of 'quasi-opposition', a sort of semi-nonsensical pseudo-inversion of roles which involves a chiasmus that does not really change anything but leaves everything the same. The following example from *The Golden Bowl* is fairly typical:

> Well, he was *of* them now, of the rich peoples; he was on their side – if it wasn't rather the pleasanter way of putting it that they were on his. (50)

It *comes to the same thing*, as it were, and the semantic difference between the first part of a chiastic structure and the second part is often very slight. There is a feeling in James's works that statements ought to be complemented with their own chiastic variations.[24] Thus in *The Sacred Fount* Mrs Briss has to complete her statement 'I've not spoken to a creature.' (184) with 'Not a creature has spoken to me.' (185). Since it takes two people to have a conversation such inversions may amount to very little in practice. Indeed it is often spelt out about such quasi-inversion that 'it comes to the same thing' as in the following example, also from *The Sacred Fount*:

> 'She's all *in* it,' he insisted. 'Or it's all in *her*. It comes to the same thing.' (59)

Against the background of such examples as these it is possible to gain an insight into the strange semantic world in which it can be claimed that 'good faith' and 'false position' come to the same thing.

> 'I think there's nothing they're not now capable of – in their so intense good faith.'
> 'Good faith?' – he echoed the words, which had in fact something of an odd ring, critically.
> 'Their false position. It comes to the same thing.' (312)

The whole question of *the similarity of the different* lies at the root of the problem of insecurity in the world of James's fiction. In James there is always a possibility that *the ostensibly different is actually the same*. The villain plays the hero and the hero plays the villain. Good is bad and bad is good. Fair is foul and foul is fair – 'it comes to the same thing'. As the governess says in *The Turn of the Screw*:

> Nothing was more natural than that these things should be the other things they absolutely were not. (30)

Possibly the extreme eagerness with which the opposition is made as total as possible has something to do with the sense that in the end it does not matter, since even in their extreme polarization the antonyms are mutually interchangeable. James's detachment led to the creation of a whole series of works in which the polarization of the antagonistic forces is total and both are equally dislikeable. The negativism of James's world comes over strongly in those stories in which the protagonist is made to choose between pest and cholera. Verena Tarrant in *The Bostonians* is faced with the choice between an ultra-feminist fanatic and a male-chauvinist reactionary. Surely the world is peopled also by other types of people than these two? But not James's world – in the world of James's fiction, if you are not one thing, you are bound to be its extreme opposite. Hyacinth Robinson in *The Princess Casamassima* faces another choice between pest and cholera. James gives such a negative picture of anarchist revolutionaries on the one hand, and of the upper-class establishment on the other, that it would have been absurd for Hyacinth to pledge his allegiance to either, and the book very properly ends with his self-immolation.

The Princess Casamassima and *The Bostonians* were concerned with politics and as we know James did not choose sides or get involved with any degree of enthusiasm in such issues.[25] But it is not only in politics that James's characters face choices between mutually contradictory alternatives which, although ostensibly very different, are yet the same in that the two alternatives are both equally bad. Catherine Sloper in *Washington Square* is torn between a tyrannical father and a silly lover, both equally dislikeable; Morgan Moreen in 'The Pupil' between a disreputable family and a hesitant tutor-friend, and so on and so forth. Why should there always be this impossible choice between alternatives of which neither is worthy of serious consideration?

The way out of hesitation in James's world is punishment of one's self. The morality is a morality of compensation and the religion is one of sacrifice. In order to make it in art the artist Félix Vendemer in 'Collaboration' has to give up his fiancée. This plot-development has numerous parallels in other James works. In order to gain something you have to give up something; that is a logical conclusion for a manner of thinking which relies on chiastic structuring in the form of the see-saw mechanism. If one is to go up, something else must go down, must it not? If something is to get better something else must get worse, must it not? Perhaps the process is reversible! Perhaps – by ensuring that something gets worse or goes down; perhaps by sacrificing something – by staying celibate, by renouncing one's native country etc. – something else may automatically get better or go up?

But what if there is a fault in the model? What if you could have had both things? Neither James nor his characters are quite sure that the chiastic see-saw model is valid logic. James felt an insecurity of choice which was not only an insecurity as to choice of actions and beliefs but even of epistemological choice. He punished his characters by putting them in situations of impossible choices. In his early career this was choices of action ('What should I do? Should I choose Olive Chancellor or Basil Ransom? Should I choose art or life?'); in his later career epistemological choices ('Are the children divine or infernal? What is true and what is false? What *is* and what *is not*?').

By the middle of his career James had found a new victim – the reader. Now the uncertainty is triple: in such works as 'The Liar', 'The Lesson of the Master', 'The Figure in the Carpet', *The Turn of the Screw* and *The Sacred Fount* the author does not know, the characters do not know and the readers do not know. How could anyone believe firmly in anything in a world where *the different is really the same*? – where the ubiquitous refrain is that 'it comes to the same thing'?

The problematical relation in James between identity and identicality is revealed in his style. It is through his difference from others that a person acquires an identity. But 'the different is really the same' in James so pronominal confusion is possible and the identity of the referent unclear. Amerigo and Adam are different people by definition, but both play the same role as objects of Maggie's love, so a 'he' could mean either. Charlotte and Maggie are certainly different persons, but they are the same in that they are both the Prince's and so a 'she' could refer to either. Maggie+Adam and Charlotte+Amerigo on the one hand, and Charlotte+Adam and Maggie+Amerigo on the other, are certainly two different sets of couples, but 'it comes to the same thing', and there is not a whit of difference between the couple of Maggie/Adam and the couple Charlotte/Amerigo and so a 'they' can refer to either in the conversations of the Assinghams.

Words belong to different types, and in speaking or writing like should be combined with like, but if 'the different is the same' then 'legitimate' and 'treachery', and 'blameless' and 'egoism', and 'good faith' and 'false position', can be oxymoronically brought together – they may seem different, but 'it comes to the same thing'.

The interchangeability of antonymic words on the sentence-level is mirrored in the interchangeability in roles of antagonistic forces on the thematic level. No matter how polarized or how different they seem they are really very similar. A perfect form of similarity is identicality. In the 'appearance and reality'-variant of chiastic inversion James often signals the interchangeability of roles through recurrent symbolic identification of the opponents with each other. It is worthwhile to look at two such cases in detail, since these may explain why Maggie is 'neither saint nor witch'[26] and why there is no difference between Charlotte and Amerigo on the one hand and Maggie and Adam on the other. The two works are 'The Liar' and *The Turn of the Screw.*

In 'The Liar' there are a number of passages in which the narrator is symbolically identified with Colonel Capadose so as to suggest the actual sameness of the seemingly different roles of the two. Lyon is repeatedly shown doing the same thing as the Colonel, as in the following passage:

> He [the Colonel] leaned forward (Lyon leaned forward to listen). (292)

The implication is that Lyon does the same as the Colonel in every respect. In that case he also lies, and the title of the story could refer to either the Colonel or to Lyon. The equation between the two men is established early in the story during a dinner-conversation when a character compares the Colonel and Lyon:

'He's [the Colonel] exceedingly clever and amusing – quite the cleverest person in the house, unless indeed you're more so.' (14)

By the end of the story the symbolic identification can be established quite openly:

Lyon imitated the Colonel (338)

Lyon is a painter, but the Colonel too is in some sense an artist. Painting-metaphors throughout the story equate Lyon and the Colonel:

'Then everything he told me last night, I now see, was tarred with that brush.' (309)

He [the Colonel] lays on colour, as it were, and what less do I do myself? (314)

These painting-metaphors suggest either that the Colonel is engaged in a harmless art rather than a vice, or else, because of the equation, they suggest that Lyon's painting is as evil as the Colonel's lying.

In fact the equation suggests both of these, i.e. both that good is bad, and that bad is good, and the reader is faced with an impossible choice. In one scene in the story Capadose is telling Lyon a tall tale about a ghost at the country-house where they are both staying.

'Oh don't go to the end of it [a corridor]!' the Colonel warningly smiled.

'Does it lead to the haunted room?' Lyon asked.

His companion looked at him a moment. 'Ah you know about that?'

'No, I don't speak from knowledge, only from hope. I've never had any luck – I've never stayed in a spooky house. The places I go to are always as safe as Charing Cross. I want to see – whatever there is, the regular thing. *Is* there a ghost here?'

'Of course there is – a rattling good one.'

'And have you seen him?'

'Oh don't ask me what *I've* seen – I should tax your credulity. I don't like to talk of these things. But there are two or three as bad – that is, as good! – rooms as you'll find anywhere.' (302)

Just as 'good' and 'bad' come to the same thing on the sentence-level in this passage so they also do on the thematic level in the entire story. Lyon and the Colonel are *the same*, which means that they are either *both* good or *both* bad.

When Lyon paints the Colonel's portrait and makes it a malicious caricature he is at the same time painting himself ('the liar') since the two men are the same. That he is in fact painting himself is suggested early in the story:

'But I've heard of you,' the lady went on. 'I know your pictures; I admire them. But I don't think you look like them.'

'They're mostly portraits,' Lyon said; 'and what I usually try for is not my own resemblance.'

'I see what you mean. But they've much more colour. Don't you suppose Vandyke's things tell a lot about him?' (286)

Despite his denial Lyon will in fact soon try for his own likeness, when he paints 'the liar'.

One half of the effect of the symbolic identification of the two men is to suggest that the Colonel's activities are harmless – since they come to the same as those of Lyon; who is on that reading a 'reliable' narrator and worthy of the readers' sympathy. But the other half suggests that Lyon's activities are the opposite of harmless, since they come to the same as those of the Colonel.[27]

At the beginning of the story there is the humorous suggestion that Lyon's portraits kill people. Lyon has come to paint Sir David, the old master of the house and Sir David has never allowed himself to be painted before.

'I'm surprised at his never having had anything done – at their waiting all these years.'

'Ah that's because he was afraid, you know; it was his pet

superstition. He was sure that if anything were done he would die directly afterwards. He has only consented to-day.'

'He's ready to die, then?'

'Oh now he's so old he doesn't care.'

'Well, I hope I shan't kill him,' said Lyon. 'It was rather unnatural of his son, to send for me.' (ibid.)

The humorous idea of Lyon's portrait killing him off is discarded as a reason for Sir David's hesitation when the old gentleman himself gives a rival explanation: he had waited because he thought that a portrait should show the mature man, with the sum of his experience. The reason for bringing in the humorous idea that Lyon's portraits have the power to kill, was of course that when regarded as a symbolic pointer the idea is not that humorous at all. Lyon's portraits *do* kill. By painting a malicious caricature of the Colonel Lyon tries to kill him in Everina's affections. This theme is taken up in a symbolic action when the Colonel slashes the portrait, during his and his wife's visit to Lyon's studio.

He [the Colonel] came up to the picture again – again he covered it with his baffled glare. 'Damn him – damn him – damn him!' he broke out once more. Yet it wasn't clear to Lyon whether this malediction had for object the guilty original or the guilty painter. The Colonel turned away and moved about as if looking for something; Lyon for the moment wondered at his intention; saying to himself the next, however, below his breath: 'He's going to do it a harm!' His first impulse was to raise a preventive cry, but he paused with the sound of Everina Brant's sobs still in his ears. The Colonel found what he was looking for – found it among some odds and ends on a small table and strode back with it to the easel. At one and the same moment Lyon recognized the object seized as a small Eastern dagger and saw that he had plunged it into the canvas. Animated as with a sudden fury and exercising a rare vigour of hand, he dragged the instrument down – Lyon knew it to have no very fine edge – making a long and abominable gash. Then he plucked it out and dashed it again several times into the face of the likeness, exactly as if he were stabbing a human victim: it had the most portentous effect – that of some act of prefigured or rehearsed suicide. In a few seconds more the Colonel had tossed the dagger away – he looked at it in this motion as for the sight of blood – and hurried out of the place with a bang of the door. (336–7)

A little later:

The portrait had a dozen jagged wounds – the Colonel had literally hacked himself to death. (337)

Lyon tries to kill the Colonel in Everina's affection with the aid of the portrait. The symbolic killing of the image on the canvas suggests that some killing takes place. But again, since the Colonel and Lyon are the same, Lyon's attempt to kill the Colonel at the same time becomes an attempt to kill himself, and the end of the story leaves it an ambiguous point which liar has been killed in Everina's affections, the Colonel or Lyon.

Lyon tried to kill Everina's love for her husband by making her ashamed of him. At the end of the story it seems that Everina *has* become ashamed, but it could be of either liar, Lyon or Capadose, or even of both. At the beginning of the story it is established in a passage of 'foretelling' that Everina's feeling of shame – which is the key-note of the whole theme of the story – could be caused by either of her two admirers:

They passed out of the dining-room, and this master of anecdote Colonel Capadose, who went among the first, was separated from his newest victim; but a minute later, before they reached the dining-room, he had come back. 'Ashmore tells me who you are. Of course I've often heard of you. I'm very glad to make your acquaintance. My wife used to know you.'

'I'm glad she remembers me. I recognised her at dinner and was afraid she didn't.'

'Ah I daresay she was ashamed,' said the Colonel with genial ease.

'Ashamed of me?' Lyon replied in the same key. (293–4)

That Lyon, not Capadose, is the one she should be ashamed of is an equally plausible interpretation as the opposite at the end of the story.

This ambiguity was signalled at the beginning of the slashing-scene by the typical Jamesian device that we dealt with in Chapter 1, i.e. the referential ambiguity of a pronoun. It is not clear whom the 'him' refers to – who should be damned.

> 'Damn him – damn him – damn him! he [the Colonel] broke out once more. Yet it wasn't clear to Lyon whether this malediction had for object the guilty original or the guilty painter. (336)

It is interesting to note here that, using the opportunity of speaking, as it were, from the point of view of the Colonel in the phrase 'the guilty painter', Lyon manages to equate the two liars through the word 'guilty' which is applied to both of them.

There is a similar confusion of pronouns earlier in the story to alert the readers' attention to the play of identities:

> 'He has been a great deal in India – isn't he rather celebrated?' she put it. Lyon confessed he had never heard of him, and she went on: 'Well perhaps he isn't; but he says he is, and if you think it that's just the same, isn't it?'
>   'If you think it?'
>   'I mean if he thinks it – that's just as good, I suppose.'
>   'Do you mean if he thinks he has done things he hasn't?' (285)

Throughout the story Lyon and the Colonel do the same thing. When Lyon lies the Colonel lies; when the Colonel lies Lyon lies. When the Colonel does not lie Lyon does not either, and when Lyon does not the Colonel does not either. During the sittings, when Lyon paints his malicious caricature – an act which amounts to a species of lying unless the Colonel really deserves it – the Colonel indulges in his favourite vice. Lyon is not content to lie through his painting during these sittings but does it verbally too.

> Lyon applied without mercy his own gift of provocation; he couldn't possibly have been in a better relation to him for that purpose. (325)

When the Colonel does not lie, the painting does not proceed. This connection between the two makes it very clear that painting the portrait is a mendacious act. The word 'act', by the way, is a favourite among the words James used for ambiguity throughout his career and in the following quotation it is used for a multiplicity of purpose. Calling the Colonel's behaviour 'acting' makes it easier to see that Lyon's act of painting comes to the same. But there is also the theatrical sense of 'acting', i.e. playing roles, pretending to be something else. In the theatrical sense both men are 'actors'.

> He encouraged, beguiled, excited him, manifested an unfathomable credulity, and his own sole lapses were when the Colonel failed, as he called it, to 'act'. He had his intermissions, his hours of sterility, and then Lyon knew that the picture also drooped. The higher his companion soared, the more he circled and sang in the blue, the better he felt himself paint; he only couldn't make the flights and the evolutions last. He lashed his victim on when he flagged; his one difficulty was his fear again that his game might be suspected. The Colonel, however, was easily beguiled; he basked and expanded in the fine steady light of the painter's attention. In this way the picture grew very fast, astonishingly faster, in spite of its so much greater 'importance,' than the simple-faced little girl's. (325)

'The Liar' is a case of incomplete chiastic inversion of the 'appearance and reality'-variety. One of James's means of suggesting the interchangeability in roles between the two antagonistic forces (the Colonel and Lyon) was the device of symbolic identification.

James's characters often do precisely the things they most condemn in others. Judged by their own standards many of them fare very badly. Many critics have noted this and studies dealing with this discrepancy have actually become quite a recognizable 'genre' in James criticism. A typical example is E. Duncan Aswell's 'James's *In the Cage*: The Telegraphist as Artist'.[28] As Aswell points out the telegraphist consistently does exactly the things she most criticizes in others. What Aswell and other critics have unveiled are in fact the surface manifestations of the underlying rule of the 'similarity of differents' in James.

The Turn of the Screw is very similar to 'The Liar'. Ostensibly it is a story about a heroic governess fighting two evil ghosts who pose a threat to two children in the governess' charge. By and by, however, it is suggested that the ghosts may in fact be rather harmless, whereas the real threat to the children may be the governess. The chiastic inversion is incomplete; though the second reading is firmly established through extensive hints it does not entirely cancel out the first alternative. The reader is faced with an impossible choice. In *The Turn of the Screw* as in 'The Liar' the interchangeability in roles between the two antagonistic forces (governess and ghosts) is signalled through a number of passages in which the governess is symbolically identified with the ghosts.   After seeing the male ghost, Peter Quint, for the second time the governess places herself exactly where he had been, and scares the housekeeper, Mrs Grose, the way the ghost had scared her:

> He was there or was not there: not there if I didn't see him. I got hold of this: then, instinctively, instead of returning as I had come, went to the window. It was confusedly present to me that I ought to place myself where he had stood. I did so; I applied my face to the pane and looked, as he had looked, into the room. As if, at this moment, to show me exactly what his range had been. Mrs Grose, as I had done for himself just before, came in from the hall. With this I had the full image of a repetition of what had already occurred. She saw me as I had seen my own visitant; she pulled up short as I had done; I gave her something of the shock that I had received. She turned white, and this made me ask myself if I had blanched as much. She stared, in short, and retreated just on *my* lines, and I knew she had then passed out and come round to me and that I should presently meet her. I remained where I was, and while I waited I thought of more things than one. But there's only one I take space to mention. I wondered why *she* should be scared. (21)

In a similar scene later on in the story the governess is identified with the female ghost Miss Jessel in the same way:

> Tormented, in the hall, with difficulties and obstacles, I remember sinking down at the foot of the staircase – suddenly collapsing there on the lowest step and then, with a revulsion, recalling that it was exactly where, more than a month before,

in the darkness of night and just so bowed with evil things, I
had seen the spectre of the most horrible of women. (58–9)

The governess is also symbolically identified with the ghosts
when the children behave towards her in the same manner as she
thinks they had behaved or behave towards the ghosts. The
governess thinks that the boy Miles has turned an 'upward look'
on Quint; the story shows him turning an upward look on the
governess:

> The shock had in truth sunk into me still deeper than I knew
> on the night when, looking out either for Quint or for Miss
> Jessel under the stars, I had seen there the boy over whose rest
> I watched and who had immediately brought in with him –
> had straightway there turned on me – the lovely upward look
> with which, from the battlements above us, the hideous
> apparition of Quint had played. (52–3)

Alternatively the governess herself does something which she has
already intimately associated with the behaviour of the ghosts.
Being bare-headed is such an action. Quint wore no hat.
Accordingly when the children go out bare-headed the governess
thinks they are under the influence of the ghosts. But when she
goes out to save them and wrest them from the influence of the
ghost, she herself goes 'with nothing on' (67). The sequence of
scenes resulting in this case of symbolic identification can be
illustrated with three quotations. First Flora goes out without a
hat:

> I had made up my mind. 'She has gone out.'
> Mrs Grose stared. 'Without a hat?'
> I naturally also looked volumes. 'Isn't that woman always
> without one?'
> 'She's with *her*?'
> 'She's with *her*!' I declared. 'We must find them.' (ibid.)

Then the governess identifies herself with the ghosts by going out
bare-headed herself:

> My companion still demurred: the storm of the night and the
> early morning had dropped, but the afternoon was damp and
> grey. I came down to the drive while she stood in the doorway.

'You go with nothing on?' (ibid.)

When she finds Flora she thinks of the girl's bare-headedness as proof of the ghostly influence, but the bare-headedness that the story shows us Flora noticing is that of the governess:

> It was Flora who, gazing all over me in candid wonder, was the first. She was struck with our bareheaded aspect. 'Why where are your things?'
> 'Where yours are, my dear!' I promptly returned.
> She had already got back her gaiety and appeared to take this as an answer quite sufficient. (70)

In the story Mrs Grose compares the present governess with the former, somewhat in the same manner that the dinner-guest in 'The Liar' compared Colonel Capadose and Lyon:

> 'What was the lady who was here before?'
> 'The last governess? She was also young and pretty – almost as young and almost as pretty, Miss, even as you.' (12)

The governess herself, too, compares herself to the ghosts in the same way as Lyon compared himself to the Colonel:

> I was queer company enough – quite as queer as the company I received; (25)

In a conversation between the governess and Mrs Grose it is ambiguously suggested that the state of affairs at Bly under the governess' regime is the same as under that of Quint.

> 'His [Quint's] effect?' she repeated with a face of anguish and waiting while I faltered.
> 'On innocent little precious lives. They were in your charge?'
> 'No they weren't in mine!' she roundly and distressfully returned. 'The master believed in him and placed him here because he was supposed not to be quite in health and the country air so good for him. So he had everything to say. Yes' – she let me have it – 'even about *them.*'
> 'Them – that creature?' I had to smother a kind of howl.

'And you could bear it?'

'No. I couldn't – and I can't now!' And the poor woman burst into tears. (27)

This could mean that the housekeeper could not bear it then, when Quint was in charge, nor bear to think about it now. But it could also mean that she could not bear it then, when Quint was in charge, nor now, when the governess is in charge, which again equates the governess and the ghost. The present time and the past are also brought together in a comparison late in the story:

'Laws!' said my friend under her breath. The exclamation was homely, but it revealed a real acceptance of my further proof of what, in the bad time – for there had been a worse even than this! – must have occurred. (49)

In a conversation after one of the appearances of the female ghost it is again suggested that the governess affects the housekeeper in the same way as the ghosts affect the governess, i.e. there is an identity of roles between governess and ghosts.

'She just appeared and stood there – but not so near.'

'And without coming nearer?'

'Oh for the effect and the feeling she might have been as close as you!'

My friend, with an odd impulse fell back a step. (31)

A little later:

Mrs Grose tried to see it. 'Fixed her?'

'Ah with such awful eyes!'

She stared at mine as if they might really have resembled them. (32)

Also:

There was a way to deal with that, and I dealt; the more readily for my full vision – on the evidence – of our employer's late clever good-looking 'own' man: impudent, assured, spoiled, depraved. 'The fellow was a hound.'

Mrs Grose considered as if it were perhaps a little a case for a sense of shades. 'I've never seen one like him. He did what he wished.'

'With *her*?'

'With them all.'

It was as if now in my friend's own eyes Miss Jessel had again appeared. (33)

When Quint appears for the third time the governess thinks the children – who have got out of bed – have again been to the garden to meet the ghost, but in a conversation between the governess and Flora the governess suggests herself as an alternative, thereby again equating herself with the ghost:

> 'You were looking for me out of the window?' I said. 'You thought I might be walking in the grounds?'
>
> 'Well, you know, I thought some one was' – she never blanched as she smiled out that at me. (42)

The governess denies that she is a 'fiend' ('As I'm not a fiend', 50), but the word again couples her with the ghosts. So do other words and epithets, in particular the prison imagery which is so prominent in the tale. The governess compares herself to a gaoler; she is 'like a gaoler with an eye to possible surprises and escapes' (54), which again links her to the ghosts, since Quint in the final scene comes 'into view like a sentinel before a prison' (85).

The bond between opposites is strong in James. James's characters often talk about their foes in affectionate terms. This on one reading is ironical, but on the other a means of symbolic identification of opposed forces with each other. In *The Turn of the Screw* the governess has by the latter half of the story become so mixed up with the ghosts that she calls them her 'friends':

> 'I only went with you for the walk,' I said. 'I had then to come back to meet a friend.'
>
> She showed her surprise. 'A friend – *you*?'
>
> 'Oh yes, I've a couple!' I laughed. (60)

In the scene by the lake the governess tries to point out Miss Jessel to Flora and Mrs Grose. But the housekeeper sees nothing and the girl turns her eyes on the governess. To the governess

Miss Jessel's appearance will be proof that she (the present governess) is sane:

> She was there, so I was justified; she was there, so I was neither cruel nor mad. She was there for poor scared Mrs Grose, but she was there most for Flora; and no moment of my monstrous time was perhaps so extraordinary as that in which I consciously threw out to her – with the sense that, pale and ravenous demon as she was, she would catch and understand it – an inarticulate message of gratitude. (71)

When Flora sees nothing (or pretends to see nothing) the governess insists in a sentence which again symbolically identifies her with the ghost:

> 'She's there, you little unhappy thing – there, *there*, and you know it as well as you know me!' (72)

Flora demands to be taken away, not from her former but from her present governess. She has a night of 'extreme unrest, a night agitated above all by fears that had for their subject not in the least her former but wholly her present governess'. (74).

The final symbolic identification of the governess with the ghosts involves the use of the typical Jamesian ambiguity-creating device of the unclear reference. Miles's 'you devil' (88) in the final scene could be directed either to Quint or to the governess.[29]

And indeed anything in *The Turn of the Screw* could be either the ghosts or the governess, because in the strange world of James's fiction it all 'comes to the same thing'. I have gone through 'The Liar' and *The Turn of the Screw* at such tiresome length because it is only against such a background as this that one can comprehend the total sameness in roles of the two antagonistic forces in *The Golden Bowl*. The two couples – Charlotte+the Prince and Maggie+her father – are opposed, but there is not a whit of difference between one and the other.

Critics have been sharply divided in opinion over *The Golden Bowl*. Two camps have come into existence. One sympathizes with Maggie and Adam, and denigrate Charlotte and the Prince in the same degree as they praise Adam and Maggie. The other faction sides with Charlotte and the Prince and accordingly make out Maggie and Adam rather monstrous.

I believe that both schools are wrong when taken separately, but that taken together they are right. In other words the divided response is precisely the right reaction to the novel. What exists in the novel is truthfully mirrored in what criticism has found; yet not in the findings of either of the schools, but in the sum of opinion of the two schools.

When critics cannot make up their minds whether Maggie is a saint or a witch a natural way out would be a compromise – that it may be true that Maggie is a saint but it is not the whole truth; or that it may be true that she is a witch but neither is that the whole truth: that neither Maggie nor Charlotte are entirely good or bad, but rather a mixture of both – in other words human.

But one wonders. It may be that Walter Wright has chosen the wrong pair of words after all, when he claims in the title of his article that Maggie is '*Neither* Saint *nor* Witch' (my italics). Maybe it is not 'neither–nor' but rather 'either–or', which is, after all, the right pair of words. Maggie (like Charlotte) is '*both–and*' – both a saint and a witch in the sense that the material for either reading is present in James's text. But what is also there in James's text, as in his thinking, is the horror of the middle ground. The pattern demands extremism, both on the sentence-level of style and on the thematic level. Oppositions in James tend to be of absolute extremes. In other words, chiastic inversion in James does not mean that a character is both good and bad in the sense of being a little of both. On the contrary such characters are *both good and bad*, but both *extremely* good and *extremely* bad, and we do not know which.

The process typical of James's thinking is to first drag the two opposites wide asunder, making them as absolutely antithetical as possible, and then to begin to create doubt as to which is which. We saw this tendency in the lability and interchangeability of terms which are each others' absolute opposites on the stylistic level of the sentence. The same tendency appears on the thematic level.

The truest response to *The Golden Bowl* is bewilderment. The novel is full of the same type of symbolic identification of opposites as those of 'The Liar' and *The Turn of the Screw*. As I pointed out in Chapter 1, the symbolic identification of the Maggie–Adam couple with the Charlotte–Amerigo one is found even in their respective relation to the central symbol of the novel, the golden bowl. When Charlotte and the Prince consider buying it they are out together, on the very eve of the Prince's and Maggie's marriage. The Prince is symbolically unfaithful to his wife with Charlotte. But when Maggie later on in the novel buys the bowl she is out hunting for a birthday present for her father. She is symbolically unfaithful to the Prince with her father. If the bowl has a crack and the crack is symbolic of the flaw in a relationship, which relationship is it? That of Maggie and Amerigo? Or of Maggie and Adam? Or of Amerigo and Maggie? Or of Amerigo and Charlotte? It is more important to note that we are made to ask these questions rather than to sort out possible answers. It should be noted that ambiguity reigns supreme in every respect. Amerigo and Charlotte may seem more guilty to begin with, but then it can be observed that Charlotte and Amerigo do not buy the bowl, whereas Maggie really does. In fact the reader's vacillation is endless and the choice impossible.

It is true that Charlotte and the Prince take advantage of their situation, but then to a large extent Maggie and her father prepare that situation for them, and almost invite them to take advantage of it. There is often this kind of strange collusion between the perpetrator and the victim of a wrong in James.[30] Potential victims perversely seek out their punishment, and those who are destined to mete out that punishment sometimes seem to do it almost reluctantly. The Prince at Matcham reflects that it would be almost ludicrous if he did not take advantage of the situation; it would be a slur on his Italian manhood.[31]

Tony Tanner in his essay 'The Fearful Self' points out that Isabel almost wilfully seeks out her punishment:

> He is a collector of things, and she offers herself up to him as a fine finished object. Isabel accepting Osmond's proposal of marriage is the uncertain self thinking it is embracing the very image of what it *seeks* to become.

It is true that the Ververs 'buy' the Prince and Charlotte. But the Prince and Charlotte on the other hand *offer* themselves precisely as things. It is true that Charlotte and Amerigo deceive Maggie and Adam. But Maggie and Adam ask for it.

This collusion between victim and victimiser existed in early James in the form of an idea that people are attracted to their opposites. In 'The Sweetheart of M. Briseux' the woman narrator says:

> We became very good friends, and it was especially for this that I liked him. Nothing is truer than that in the long run we like our opposites; they're a change and a rest from ourselves.[33]

At that time James's world was sane enough for the story to end with the girl's rejection of her fiancé Harold who is an early avatar of Gilbert Osmond. But the masochistic tendencies in James, which later make his victims seek out their misfortune, does not have an alternative in the form of an affirmation of happiness; only in an alternative type of sterility. Taking 'sterility' even literally it is symptomatic that the heroine in 'The Sweetheart of M. Briseux' remains a spinster. It is possible to understand those James works in which the characters make their sacrifice for a valid reason. But James's characters do not really need a reason.

The strange cooperation between victim and victimizer shows us another way in which something 'comes to the same thing'. It reveals yet another type of uncertainty – uncertainty as to reasons. Things happen in James's world, but it is not clear why. Osmond acquires Isabel, but it is not clear whether this is a result of Osmond's and Madame Merle's sinister machinations, or a result of Isabel's own perversity. Charlotte and Amerigo deceive Maggie and Adam, but it is not clear whether they are driven to it, or whether they manoeuvre themselves into a position to do it. There often seems to be a reciprocity of matching reasons, with both sides equally responsible.

James's fiction sometimes becomes a pleasant world of pseudo-binarity, pseudo-choices, quasi-opposition, seeming dichotomies and false dualities – all really, in the end, 'coming to the same thing'. A number of James's characters make inversion a tool in a curious epistemology in which hypotheses are always verified no matter what result a test yields. The telegraphist of *In the Cage*, the governess in *The Turn of the Screw* and the week-end guest of *The Sacred Fount* are all 'scientist-figures' in quest of knowledge.[34] But their methods of verifying their respective hypotheses are exceedingly strange, and the strangest feature of all is their use of a kind of private 'inversion-rule' according to which any phenomenon may mean the opposite of what it seems to mean. Thus their tests all really have only one outcome, in other words the characters will always be able to find reasons to think whatever they wish to think. There is no real possibility of difference, in the end everything 'comes to the same thing'.

The uses of *pseudo-difference* are extensive and varied in James. In Chapter 1 I commented on the fact that Maggie's behaviour has to be the same whether she undertakes to lie for the sake of her father or with the aim of winning Amerigo back. Insecurity in connection with the similarity–difference opposition can be either a doubt whether the seemingly different is actually similar or whether the seemingly similar is actually different. Many James characters use various forms of self-deception to create a private 'difference' in what to the outside world, including the reader, remains one and the same thing. A typical form of such self-deception is impersonation in the form of private role-playing. When James's characters want to do something particularly dubious they cast themselves in some role, acquiring a second, 'theatrical', identity in the fashion of Walter Mitty; but with the difference that whereas Walter Mitty only day-dreams, some of James's characters become momentarily schizophrenic enough to act in their assumed identity not only in their thoughts but in their reality as well. When the telegraphist of *In the Cage* tortures the male hero Captain Everard, and prolongs her sadistic enjoyment by withholding the information he desires as long as possible, she thinks of herself as a terrible young clerk at Paddington or Knightsbridge.[35] Thus, for herself, there is *difference*. There is one nice, compassionate young woman, i.e. her picture of herself, and there is another nasty one from Paddington or Knightsbridge who likes to torture Everard. But these two are *one and the same person*, and Everard can hardly be aware that the blame for her spells of nasty behaviour should be attributed to the Paddington or Knightsbridge clerk she impersonates. To him she is one person.

The structure of chiastic inversion involves the idea of *reciprocity*. This idea in turn must inevitably involve the idea of *similarity*. If A can become what B is and B can become what A is, this must mean that they are *similar* since they can take each other's roles. But insofar as they have separate identities, which by definition they should, then they must also somehow be *different*. In the pattern of chiastic inversion the whole relation of similarity to difference is mysterious, and it is symptomatic that the questions readers are made to ask about *The Golden Bowl* concern precisely *similarity* and *difference*.

Charlotte and Maggie are similar in that both deceive and lie, Charlotte during the first half of the novel and Maggie during the second. The critics who side with Maggie hold Charlotte's deception against her. But if lying is such a bad thing when Charlotte does it, how comes it to be such a good thing when Maggie does it? Or, conversely, if it is such a good thing when Maggie does it, was it really so bad when Charlotte did it? The critics who side with Charlotte hold Maggie's lying against *her*. But again the corresponding questions, with the necessary substitutions, can be asked. Indeed the questions are asked not only by the reader but by the characters in the novel as well. The Prince at the beginning of Chapter XXI hypothetically attributes such a question to Fanny Assingham:

> 'Ah, if it would have been so bad for them, how can it be so good for you?' (282)

It seems that in order to come down squarely on one side or the other the reader must be willing to adopt the same type of double-standards as those that are cherished by some of James's most questionable characters. One has to adopt the sort of chiastic double-think according to which a bad thing is good (when done by one's own side) and a good thing bad (when done by the other side). This kind of chiastic thinking depends on a capacity for inversion (cf. the capacity for sudden shifts of allegiance in *1984*, where a friendly foreign power can instantly become the enemy and the enemy a friend), and a tolerance of oxymoronic contradiction ('war is peace'). Double-think is not foreign to some of James's characters. There is clearly a close relationship between double-think in Orwell and the Jamesian 'double-exposure'-works we have been discussing.

But even though some of James's characters are capable of double-think I think it is debatable to what extent James suggested that the reader should applaud them for it and share their mental activity. The James characters who delude themselves are *shown to be doing so* and that undermining is after all James's work too. Steering away from the Scylla of believing unconditionally in James's doubtful characters we should perhaps not turn too sharply and run into the Charybdis of entirely disbelieving. Rather we should stay in the Jamesian thematic mainstream of doubt, vacillation, hesitation and uncertainty.

The reason why critics, collectively speaking, have not known whether to side with Maggie or Charlotte is that James himself does not know. Throughout the novel he stresses the similarity in the actions of the one pair (Charlotte–Amerigo) and the other (Maggie–Adam). They are both shown in the same relation to the bowl; both couples are repeatedly said to be acting in 'good faith' etc. The characters are shown doing the same thing not only simultaneously (for instance preferring their illegitimate partners to their legitimate) but also in turns, which leads to a number of 'turning of the tables'-inversions. During the early part of the second half of the novel Maggie had felt threatened by Charlotte; at the end she turns the tables and threatens *her*. In the following quotation the two antagonistic forces in *The Golden Bowl*, Maggie and Charlotte, are symbolically identified quite in the manner in which the governess and the ghosts were symbolically identified in *The Turn of the Screw*:

> The resemblance had not been present to her on first coming out into the hot, still brightness of the Sunday afternoon – only the second Sunday, of all the summer the Principino, had practically been without accessions or invasions; but within sight of Charlotte, seated far away, very much where she had expected to find her, the Prince fell to wondering if her friend wouldn't be affected quite as she herself had been, that night on the terrace, under Mrs Verver's perceptive pursuit. The relation, to-day, had turned itself round; Charlotte was seeing her come, through patches of lingering noon, quite as she had watched Charlotte menace her through the starless dark; and there was a moment, that when the interval was bridged by a recognition not less soundless, and to all appearance not less charged with strange meanings, than that of the other occasion. The point, however, was that they had changed places; (550–1)

The relation has turned itself round and they have changed places and roles. The same inverted distribution of roles, with Maggie as the pursuer and Charlotte as the pursued, also occurs later in the chapter when Maggie comes round to bring Charlotte the right volume of the three-decker novel:

> She passed again through the house, unchallenged and emerged upon the terrace, which she followed, hugging the shade, with that consciousness of turning the tables on her friend which we have already noted.
> . . .
> It was a repetition more than ever then of the evening on the terrace; the distance was too great to assure her she had been immediately seen, but the Princess waited, with her intention, as Charlotte on the other occasion had waited – allowing, oh allowing, for the difference of the intention! Maggie was full of the sense of *that* – so full that it made her impatient; whereupon she moved forward a little, placing herself in range of the eyes that had been looking off elsewhere, but that she had suddenly called to recognition. (560-1)

Maggie may be full of her sense of difference in this passage, but even Maggie later speculates on similarities; whether Charlotte's loss of Amerigo is not as terrible as her own near-loss of him had been ('It's *always* terrible for women', 589).

It is possible that James's pattern of symbolic identification of the illegitimate couples in *The Golden Bowl* includes not only an appreciation of the neatness of the symmetry but also some traces of the element that I earlier mentioned as a major ingredient in chiastic inversion, i.e. humour. There are some strange correspondences in *The Golden Bowl* which could be explained as humorous instances of symbolic identification. During their visit to the shop in Bloomsbury Charlotte and the Prince abstain from giving each other presents. Charlotte does not accept a present from the Prince because she does not know how she could wear it:

> 'There's nothing here she could wear.'
> It was only after a moment that her companion rejoined. 'Is there anything – do you think – that you could?'
> It made her just start. She didn't, at all events, look at the objects; she but looked for an instant very directly at him. 'No.'

'Ah!' the Prince quietly exclaimed.

'Would it be,' Charlotte asked, 'your idea to offer me something?'

...

She had another pause, while the shopman only waited. 'If I were to accept from you one of these charming little ornaments as you suggest, what should I do with it?'

He was perhaps at last a little irritated; he even – as if he might understand – looked vaguely across at their host. 'Wear it, *per Bacco!*'

'Where then, please? Under my clothes?' (118)

The ornament would be a symbol of their illicit relationship and therefore it could not be worn by Charlotte except perhaps under her clothes. With this scene in mind the reader cannot but be puzzled by a passage much later, in Chapter XXX, in which we learn that *Maggie* does wear an ornament under her clothes:

'What I've always been conscious of is your having concealed about you somewhere no small amount of character; quite as much in fact,' Fanny smiled, 'as one could suppose a person of your size able to carry. The only thing was,' she explained, 'that thanks to your never calling one's attention to it, I hadn't made out much more about it, and should have been vague, above all, as to *where* you carried it or kept it. Somewhere *under*, I should simply have said – like that little silver cross you once showed me, blest by the Holy Father, that you always wear, out of sight, next to your skin.' (417)

I cannot help feeling that James is being funny here, and that it is not so much Maggie's relationship with the Holy Father in the Vatican that the ornament symbolizes, but rather her relationship with a father at much closer quarters, who is 'holy' to her in a different sense. One almost feels guilty noticing such correspondences as this one and not quite sure whether one is not reading things into the text. But considering the anatomy of James's sense of humour the idea is not too far-fetched. James's play with names – to mention only one example – reveals a sense of humour which could have produced such results as this – if it is indeed meant to be humorous, as I think.

Chiastic inversion reflects a world of semantic chaos. In a

world where 'fair is foul and foul is fair' there is no semantic *order* or *stability* and the semantic anarchy of this opening line of *Macbeth* reflects the social, political and emotional chaos depicted in the play. It is significant that the tyranny depicted in Orwell's *1984* and *Animal Farm* relies on *lability* as one of its main tools of oppression. To Aldous Huxley, in *Brave New World*, the totalitarian threat lies in *stability*; the society he depicts is frighteningly stable. In contrast the means of repression in Orwell's world is *change*. In *Animal Farm*, for instance, the commandments of 'animalism' are gradually *changed* one by one. Lability is frightening to Orwell, and semantic lability is as frightening as political and social lability. Words should have stable meanings, it should be impossible to say 'war is peace'.

In *Animal Farm* everything that the animals have achieved is destroyed through change and lability. Possibly the worst form of lability to Orwell was semantic chaos and he again and again returned to the theme of the corrupting influence of linguistic lability. Insecure language reflects an insecure world.

There are similarities between the insecure language depicted by Orwell and the Jamesian mannerisms we have been discussing. Even though the insecurity of James's world is of a totally different kind from that of Orwell, there are nevertheless some parallels. But the attitude of Orwell to the world he had created in his fiction was one of unmitigated horror. The degree of consciousness in Orwell is high; he knew what he was doing, and he knew what he wanted the reader to think. James's attitude on the other hand is difficult to make out. It also seems to vary, and often one does not know whether he had an attitude at all. It is obvious that Orwell is scared stiff by the rewriting of history in *1984*, but what is James's attitude to the rewriting of history in 'Maud-Evelyn' for instance?

James's attitude to the semantic lability in his works is not very clearcut and in the end one has to conclude that the insecurity manifested in the stylistic mannerisms connected with chiastic inversion is also, at least to some extent, a reflection of the author's own insecurity.

Chiastic inversion primarily creates ambiguity but as I said in the Introduction ambiguity and intensity usually coexist. In chiastic inversion the copresence of ambiguity and intensity is evident even in the tell-tale device of italicization – a typographic device used to achieve some intense emphasis in the chaos of switches and inversions. It is almost impossible to sum up the chart of a chiastic situation or development without using italicization, cf. James's idea of *The Sacred Fount* in his *Notebook*-entry:

> ... When he reaches the age that *she* was (on their marriage) she has gone back to the age that *he* was ...[36]

Intense emphasis is necessary in a world which is semantically chaotic and ambiguous. But by its very presence even intensity ultimately adds to the feeling of uncertainty.

Conclusion

What sort of a world is it then, the world of Henry James's fiction?

It is a world characterized by *insecurity*; which is manifested in style in ambiguity- and intensity-creating devices. It is a world where you do not know *who is who* (Chapter 1, referential ambiguity in pronouns). It is a world where *nothing is ever final* (Chapter 2, end-linking). It is a world where *statements cannot be trusted*, even though they be made with special intensity and emphasis (Chapter 3, emphatic affirmation). It is a world where it is hoped, and yet at the same time doubted, that *language can govern reality* (Chapter 4, the 'finding a formula'-formula). It is, finally, a world where you do not know *who does what to whom, or why* (Chapter 5, chiasmus).

Of all features of James's style *chiasmus* is the most important. Chiasmus in James is not only decorative or ornamental. It influences not only *how* James writes, but *what* he writes. Furthermore, it influences what he *thinks*, and even what he *perceives*.

Chiasmus should be seen as hierarchically superior to the devices or idiosyncrasies dealt with in Chapters 1–4. Chiasmus is a figure of repetition, even though it is a special variety, in that the second half of a chiasmus not only repeats the two main elements of the first half but also inverts their order (a b – b a). Repetition, we recall, was also the main principle in end-linking (Chapter 2), and in emphatic affirmation (Chapter 3). But the devices dealt with in the earlier chapters of this study are related to chiasmus in many more ways than this. The structure of end-linking, for instance, could be given as '...a,a ...!' and the structure of chiasmus as, say, 'b a,a b'. In end-linking, as in chiasmus, there is a break in the middle, often marked in writing with a comma, and two similar elements on either side of the break. End-linking is thus, in a sense, the middle part of a chiasmus. One may regard many cases of end-linking as incipient cases of chiasmus; chiasmus that never materialized fully.

As to referential ambiguity in pronouns and chiasmus there is a link between these two as well. The most important variety of chiasmus of all is what I would like to call *existential chiasmus*, i.e. chiasmus that makes use of the verb *to be*, as in the example 'fair is foul and foul is fair'. This variety of chiasmus is doubly destructive of stability, because it creates doubt about categories – and the boundaries and differences between them – in two ways: firstly, because the elements are capable of taking each other's roles and positions (which means that they must be somehow similar), and secondly, through the verb 'to be', which expresses identity or identicality.

James was a dualist and preferred to have *two* of anything – if only he could – rather than any other number (such as, for instance, one, three, four etc.). Thus in *The Golden Bowl*, for instance, there are *two* men and *two* women. But, furthermore, whenever he had two of anything he would never for long be sure about which was which – because of the corrupting influence of the existential formula 'a is b, and b is a'. Therefore, in *The Golden Bowl*, where there are *two* men, Amerigo and Adam, the existential formula – always at the back of James's mind – semi-consciously insists that 'Amerigo is Adam, and Adam is Amerigo'. If that again is so, then there is really no reason why they, or either of them (no matter which), should not be referred to by the pronoun 'he'. Who cares about possible referential ambiguity! 'It comes to the same thing', does it not? It must – if 'Adam is Amerigo, and Amerigo Adam'.

This may all sound strange, but such is the relationship between referential ambiguity in pronouns and chiasmus.

In Chapter 4 I mention briefly Henry James's curious brand of pragmatism and the strange relationship between the brothers. Actually the relationship is not all that strange, because William's philosophy is of a curious brand too. Whoever invented the old joke that 'Henry's novels read like philosophy and William's philosophy like novels', must have had an extraordinarily deep, intuitive insight into the psyche of both men. In structure the joke is a chiasmus, and this is highly appropriate, since both men were what we may call *chiasticists*. In

William's philosophy we often find observations such as the claim that we 'do not cry because we are sorry; but are sorry because we cry'. A chiasticist feels he has to *complement* any given statement with its own inversion – only thus is symmetry achieved. (And without symmetry the chiasticist is never satisfied.)

William's entire philosophy of pragmatic truth and reality springs from this. In distributing importance and emphasis to either half of such pairs as the self and the other, the subjective and the objective, tychism and synechism, it seemed to William James that European philosophy consistently favoured the latter. That was intolerable! The symmetry had to be restored and the balance redressed, so William James decided complementarily to stress the former. Thus, on the intellectual matrix of chiasticism, William James creates his pragmatist philosophy, according to which truth and reality is not only something that the environment imposes on the individual, but also something that the individual imposes on the environment.

As I already said William and Henry were, after all, brothers, and it is no wonder that Henry too created characters (such as the week-end guest) who think they can 'engender truth' on reality. In a large measure the brothers probably inherited it all from their father. Caring about supplying a missing complementary inversion (to make chiastic symmetry complete) often, in practice, means fighting for the underdog. That is an activity typical of rebels and outcasts. They and society are antithetical. What is good to society seems bad to them; what is bad to society seems good to them. Hence oxymoron etc., but hence also chiasmus itself, and hence such philosophies as pragmatism.

If we go a little further into this we shall also see how another aspect of end-linking – namely the implied self-sufficiency inherent in it – fits the puzzle:

Chiasmus is an example of *bilateral symmetry*, and *relativism* is a function of symmetry. This is where James's relativism comes from. A chiasticistic universe is *incurvatus in se*, self-sufficient, self-generating and self-perpetuating. In a chiasmus the two halves are each other's inversions; each other's mirror-images. The *direction* within a chiasmus is towards the middle. It is *reflected* there.

Chiasmus is therefore typical of *narcissistic* people who have trouble with their relations to the outside world and to other people and would like to see in other people primarily a reflection of themselves. They would like to see a mirror-image, as from the surface of a well. In the Narcissus-myth, we recall, the name of the nymph who loved Narcissus was 'Echo'. An *echo* is a repetition that returns to its source. A mirror-image is also a repetition that returns to its source. In a chiasmus the second half is a repetition of the first half, but with the order of the two main elements inverted, so that the meaning of the second half returns to its source in the first half. In a chiasticistic universe only *relations* exist; nothing exists absolutely.

Chiasmus expresses the principle of *reciprocity*, as in the following example: 'Jack loves Jill and Jill Jack'. James sometimes uses chiastic constructions to express achieved reciprocity, for instance in the 'erotic passage' in *The Golden Bowl*: 'their pressure their response and their response their pressure' (p. 265). But far more often one finds that the principle of mutuality inherent in chiasmus *creates problems* for the chiasticists, both in their own private lives and in the lives of their characters in fiction. (I am now talking about a chiasticist tendency generally, and not specifically about James.)

To a chiasticist there is any number of things that can go wrong in his relations with others. There may be Somebody he would love, but he cannot love Somebody until Somebody also loves *him* – that rule is dictated by the demands of reciprocity. If he then looks to see whether Somebody shows any signs of loving him, and he does not perceive any clear signs, that must mean – must it not? – that Somebody *hates* him (– this follows from the rule of obligatory extremism, the 'horror of the middle ground'; if you are not one thing you are bound to be its extreme opposite). If, therefore now, Somebody – as it seems – *hates* him, why then *he* must hate *Somebody*. This the chiasticist then accordingly proceeds to do; and so on, and so forth, *ad infinitum*.

Because of the rule of reciprocity inherent in chiasmus, chiasticists are always dissecting their relationships with others with pathological intensity, looking for the smallest signs of presence or absence of reciprocity. And the smallest possible observations of signs of change may cause grotesquely disproportionate reactions. This greatly encourages paranoia. It also encourages other things such as solipsism, megalomania, manic-depressive see-saw changes in mood etc. It is paradoxical that the *sensitivity*, which is the greatest gift of many of these chiasticists in their career as literary artists, is also at the same time a curse.

The only really perfect partner for a chiasticist is *his own self.* We can now see James's revisions in their proper chiasticistic context. The way out of the difficulties created by the principle of reciprocity is to split the self and let the halves communicate. In James's revisions we see a dialogue between James and James; James-now talks to James-then.

When a chiasticist is in the process of writing a text, he avoids putting the himself of the current sentence in relation to the outside world by basing the sentence directly on its referent. There is a far better solution on offer. By relating the present sentence to the previous through repetition, the chiasticist can associate with a perfect partner – himself. Hence end-linking.

Critics often instinctively use words beginning in 'idio-' about chiasticists. About James, for instance, it is frequently said that his style is 'idiosyncratic'. The use of these words beginning in 'idio-' recognizes the importance of the 'self' in the case of these authors – the self-'everything', including self-sufficiency, that stems from chiasticism.

We remember how often James in his prefaces (to the New York Edition) congratulates himself on solving some difficulty. Well, *he* himself says that the difficulty was there; *he* himself is the sole judge of whether it was solved or not, and so on. It is the most solitary kind of *solitaire.* You put up the dummies you shoot down, and you make stepping-stones of your dead selves.

Like James himself his characters also self-sufficiently engage in zig-zagging dialectics (the governess, the week-end guest etc.). These characters are guilty of several fallacies in their logic, such as that of the undistributed middle and the vicious circle. These fallacies result from chiasticism. Chiasmus is about *order*, in the sense of sequential order, i.e. what comes first and what comes after. Chiasmus negates order, because the order of each half neutralizes the order in the other half. In a chiasticist universe you may freely vacillate between any two of anything – indeed you *should.*

Empiricist methodology forbids switches of order. You are supposed to proceed from test to result, from sampling to analysis, from evidence to conclusion, from hypothesis to test, etc. You are not allowed to switch around every now and then – that leads precisely to the vicious circle and to the undistributed middle. The week-end guest, the governess and the telegraphist are guilty of these fallacies because they are consequences of the nature and function of chiasmus, which is a pattern of thought these characters make frequent use of.

Let us now see how the strange collusion between victim and victimizer, which is so typical in James, also follows from the nature and function of chiasmus.

Chiasmus, as I said, is an example of bilateral symmetry, and relativism is a function of symmetry. The relation between symmetry and asymmetry is problematical to a chiasticist. Our universe is to a large extent based on asymmetry. Our moral sense, for instance, demands that we should asymmetrically take sides *for* the tortured, *against* the torturer. This a chiasticist cannot do – hence his deficiency in moral sense, his callousness, and his seeming cruelty. There is no asymmetry (i.e. difference in importance, weight, precedence, preferability, *order*) between a torturer and a tortured to a chiasticist; the existential formula negates that difference: 'Torturer is tortured and tortured torturer'; 'To torture is to be tortured and to be tortured is to torture'.

Because of this James can never really see any difference, e.g. between the parties in *The Golden Bowl*: 'To be deceived is to deceive, and to deceive is to be deceived'; 'To buy as goods is to be bought as goods, and to be bought as goods is to buy as goods' – subject is object and object is subject.

Chiasmus negates the difference between subject and object, between left and right, between beginning and end, between before and after, between active and passive. In a chiasmus there is properly speaking no right or left; there is no before or after; no beginning nor end. Whatever one half of the chiasmus says, the other contradicts it. Chiasmus creates lability, balance and equilibrium.

Chiasmus destroys the distinction between subject and object in English, because chiasmus is about sequential order, and in English what is subject and what is object is determined through word-order. What comes first is subject and what comes after is object, if the sentence is spoken. If the sentence is written what is left in the sentence is subject and what is right is object. Analytical languages, such as English, indicate the subject- and object-functions mainly through word-order, whereas synthetic languages, such as Latin or Finnish, indicate them mainly

through case. This means that chiasmus is vastly more important in analytical languages than in synthetic. In synthetic
languages chiasmus is something primarily *decorative* or *ornamental* – this is why the ancient authors had practically nothing to
say on the subject of chiasmus which is interesting or relevant to
a speaker of English. In an analytical language again chiasmus is
something primarily *philosophical* or *psychological* – which is why I
think it appropriate to use such words as 'psychomorphology' in
describing how a chiasmus-addict thinks. Knowledge of the way
chiasmus works is a key to the mind of a chiasticist. If you
understand chiasmus, you understand James.

In the sentence 'Jack loves Jill' we know that 'Jack' is the one
doing the loving (subject), and 'Jill' the one being loved (object),
because 'Jack' occurs left and 'Jill' right in the sentence. If we
want to say that 'Jill' is the one doing the loving, and 'Jack' the
one being loved, we reverse the order: 'Jill loves Jack', and to
express reciprocity we use chiasmus: 'Jack loves Jill, and Jill
Jack'. But to an ambilateralist mind such as James's that is all
very difficult.

The destruction of his capacity for asymmetrical thinking in a
chiasticist, through the obligatory absolute ambilateralism inherent in chiasmus, has consequences so vast and far-reaching
that they can hardly be comprehended at first – the mind
boggles. The problem of the strange collusion between victimizer
and victim in James's fiction is only *one* result of chiastic
obligatory symmetry and ambilateralism, and that alone is
sufficient to keep one puzzled almost for ever.

In the five chapters of this study I have occasionally made
evaluative comments on James's works. Perhaps some readers
would like more comments on how I think chiasmus affected the
quality of James's work.

I feel, however, that so many good critics have said so many
things in evaluation of James's work that I cannot add very
much here. What I *am* saying is – obviously – that whatever
James is he is to a large extent thanks to chiasticism. There are
negative as well as positive features to chiasticism. Chiasticism
leads to insecurity, and there are many facets of insecurity too.
Doubtless insecurity is in one sense something very negative. It
may mean hesitation, moral and intellectual cowardice, self-
destructiveness and sterility. But it may also mean sensitivity,
humility, flexibility and open-mindedness. We must all decide

for ourselves.

The results of my investigation of James's psychomorphology has some consequences for my view of James scholarship. Like Shlomith Rimmon, Dorothea Krook and others, I too can no longer believe in the efforts of those critics who try to argue cases based on compromise. These critics hope for sanity; but chiasticism does perhaps not quite allow it. Dualist extremism plus vacillation is the structural backbone of chiasticism, and although chiasticists constantly long for compromise, union, fusion, synthesis, *via media*, etc., they can never reach any of these because it is in the nature of chiasticism both to create the longing for them and at the same time to frustrate that same longing. Chiasticists dream of synthesis, but they visualize it in terms of a middle between two extremes, so that the very idea nevertheless presupposes the poles, and therefore constantly defeats itself. Hence the sterility of James's world. In the world of a chiasticist opposites seldom meet and unite; and a chiasticist sees most things in life as opposites – including men and women.

Another genre of James criticism that I no longer trust is works aimed at establishing James's 'views', his 'philosophy', his 'morals' etc. These attempts are misguided. One can write a catalogue of James's subjects, but never of his specific opinions on them, unless it be a catalogue where opinions come in pairs, of which each half negates the other. Whatever James says in one place in his writings can usually be found contradicted somewhere else. Indeed this has to be so since chiasticist relativism dictates that nothing exists unless complemented with its own antithetical inversion.

What I have said in this conclusion may all sound hyperbolic. To a large extent perhaps it is. But there is no other way of writing about these things, and what I am saying is, I think, true in some basic sense even though it should not be true in every single instance of application.

To sum up therefore: The world of Henry James's fiction is rich and varied. But if one had to characterize it, using one single word, a study of some typical stylistic devices seems to suggest that a fairly good description would be the word that I decided to put into the title – 'insecure'.

Notes and References

INTRODUCTION

1. Quotes, with page numbers given within parentheses in the text, from Henry James, *The Golden Bowl*, in Leon Edel (ed.), *The Bodley Head Henry James, vol. ix, The Golden Bowl* (London: Bodley Head, 1971).
2. Leon Edel and Gordon N. Ray (eds), *Henry James and H.G. Wells: A Record of their Friendship, their Debate on the Art of Fiction, and their Quarrel* (London: Rupert Hart-Davis, 1958) p. 267.
3. E.g. the unsigned review in *Saturday*, March 1905, xcix, 383–4; reprinted in Roger Gard (ed.), *Henry James: The Critical Heritage* (London: Routledge & Kegan Paul, 1968) pp. 381–4, p. 381 'intensity', p. 383 'Hence it is that one has come to measure Mr. James's success by the amount and intensity of dramatic action which a theme will yield him'.
4. Philip Grover, *Henry James and the French Novel: A Study in Inspiration* (London: Paul Elek, 1973) p. 176.
5. Wilson's article 'The Ambiguity of Henry James' was first published in *Hound and Horn*, 7 (April–June 1934) 385–406. A revised version Gerald Willen (ed.), *A Casebook on Henry James's 'The Turn of the Screw'* 2nd edn (New York: Thomas Y. Crowell, 1969) together with the story, some critical articles and other relevant material.
6. Jean Frantz Blackall, *Jamesian Ambiguity and* The Sacred Fount (Ithaca: Cornell University Press, 1965).
7. Charles Thomas Samuels, *The Ambiguity of Henry James* (Urbana: University of Illinois Press, 1971).
8. Shlomith Rimmon, *The Concept of Ambiguity – the Example of James* (Chicago and London: University of Chicago Press, 1978).
9. For a list of criticism on *The Golden Bowl*, see Beatrice Ricks (comp.), *Henry James: A Bibliography of Secondary Works*, The Scarecrow Author Bibliographies, no. 24 (Metuchen: Scarecrow Press, 1975) pp. 70–8.

CHAPTER 1: REFERENTIAL AMBIGUITY IN PRONOUNS

1. James 'ciphering out' – F.O. Matthiessen and Kenneth B. Murdock (eds), *The Notebooks of Henry James* (New York: Oxford University Press, 1947) p. 236; hereafter cited as *Notebooks* – the plot of *What Maisie Knew* let events develop out of the requirements of his abstractions – '. . . for a proper symmetry the second

194   *The Insecure World of Henry James's Fiction*

parent should marry too . . .', Henry James, *The Art of the Novel: Critical Prefaces*, introd. Richard P. Blackmur (New York: Charles Scribner's Sons, 1962) p. 140 hereafter cited as Blackmur. James's tendency towards strict abstraction was so strong that for the plan of *The Awkward Age* he actually drew a diagram (Blackmur, p. 110).

2. Though of course the greatest intensity comes from our interest in the two interlocking triangular dramas. Cf. Leon Edel's introduction to the Bodley Head edition, pp. 7–13.

Although the frame for the drama is quadragonal, the drama itself is doubly triangular. Thus many of the symbols build on the number 3 rather than four – the bowl breaks into three fragments; the three-decker novel etc.

3. *Notebooks*, p. 131.

4. According to Maggie, p. 480.

5. Afraid that some readers might miss the pattern James gives them a verbal nudge by having the correspondence signalled through the repetition of the word 'prowl'. Maggie uses the word first: 'It's the golden bowl, you know, that you saw at the little antiquario's in Bloomsbury, so long ago – when you went there with Charlotte, when you spent hours with her, unknown to me, a day or two before our marriage. It was shown you both, but you didn't take it; you left it for me, and I came upon it, extraordinarily, through happening to go into the same shop on Monday last; in walking home, in prowling about to pick up some small old thing for father's birthday . . .' (p. 477). The Prince repeats the word: 'We went forth together and we looked; we rummaged about and, as I remember we called it, we prowled;' (ibid.). Attention is specifically drawn to the word. To point to symbolic patterns through the repetition of a word or phrase is a frequent technique in James. The word 'prowl' is used repeatedly in scenes connected with the bowl.

6. James used the ambiguity in 'marry' (either 'marry someone' or 'marry someone to someone') in many works, e.g. *The Awkward Age*. It is therefore obvious that his repeated play on 'marry' in *The Golden Bowl* is intentional. Cf. e.g. Adam '. . . if he had consented to marry his daughter . . .' (p. 145).

7. When Adam marries Charlotte one reason is that Charlotte is about the only woman that *Maggie* would accept: '. . . [Fanny] seemed to feel sure Maggie would accept Charlotte, or whereas I didn't quite make out either what other woman, what other *kind* of woman, one could think of her accepting' (p. 322). Thus the marriage suited Charlotte (with an eye on Amerigo), Amerigo (waiting for Charlotte), Adam (pleasing his daughter) and Maggie (pleasing her father). It suited everyone – for a time.

8. In addition we have the Assinghams to reckon with; Fanny being enamoured with the Prince and Bob with Charlotte etc.

9. See Jan G. Koiij, *Ambiguity in Natural Language: An Investigation of Certain Problems in Its Linguistic Description*, North-Holland Linguistic Series, 3 (Amsterdam: North-Holland, 1971) p. 110 & *passim*.

10. A critic in *Bookman* (America; January 1905, xx, 418–9) wrote: 'Fully half of *The Golden Bowl* consists of notes which he ought in conscience to have destroyed, and of details the bare mention of which misleads by a sense of their importance' (Gard, *Henry James: The Critical Heritage*, p. 391). This critic obviously thought that literature should be product rather than process. Other critics (e.g. Gard, *Henry James: The Critical Heritage*, p. 380; Unsigned review, *Athenaeum*, March 1905, 4038, 332) wish the book had been twice as long.

Criticism against James's habit of putting in the problems and the whole history of their solution rather than merely the result, is often connected with the general accusation that James was all form and no content.

11. Henry James, *The Turn of the Screw*, A Norton Critical Edition, Robert Kimbrough (ed.) (New York: W.W. Norton, 1966), p. 12. Page numbers hereafter given within parentheses in the text.

12. James used this ambiguity elsewhere. There is an exact parallel in *Confidence*. See Ralf Norrman, *Techniques of Ambiguity in the Fiction of Henry James: With Special Reference to* In the Cage *and* The Turn of the Screw, Acta Academiae Aboensis, Ser. A Humaniora, vol. 54, no. 2 (Åbo: Åbo Akademi, 1978), pp. 104–5; hereafter referred to as Norrman.

13. See Norrman, Chapter 3, section 4 and *passim*. Insistent avoidance of pronouns is as important as insistent use; cf. Carlo Izzo, 'Henry James Scrittore Sintattico', *Studi Americani*, 2 (1956), p. 133.

14. Robert G. Johnson, 'A Study of the Style of Henry James's Late Novels', Diss. (Bowling Green State University, 1971), pp. 83–4. See also pp. 38–47 and p. 97. On pronouns see also Rimmon, *The Concept of Ambiguity*, pp. 74–5; 110–12; 198–202; 221; 151–4.

15. A number of critics, including myself, have long been arguing against an automatic assumption that James's ambiguities *can* and *should* always be interpreted. Shlomith Rimmon's book, for instance, argues very convincingly that in a number of works the choice between alternatives is an impossible one.

16. Authors sometimes find it convenient to manipulate the context so that normal grammatical rules are neutralized and a desired ambiguity is created. An elegant example of this is Mark Twain's *Huckleberry Finn*, Chapter 31, 'You Can't Pray a Lie' where Twain creates ambiguity through a clash of two grammars and their respective rules for the regulation of the referent of relative clauses.

> That's just the way: a person does a low-down thing, and then he don't want to take no consequences of it. Thinks as long as he can hide, it ain't no disgrace. That was my fix exactly. The more I studied about this the more my conscience went to grinding me, and the more wicked and low-down and ornery I got to feeling. And at last, when it hit me all of a sudden that here was the plain hand of Providence slapping me in the face and letting me know my wickedness was being watched all the time from up there in heaven, whilst I was stealing a poor old woman's nigger that hadn't ever done me no harm, and now was showing me there's One that's always on the lookout, and ain't a-going to allow no such miserable doings to go only just so fur and no further, I most dropped in my tracks I was so scared. Well, I tried the best I could to kinder soften it up somehow for myself by saying I was brung up wicked, and so I warn't so much to blame; but something inside of me kept saying, 'There was the Sunday-school, you could 'a' gone to it; and if you'd 'a' done it they'd 'a' learnt you there that people acts as I'd been acting about that nigger goes to everlasting fire.' (Mark Twain, *The Adventures of Huckleberry Finn*, introd. Lionel Trilling [New York: Rinehart, 1954], p. 213)

This is the central scene in the book when Huck is beset by doubts and contemplates morality and finally decides to go to hell rather than do the right thing and give the negro Jim up to his owner, Miss Watson. There are two kinds of morality in the scene: ostensible, codified, legitimate morality according to which Huck ought to give Jim up; and natural morality according to which he ought to behave precisely as he does, i.e. let Jim go. Irony in the scene is created by an inversion so that a very moral decision – to let Jim escape – has to be reached via a decision to be immoral and go to hell. The focal point of this chapter is the phrase '. . . whilst I was stealing a poor old woman's nigger that hadn't ever done me no harm . . .'.

The rules governing relative clauses in Huck's grammar are not as formalized as in standard American. In Huck's grammar the rule about relative clauses is that they refer to whatever preceding element it is semantically natural they should refer to, i.e. in this case 'old woman' (Miss Watson) and the meaning is 'Miss Watson (old woman) who had never done me any harm'. But in standard American English the rule about a that-clause is not a pragmatic one, as in Huck's dialect, but a formal one, namely that such relative clauses refer to the immediately preceding element, which in this case is 'nigger'. Through the distractive influence of the foreign grammar of standard English there is therefore a secondary meaning where 'that' refers to 'nigger', i.e. 'a nigger (Jim) who had never done me any harm'.

The two grammars clash and this creates the ambiguity. The ambiguity was desirable for Twain because he operated with two kinds of morality and he wanted the alternative kind (Huck's 'natural' morality) to run as an ironic undercurrent in every line that ostensibly endorses the false, official morality of society. It was true from one point of view that Miss Watson had not done him any harm – a view supported by Huck's grammar. On the other hand neither had Jim done him any harm – a view supported by the grammar of standard English.

This type of ambiguity is fairly widespread. Even authors who are not famous for subtleties and ambiguities make occasional use of it, as, for instance, Dickens in *Nicholas Nickleby*, Chapter 8: 'and that he will love Master Squeers, and not object to sleeping five in a bed, which no Christian should'. (Charles Dickens, *Nicholas Nickleby*, Michael Slater (ed.) (Harmondsworth: Penguin 1978; first pub. 1839) p. 159). To the speaker it is 'objecting' that no Christian should, but to the author and to the readers, it is 'sleeping five in a bed' that no Christian should.

It is the privilege of literary authors to manipulate grammatical rules to achieve a desired effect and Henry James made use of this privilege very extensively, particularly in connection with rules on pronominal antecedents. 17. In the same underhand way James introduces the word 'engaged' which is meant to suggest more than it stands for in its strict textual sense. When James writes 'He was engaged . . .' the reaction he wants us to have as readers is the thought that Amerigo is engaged, not only 'in the policy of not magnifying', but also engaged 'to be married to Maggie'. The disruption of the sentence-structure through the parenthesis 'as hard as possible' facilitates the drift of our thoughts in this direction. This type of ambiguity is related to the type of equivocation which depends on a silent, private continuation of a statement, a mental reservation, that often reverses the sense of what has been said aloud. The ambiguity-creating device is used very frequently in low-class theatre where the beginning of a sentence is first structured so as to guide the thoughts of the audience towards an indecency only to cancel the sense at the end with a word or phrase that makes the meaning of the whole sentence innocent. The last part should preferably be short and it is preceded by a suspense-creating pause, often achieved by the insertion of a parenthetical phrase which disrupts the sentence-structure.

A variation of this humorous ambiguity is when a character in comedy realizes that he has said something unsuitable and saves the situation by adding a phrase that changes the meaning.

18. In this scene, however, we are also given the first foretaste of Adam's future emancipation – if that is the word – from fatherhood in the following remark: '"Can't a man be, all his life then," he almost fiercely asked, "anything but a father?"' (ibid.).

19. 'The whole situation works in a kind of inevitable rotary way – in what would be called a vicious circle.' (*Notebooks*, p. 130).

20. Gard, *Henry James: The Critical Heritage*, p. 386.

21. Gard, *Henry James: The Critical Heritage*, p. 500.

22. Gard, *Henry James: The Critical Hertage*, pp. 483–4.

23. Edmund Nierlich, *Kuriose Wirklichkeit in den Romanen von Henry James: Ein Methodischer Beitrag zur Werkanalyse in der Literaturwissenschaft*. Studien zur Germanistik, Anglistik und Komparatistik: Herausgegeben von Armin Arnold und Alois M. Haas, Band 17 (Bonn: Bouvier Verlag Herbert Grundmann, 1973), p. 115.

24. Robert L. Gale, *Plots and Characters in the Fiction of Henry James* (Hamden Ct: MIT Press, 1972), p. 30. Cf. Norrman, p. 151.

25. James prepared the reader for this in Chapter XVII where the Prince is struck dumb with a 'congruity' (252). He misses Maggie; he would have liked to have tea with her, but she is absent. Instead Charlotte comes along to fill the gap in his life. The scene is a masterstroke. At the very point when the Prince's behaviour is least defendable (when he and Charlotte decide to make a move) it is suggested that Maggie is partly to blame. His longing for Maggie foreshadows the end of the novel. The Prince's character is brought out by the events of the plot. His missing Maggie before Charlotte comes is almost like a cry of help before fate points its finger in another direction: 'if you miss one woman here is another!'

26. Such is the symmetry of the situation that as long as Maggie does not accept the legitimate set unreservedly Amerigo and Charlotte can always turn the tables on her. In Chapter XIV Fanny disapproves of Charlotte staying with Amerigo at the party when Maggie has gone to take care of Adam. Fanny thinks Charlotte ought to be with her husband. Charlotte turns the tables, reminding Fanny that in that case Maggie ought to as well '. . . seeing, especially, that the daughter has a husband of her own in the field'. (224).

27. Donald L. Mull, *Henry James's 'Sublime Economy': Money as Symbolic Center in the Fiction* (Middleton: Wesleyan University Press, 1973), p. 158.

See also F.O. Matthiessen, *Henry James: The Major Phase* (New York: Oxford University Press, 1963): 'James means to convey thus the rare inclusiveness of her generosity; . . .' (p. 97); Oscar Cargill, *The Novels of Henry James* (New York: Macmillan, 1961), pp. 409–10; Frederick C. Crews, *The Tragedy of Manners: Moral Drama in the Later Novels of Henry James* (New Haven: Yale University Press, 1957): 'The Christlike size of Maggie's love . . .' (p. 106). Cf. also Samuels, *The Ambiguity of Henry James*, pp. 218–9.

28. See e.g. Samuels, *The Ambiguity of Henry James*, pp. 223–4.

29. Samuels, *The Ambiguity of Henry James*, p. 224.
30. There is a similar passage in Chapter XXX:

> 'Conspiring – so far as *you* were concerned – to what end?'
> 'Why, to the obvious end of getting the Prince a wife – at Maggie's expense. And then to that of getting Charlotte a husband at Mr Verver's.' (427–8)

Presumably the sense of the phrase 'at someone's expense' here is that for Maggie to marry Amerigo and Adam to marry Charlotte is an 'expense' or a depletion of their resources. There are places in James where such ideas of marriage occur, e.g. *The Aspern Papers* or 'The Figure in the Carpet' or those stories such as 'The Lesson of the Master' and 'The Author of Beltraffio' in which marriage seems to be antithetical to artistic creativity. Is it too fanciful an idea to see a verbal play here – to think that James confuses us so that for a moment wife and husband apply to Charlotte and Amerigo (Amerigo getting Charlotte for a 'wife' and Charlotte Amerigo for a 'husband') at the expense of their real wife and husband respectively? In any case the play on the word *expense* continues. On p. 529 it is Maggie, not Charlotte, who goes on at Adam's expense.
31. It is this type of ambiguity that makes one wish, as a reviewer wrote (Gard, *Henry James: The Critical Heritage*, p. 380), that James had given us two more volumes, one from Adam's point of view and one from Charlotte's.
32. One of the reader's problems in *The Golden Bowl* is to decide on an attitude towards Maggie's self-centredness, the selfishness that once is referred to as her 'blameless egoism'.

Self-erasing combinations like this, Jacobean oxymoron, are very frequent. James often planted them intentionally so as to create ambiguity through the reader's vacillation between the sense of one half and that of the other in the combination. Sometimes James is highly amused by oxymoron and his 'blameless egoism' may be as intentional as Melville's 'sinister dexterity'. See Norrman, Chapter 2, 'self-erasing combinations'.

But in the last analysis these self-erasing combinations were also inevitable in late James and they reveal a basic sense of insecurity in James's world. This will be dealt with at length in Chapter 5.

The fondness of oxymoron, paradoxes and antitheses in James is so strong that it begins to colour the language of his critics. When an early critic called James 'ardently frigid' (Gard, *Henry James: The Critical Heritage*, p. 418; W.C. Brownell, 'Henry James', *Atlantic*, April 1905, xcv, 496-519) he was probably unconsciousy imitating the man whose work he was attacking.
33. See Norrman, pp. 67–70.

CHAPTER 2: END-LINKING

1. See Nils Erik Enkvist, *Linguistic Stylistics*, Janua Linguarum, Studia Memoriae Nicolai Van Wijk Dedicata, Series Critica 5, Werner Winter (ed.) (The Hague–Paris: Mouton, 1973), pp. 110–26.
2. Grover, *Henry James and the French Novel*, p. 183.

3. Edel and Ray, *Henry James and H.G. Wells*, p. 248. From H.G. Wells, 'Of Art, of Literature, of Mr. Henry James', *Boon, The Mind of the Race, The Wild Asses of the Devil*, and *The Last Trump* (London, 1915), pp. 84–128.

4. Willen, *Casebook*, p. 125.

5. Wells left no doubt that he saw the superficiality as negative: 'He has, I am convinced, one of the strongest, most abundant minds alive in the whole world, and he has the smallest penetration. Indeed, he has no penetration. He is the culmination of the Superficial type. Or else he would have gone into philosophy and been greater even than his wonderful brother ... But here he is, spinning about, like the most tremendous of water-boatmen – you know those insects? – kept up by surface tension. As if, when once he pierced the surface, he would drown. It's incredible. A water-boatman as big as an elephant. I was reading him only yesterday – "The Golden Bowl"; it's dazzling how never for a moment does he go through.' (Edel and Ray, *Henry James and H.G. Wells*, pp. 245–6).

6. For the intensifying effect of repetition see Gunnar Persson, *Repetition in English: Part I: Sequential Repetition*, Act . Universitatis Upsaliensis, Studia Anglistica, Upsaliensia 21 (Uppsala, 1974). On James's use of key-words see Norrman, Chapters 2–3.

7. See e.g. Stephen Ullmann, *Meaning and Style: Collected Papers* (Oxford: Basil Blackwell, 1973), pp. 54–6.

8. For 'theme' and 'rheme' I shall here use a positional surface definition; 'thematic' parts of the sentence are usually found at the beginning of a sentence; 'rhematic' at the end. 'Sentence' will be used in several senses – the context or the example will show which is intended.

9. R.W. Short, 'The Sentence Structure of Henry James', *American Literature*, 18 (May 1946), no. 2, p. 80. My argument here may seem to contradict that of Short who writes: 'Good conventional prose structurally resembles a chain of links, in which the links may represent sentences, each tied to the preceding one, or paragraphs, each likewise tied to the preceding one. With numerous exceptions, we discover the relationship of one unit with an earlier unit by tracing back, link by link, the orderly chain of argument. The prose of James progresses much less simply.' (ibid.). As will be shown, however, even the concatenation of sentences in James is somehow 'fluid' or quasi, so that Short is essentially right even though links exist, and exist in abundance, in James's prose.

10. Henry James, *The Wings of the Dove*, vol xxxi of *The Novels and Stories of Henry James* (London: Macmillan, 1923), p. 239, my italics. This edition hereafter cited as *Novels and Stories*.

11. Carlo Izzo, 'Henry James, Scrittore Sintattico', p. 140. Again, though Short's and Izzo's comments may seem incompatible this is not really so. Izzo sees the concatenation as a manifestation of James's 'logica della fantasia'. He seems to argue that end-linking is something from normal prose that remains; almost against James's will as it were, after James's attempts to denaturate himself. But is it not the case that James appropriates end-linking too and makes it a device completely his own? End-linking does not function the same way textually in James as in other authors.

12. Clara F. McIntyre, 'The Later Manner of Mr. Henry James', *Publications of the Modern Language Association of America (PMLA)*, 27 (September 1912), no. 3, pp. 366–7. Gard, *Henry James: The Critical Heritage*, p. 499.

13. All related devices (apposition etc.) are used in James with a particular

insistency. The study of parataxis, coordination and apposition in James's style is a long chapter which is by no means finished yet. For a good study of one aspect of parataxis (the parenthesis) see Mary Carolyn McGinty, *The Jamesian Parenthesis: Elements of Suspension in the Narrative of Henry James's Late Style* (Diss., The Catholic University of America, 1964).

14. Witness the frequency of such phrases as 'unless, she amended with a further thought . . .' James comments on the Prince's 'inability, in any matter in which he was concerned, to conclude' and, predictably, the critics pounce on this phrase to say that it could also be applied to the author himself. Cf. Gard, *Henry James: The Critical Heritage*, p. 383. Cf. also James's comment on relations which 'stop nowhere', Blackmur, p. 5.

15. Sister McGinty found that 75.4 per cent of the parentheses she studied in *The Ambassadors* were resumptive and 24.6 per cent progressive. Out of 460 resumptive suspensions the resumptive effect was proximate in 224, the suspensions repeating the final element of the suspended meaning, and in 236 remotely resumptive, the suspensions repeating some other meaning still within the preceding context of the sentence.

The resumptive meaning in 196 suspensions were repetitions of exact lexical units used in the suspended meaning (there were also referential and hyponymic links). See McGinty, especially pp. 76–83, but also the conclusion pp. 120–4.

16. On dictation and James's style see McGinty, *The Jamesian Parenthesis*, p. 2.

17. Sister McGinty too uses the word 'intense' commenting on end-linking: ('. . . of the *grounds – grounds* all handled and . . .'; 'the effect of the repetition here is intensifying emphasis and clarification'.).

18. Gard, *Henry James: The Critical Heritage*, p. 382. (Unsigned review, *Saturday*, March 1905, xcix, 383–4).

19. Gard, *Henry James: The Critical Heritage*, p. 384.

20. Gard, *Henry James: The Critical Heritage*, p. 383.

21. The image of a labyrinth probably suggests itself to so many critics largely because of the density of inter-sentence links, particularly end-linking; 'labyrinth' and 'serpentine'; Gard, *Henry James: The Critical Heritage*, p. 428 (W.C. Brownell, 'Henry James', *Atlantic*, April 1905, xcv, 496–519. Charles du Bos grouped James with Donne and Browning calling him a 'génie labyrinthique' (Angelo Philip Bertocci, *Charles du Bos and English Literature: A Critic and his Orientation* [New York: King's Crown Press, 1949] p. 199).

22. *The Works of Mark Twain: Roughing It* with an introduction and explanatory notes by Franklin R. Rogers; Text Established and Textual Notes by Paul Baender, The Iowa Center for Textual Studies (Berkeley, Los Angeles, London: University of California Press, 1972), pp. 344–5.

23. Ernst Kris, *Psychoanalytic Exploration in Art* (London: George Allen & Unwin, 1953). Chapter 10, 'Aesthetic Ambiguity,' written in collaboration with Abraham Kaplan, p. 246.

24. Seymour Chatman, *The Later Style of Henry James*, Language and Style Series II, general ed. Stephen Ullmann (Oxford: Basil Blackwell, 1972).

25. Of course, with the fondness for antithesis that is so typical of James's mind, antonymy is also a good link. Oppositeness is in itself a relation, a link as good as any in James. See Chapter 5.

26. On the heightened cliché in James see David Lodge, *Language of Fiction: Essays in Criticism and Verbal Analysis of the English Novel* (London: Routledge &

Kegan Paul, 1966) p. 196.

27. Barry Menikoff's article might suggest that pronominal theme to theme repetition is frequent in James. However, we need only make two observations here. Work-initial cataphoric pronominal reference ('She waited, Kate Croy ...') is habitual in late James and fits in well with his other techniques. Secondly, as Johnson, *A Study of the Style of Henry James's Late Novels*, demonstrates, James uses pronouns often during his late period, and more often than earlier. Barry Menikoff, 'The Subjective Pronoun in the Late Style of Henry James', *English Studies*, 52 (October, 1971), no. 5, 436–41.

28. E.g. Leon Edel, 'To the Poet of Prose', *Modern Fiction Studies*, 12 (Spring 1966), no. 2, p. 5.

29. Morris W. Croll, 'The Baroque Style in Prose', in Kemp Malone and Martin B. Rund (eds), *Studies in English Philology*, A Miscellany in honor of Frederick Klaeber (Minneapolis: University of Minnesota Press, 1929), pp. 427–56. Could not the following passage have been written about James as well?

> The two passages, in short, are written as if they were meant to illustrate in style what Bacon calls 'the method of induced knowledge', either they have no predetermined plan or they violate it at will; their progression adapts itself to the movements of a mind discovering truth as it goes, thinking while it writes. At the same time, and for the same reason, they illustrate the character of the style that we call 'baroque'. See, for instance, how symmetry is first made and then broken, as it is in so many baroque designs in painting and architecture; how there is a constant swift adaptation of form to the emergencies that arise in an energetic and unpremeditated forward movement; and observe, further, that these signs of spontaneity and improvisation occur in passages loaded with as heavy a content as rhetoric ever has to carry. That is to say, they combine the effect of great mass with the effect of rapid motion; and there is no better formula than this to describe the ideal of the baroque design in all the arts (pp. 442–3).

30. Croll, 'The Baroque Style in Prose', p. 428.

31. Croll, 'The Baroque Style in Prose', p. 430.

32. 'The members of this period stand farther apart from another than they would in a Ciceronian sentence; there are no syntactic connectives between them whatever ...' (p. 429); 'In all of these passages, as in the period quoted from Wotton, there are no two main members that are syntactically connected.' (p. 432) etc.

33. The effect is 'intense' because the reader has to note the links for himself. The author does not signal through argument markers, what the textual position of each sentence will be. He could have written 'The world that I regard is myself', *in other words* 'it is the microcosm ...' thereby signalling explicitly to the reader that the second member will be a variation of the first. But he preferred not to. James also often suppressed such signals (– and in some cases, when they are used they are used unorthodoxly). Ellipsis is a phenomenon that contributes greatly to intensity (and also to obscurity).

34. Croll, 'The Baroque Style in Prose', p. 433.

35. Croll, 'The Baroque Style in Prose', p. 447.

36. Ibid. This is true on the stylistic level. In their overall structure James's works were of course very carefully planned.

37. Card-playing metaphors should be expected in this novel in which a game of bridge is going on in one of the crucial scenes. Bridge – four persons – suits the set-up of the novel; 'advantage' could refer to tennis doubles – with switched partners – but perhaps the connotations are not that specific. A game which would be very true in spirit to the latter half of the novel is poker, which depends a lot on not letting the other players guess what cards you hold and yourself trying to guess what cards they hold. An early reviewer of *The Golden Bowl* in the *Times Literary Supplement*, February 1905, 47, spontaneously used card-playing metaphors in his text. Gard, *Henry James: The Critical Heritage*, pp. 374–5.

CHAPTER 3: EMPHATIC AFFIRMATION

1. 'Yes' is typically used in *The Golden Bowl* as the beginning of a more expanded answer. Often this answer amounts to a qualification or an evasion. Thus there is an inflationary shift so that affirmation demands emphatic repetition and 'yes' almost stands for 'no'.

2. Gard, *Henry James: The Critical Heritage*, p. 495.

3. It is, as he wrote to his brother, a matter of what he *could*, but also at the same time of what he *would*.

4. Tuomo Laitinen, *Aspects of Henry James's Style* (Helsinki: Suomalainen tiedeakatemia, 1975), pp. 21–7.

5. Norrman, pp. 29–31 and *passim*.

6. Naturally with the necessary changes of pronouns. Pronominal transformations (and corresponding changes of verbs etc.) will be taken for granted and ignored from now on.

7. See J.L. Austin, *How to do Things with Words: The William James Lectures delivered at Harvard University in 1955* (New York: Oxford University Press, 1965).

CHAPTER 4: THE 'FINDING A FORMULA'-FORMULA

1. William Dean Howells, 'Editha', in Willard Thorp (ed.), *Great Short Works of American Realism* (New York: Harper & Row, 1968), pp. 210–24.

2. *Novels and Stories*, 17, p. 321.

3. Henry James, *In the Cage & Other Tales*. Morton Dauwen Zabel (ed.) (New York: W.W. Norton, 1969), p. 205.

4. Willen, *Casebook*, pp. 147–8.

5. See John E. Tilford, Jr., 'James the Old Intruder', *Modern Fiction Studies*, 4 (Summer 1958), no. 2, 157–64.

6. Cf. Tony Tanner, *The Reign of Wonder: Naivety and Reality in American Literature* (Cambridge University Press, 1965), pp. 310–19.

7. *Novels and Stories*, 29, p. 168.

8. William James, *Pragmatism: A New Name for Some Old Ways of Thinking; Together with Four Related Essays Selected from* The Meaning of Truth (New York:

Longmans, Green, 1943), p. 233.
9. Cf. W. James, *Pragmatism*, p. 51.
10. Percy Lubbock (ed.), *The Letters of Henry James* (London: Macmillan, 1920), ii, p. 85.
11. There is a rich literature on Henry's pragmatism. See Richard A. Hocks, *Henry James and Pragmatistic Thought: A Study in the Relationship between the Philosophy of William James and the Literary Art of Henry James* (Chapel Hill: University of North Carolina Press, 1974); Edward Rich. Levy, 'Henry James and the Pragmatic Assumption: The Conditions of Perception', Diss. (University of Illinois, 1964); James Edwin Woodard, Jr., 'Pragmatism and Pragmaticism in James and Howells', Diss. (University of New Mexico, 1969); Eliseo Vivas, 'Henry and William: (Two Notes)', *The Kenyon Review*, 5 (Autumn 1943), no. 4, 580–94; John Henry Raleigh, 'Henry James: The Poetics of Empiricism', *PMLA*, 66 (March 1951), no. 2, 107–23; Henry Bamford Parkes, 'The James Brothers', *The Sewanee Review*, 56 (April–June 1948), no. 2, 323–8; William McMurray, 'Pragmatic Realism in *The Bostonians*', *Nineteenth-Century Fiction*, 16 (March 1962), no. 4, 339–44; Joseph J. Firebaugh, 'The Pragmatism of Henry James', *The Virginia Quarterly Review*, 27 (Summer 1951), no. 3, 419–35. On the relationship between the brothers see e.g. Leon Edel, *Henry James: The Untried Years 1843–1870* (London: Rupert Hart-Davis, 1953), *The Conquest of London 1870–1883* (1962), *The Middle Years 1884–1894* (1963), *The Treacherous Years 1895–1901* (1969), *The Master 1901–1916* (1972); F.O. Matthiessen, *The James Family: Including Selections from the Writings of Henry James, Senior, William, Henry & Alice James* (New York: Alfred A. Knopf, 1948); Gay Wilson Allen, *William James: A Biography* (London: Rupert Hart-Davis, 1967). Henry James's knowledge of philosophy in the ordinary sense of the word was shallow. But naturally William's friends were also Henry's friends. On the relations of the James family with Chauncey Wright, Oliver Wendell Holmes, Jr. and Charles Sanders Peirce see Ralph Barton Perry, *The Thought and Character of William James: As revealed in Unpublished Correspondence and Notes, Together With His Published Writings*, vol. I, 'Inheritance and Vocation', vol. II, 'Philosophy and Psychology' (London: Humphrey Milford: Oxford University Press, 1935), also in briefer version *The Thought and Character of William James* (Cambridge: Harvard University Press, 1948). Cf. also Levy, pp. 7–24.

CHAPTER 5: CHIASTIC INVERSION, ANTITHESIS AND OXYMORON

1. E.M. Forster, *Aspects of the Novel* (London: Edward Arnold, 1958), pp. 140–50.
2. Edmund Wilson, 'The Ambiguity of Henry James', pp. 115–53 in Willen, *Casebook*, p. 123.
3. *Notebooks*, pp. 150–1.
4. *Notebooks*, p. 275.
5. Henry James, *The Sacred Fount*, introd. Leon Edel (London: Rupert Hart-Davis, 1959), p. 9.
   The Sacred Fount is problematical in that the narrator's theory seems to be

undermined in several ways. It is not clear whether he might be wrong because there are no vampire–victim relationships at all; or whether he might be wrong because, although vampire–victim relationships do exist, he has got hold of the wrong set.

6. Arthur Koestler, *The Act of Creation* (London: Hutchinson, 1964) p. 33.

7. T.S. Eliot, 'On Henry James: In Memory', in F.W. Dupee (ed.), *The Question of Henry James: A Collection of Critical Essays* (New York: Henry Holt, 1945), p. 110.

8. There are a number of good studies on James's names. See Richard Gerber, 'Die Magie der Namen bei Henry James', *Anglia*, 81 (1963), no. 1/2, esp. pp. 189–91. See also Robert L. Gale, 'Names in James', *Names*, 14–15 (June 1966), 83–108; Joseph M. Backus,'"Poor Valentin" or "Monsieur le Comte": Variation in Character Designation as Matter for Critical Consideration in Henry James' *The American*, *Names*, 20–21 (1972–3), 47–55; Evelyn J. Hinz, 'Henry James's Names: Tradition, Theory, and Method', *Colby Library Quarterly*, 9 (September 1972), no. 11, 557–78; Joyce Tayloe Horrell, 'A "Shade of a Special Sense": Henry James and the Art of Naming', *American Literature*, 42 (May 1970), no. 2, 203–220.

9. Particularly repetition of the labial consonant [b].

10. *Novels and Stories*, 20, p. 102 and *passim*.

I have not been able to ascertain whether the name Guy may have been chosen ironically. The slang meaning 'man' existed at this time even though it may not have been common.

11. James's usual onomastic method of putting servants in their place was to give them harsh-sounding names that grate on the ear. For butlers we have Banks, Bates, Gotch, Tatton, and Withers; governesses Mrs. Hack, Miss Steel, Miss Teagle, and Mrs. Wix; nurses Bald, Boggle, Moddle, Mumby, and Ruddle.

But moving around Europe James must have been amused by the incongruity between language and reality in the cases of servants with classical or otherwise literarily allusive names, and he gave servant-characters in his fiction such names as Alcibiade, Assunta, Augustine, Azarina, Belinda, Celestine, Celsomine, Cynthia, Eugenio, Olimpia, and Zenobie. Cf. Gale, 'Names in James', pp. 100–1.

12. *Novels and Stories*, 23, p. 306.

13. Cf. Edmund Wilson in Willen, *Casebook*, pp. 148–9.

14. *Novels and Stories*, 17, p. 319.

15. *Novels and Stories*, 20, p. 281.

16. Cf. Simon Nowell-Smith, *The Legend of the Master* (London: Constable, 1947), p. xxiii. See also pp. xxvi–xxvii.

17. Ibid. p. xxiii.

18. That characters and author speak alike becomes apparent from a comparison of the preface of *The Golden Bowl* with the book itself. The same mannerisms characterize the style of both. Antithesis for instance, which is so typical of the text itself, occurs in the very first sentence of the preface exactly in the form it often has in the text of the novel itself:

> Among many matters thrown into relief by a refreshed acquaintance with *The Golden Bowl* what perhaps stands out for me is the still marked inveteracy of a certain indirect and oblique view of my presented action;

unless indeed I make up my mind to call this mode of treatment, on the contrary, any superficial appearance notwithstanding, the very straightest and closest possible. (15).

19. See e.g. F.W. Dupee, *Henry James* (London: Methuen, 1951), p. 13; or Van Wyck Brooks, *The Pilgrimage of Henry James* (London: Jonathan Cape, 1928), p. 4.

20. Cf. Rimmon, *The Concept of Ambiguity*, p. 216.

21. Quotations from Henry James, *The Sacred Fount*, p. 198.

22. Henry James, *The Complete Tales of Henry James*, ed. and introd. Leon Edel (London: Rupert Hart-Davis, 1962–4), 3, p. 56.

23. Henry James, *The Awkward Age*, The Norton Library (New York: W.W. Norton, 1969), p. 255.

24. The symmetry between the first half and the second half of a chiastic structure involves the idea of *reciprocity*, and reciprocity in turn involves the idea of similarity. It is not surprising that the roles of the characters in *The Golden Bowl* should be similar since the plan of the book is two symmetrical halves, the point of inversion occurring in the middle. Even in his comments in the preface James inevitably slips into chiasmus in his sentences when he describes the symmetry of the novel:

It is the Prince who opens the door to half our light upon Maggie, just as it is she who opens it to half our light upon himself; (18)

25. With the exception of his last few years during the war when he did get deeply involved in the allied cause.

26. Walter Wright, 'Maggie Verver: Neither Saint Nor Witch', in Tony Tanner (ed.), *Henry James: Modern Judgements* (London: Macmillan, 1968), pp. 316–26.

27. In other words, the narrator in this story could be 'unreliable' in several ways: either in the sense that the Colonel is not as bad as he seems, or else that the Colonel is bad but Lyon equally bad.

28. E. Duncan Aswell, 'James's *In the Cage*: The Telegraphist as Artist', *Texas Studies in Literature and Language*, 8 (Fall 1966), no. 3, 375–84.

29. For a study of this aspect of *The Turn of the Screw*, see Norrman, pp. 52, 89–93, 150–80 and *passim*; and E. Duncan Aswell, 'Reflections of a Governess: Image and Distortion in "The Turn of the Screw"', *Nineteenth-Century Fiction*, 23 (June 1968), no. 1, 49–63. In the fifties and sixties critics tended to see these passages of symbolic identification in terms of limited, momentary irony, see e.g. Oscar Cargill, 'Henry James as Freudian Pioneer', *Chicago Review*, 10 (Summer 1956), no. 2, p. 21, and Marius Bewley, *The Complex Fate: Hawthorne, Henry James and Some Other American Writers* (London: Chatto and Windus, 1952), pp. 109–111. Since the late sixties, however, critics have gradually begun to realize that the pattern reveals something far more essential and important. See Paul N. Siegel, '"Miss Jessel": Mirror Image of the Governess', *Literature and Psychology*, 18 (1968), no. 1, 30–8, and Juliet McMaster, 'The Full Image of a Repetition in *The Turn of the Screw*', *Studies in Short Fiction*, 6, (Summer 1969), no. 4, 378–82.

30. On the interchangeability of victim and victimizer see also Rimmon, *The Concept of Ambiguity*, pp. 206–7.

31. The end of Chapter XX.

32. Tony Tanner, 'The Fearful Self: Henry James's *The Portrait of a Lady*', in *Henry James: Modern Judgements* (Nashville/London: Aurora Publishers, 1970), 141–59, p. 148. In fact Tanner convincingly makes out very much the same similarity between the opposites of Isabel and Osmond as can be made out between e.g. the governess and the ghosts in *The Turn of the Screw*.

> Osmond is an egotist, but so, we are told, is Isabel; he is cold and dry, but so is she; he pays excessive attention to appearances rather than realities, and up to a point so does she (I will return to this); he prefers art to life, and so does she; he has more theories than feelings, more ideals than instincts and so does she. (ibid.)

33. Henry James, *Complete Tales*, 3, p. 64.
34. Cf. Norrman, pp. 40–50.
35. Cf. Norrman, p. 149.
36. *Notebooks*, p. 150.

List of Works Cited

Allen, Gay Wilson, *William James: A Biography* (London: Rupert Hart-Davis, 1967).

Aswell, E. Duncan, 'James's *In the Cage*: The Telegraphist as Artist', *Texas Studies in Literature and Language*, 8 (Fall 1966), no. 3, 375–84.

—— 'Reflections of a Governess: Image and Distortion in "The Turn of the Screw"', *Nineteenth-Century Fiction*, 23 (June 1968), no. 1, 49–63.

Austin, J.L., *How to do Things with Words: The William James Lectures delivered at Harvard University in 1955* (New York: Oxford University Press, 1965).

Backus, Joseph M., '"Poor Valentin" or "Monsieur le Comte": Variation in Character Designation as Matter for Critical Consideration in Henry James' *The American*, *Names*, 20–21 (1972–3), 47–55.

Bertocci, Angelo Philip, *Charles du Bos and English Literature: A Critic and his Orientation* (New York: King's Crown Press, 1949).

Bewley, Marius, *The Complex Fate: Hawthorne, Henry James and Some Other American Writers* (London: Chatto & Windus, 1952).

Blackall, Jean Frantz, *Jamesian Ambiguity and* The Sacred Fount (Ithaca: Cornell University Press, 1965).

Brooks, Van Wyck, *The Pilgrimage of Henry James* (London: Jonathan Cape, 1928).

Cargill, Oscar, 'Henry James as Freudian Pioneer', *Chicago Review*, 10 (Summer 1956), no. 2, 13–29.

—— *The Novels of Henry James* (New York: Macmillan, 1961).

Chatman, Seymour, *The Later Style of Henry James*, Language and Style Series II. Stephen Ullmann (gen. ed.) (Oxford: Basil Blackwell, 1972).

Crews, Frederick C., *The Tragedy of Manners: Moral Drama in the Later Novels of Henry James* (New Haven: Yale University Press, 1957).

Croll, Morris W., 'The Baroque Style in Prose', in Kemp Malone and Martin B. Rund (eds), *Studies in English Philology*. A Miscellany in honor of Frederick Klaeber (Minneapolis: University of Minnesota Press, 1929).

Dickens, Charles, *Nicholas Nickleby*, ed., introd. and notes Michael Slater (Harmondsworth: Penguin, 1978).

Dupee, F.W., *Henry James* (London: Methuen, 1951).

—— *The Question of Henry James: A Collection of Critical Essays* (New York: Henry Holt, 1945).

Edel, Leon and Gordon N. Ray (eds), *Henry James and H.G. Wells: A Record of their Friendship, their Debate on the Art of Fiction, and their Quarrel* (London: Rupert Hart-Davis, 1958).

Edel, Leon, *Henry James: The Untried Years 1843–1870* (London: Rupert Hart-Davis, 1953), *The Conquest of London 1870–1883* (1962), *The Middle Years 1884–1894 (1963)*, *The Treacherous Years 1895–1901* (1969), *The Master 1901–1916* (1972).

────── 'To the Poet of Prose', *Modern Fiction Studies*, 12, (Spring 1966), no. 2.

Eliot, T.S., 'On Henry James: In Memory', in F.W. Dupee (ed.), *The Question of Henry James: A Collection of Critical Essays.*

Enkvist, Nils Erik, *Linguistic Stylistics*, Janua Linguarum, Studia Memoriae Nicolai Van Wijk Dedicata, Series Critica 5, ed. Werner Winter (The Hague–Paris: Mouton, 1973).

Firebaugh, Joseph J., 'The Pragmatism of Henry James', *The Virginia Quarterly Review*, 27 (Summer 1951), no. 3, 419–35.

Forster, E.M., *Aspects of the Novel* (London: Edward Arnold, 1958).

Gale, Robert L., 'Names in James', *Names*, 14–15 (June 1966), 83–108.

────── *Plots and Characters in the Fiction of Henry James* (Hamden Ct: MIT Press, 1972).

Gard, Roger (ed), *Henry James: The Critical Heritage* (London: Routledge & Kegan Paul, 1968).

Gerber, Richard, 'Die Magie der Namen bei Henry James', *Anglia*, 81 (1963), no. 1/2, 175–97.

Grover, Philip, *Henry James and the French Novel: A Study in Inspiration* (London: Paul Elek, 1973).

Hinz, Evelyn J., 'Henry James's Names: Tradition, Theory, and Method', *Colby Library Quarterly*, 9 (September 1972), no. 11, 557–78.

Hocks, Richard A., *Henry James and Pragmatistic Thought: A Study in the Relationship between the Philosophy of William and the Literary Art of Henry James* (Chapel Hill: University of North Carolina Press, 1974).

Horrell, Joyce Tayloe, 'A "Shade of a Special Sense": Henry James and the Art of Naming', *American Literature*, 42 (May 1970), no. 2, 203–220.

Howells, William Dean, 'Editha', in Willard Thorp (ed.), *Great Short Works of American Realism* (New York: Harper & Row, 1968).

Izzo, Carlo, 'Henry James Scrittore Sintattico', *Studi Americani*, 2 (1956), 127–42.

James, Henry, *The Art of the Novel: Critical Prefaces*, introd. Richard P. Blackmur (New York: Charles Scribner, 1962).

────── *The Awkward Age*, The Norton Library (New York: W.W. Norton, 1969).

────── *The Complete Tales of Henry James*, ed. and introd. Leon Edel (London: Rupert Hart-Davis, 1962–4).

────── *The Golden Bowl*, The Bodley Head Henry James, vol ix, ed. Leon Edel (London: The Bodley Head, 1971).

────── *In the Cage & Other Tales*, ed. and introd. Morton Dauwen Zabel (New York: W.W. Norton, 1969).

────── *The Novels and Stories of Henry James* (London: Macmillan, 1922).

────── *The Sacred Fount*, introd. Leon Edel (London: Rupert Hart-Davis, 1959).

────── *The Turn of the Screw*, A Norton Critical Edition, ed. Robert Kimbrough (New York: W.W. Norton, 1966).

James, William, *Pragmatism: A New Name for Some Old Ways of Thinking; Together with Four Related Essays Selected from* The Meaning of Truth (New York: Longmans, Green, 1943).

Johnson, Robert G., 'A Study of the Style of Henry James's Late Novels' (Diss., Bowling Green State University, 1971).

Koestler, Arthur, *The Act of Creation* (London: Hutchinson, 1964).

Koiij, Jan G., *Ambiguity in Natural Language: An Investigation of Certain Problems in*

Its Linguistic Description, North-Holland Linguistic Series, 3 (Amsterdam: North-Holland, 1971).

Kris, Ernst, *Psychoanalytic Exploration in Art* (London: George Allen & Unwin, 1953).

Laitinen, Tuomo, *Aspects of Henry James's Style* (Helsinki: Suomalainen tiedeakatemia, 1975).

Levy, Edward Rich., 'Henry James and the Pragmatic Assumption: The Conditions of Perception' (Diss., University of Illinois, 1964).

Lodge, David, *Language of Fiction: Essays in Criticism and Verbal Analysis of the English Novel* (London: Routledge & Kegan Paul, 1966).

Lubbock, Percy (ed.), *The Letters of Henry James* (London: Macmillan, 1920).

McGinty, Mary Carolyn, 'The Jamesian Parenthesis: Elements of Suspension in the Narrative of Henry James's Late Style' (Diss., The Catholic University of America, 1964).

McIntyre, Clara F., 'The Later Manner of Mr. Henry James', *PMLA*, 27 (September 1912), no. 3.

McMaster, Juliet, 'The Full Image of a Repetition in *The Turn of the Screw*', *Studies in Short Fiction*, 6 (Summer 1969), no. 4, 377–82.

McMurray, William, 'Pragmatic Realism in *The Bostonians*', *Nineteenth-Century Fiction*, 16 (March 1962), no. 4, 339–44.

Matthiessen, F.O., *Henry James: The Major Phase* (New York: Oxford University Press, 1963).

—— *The James Family: Including Selections from the Writings of Henry James, Senior, William, Henry & Alice James* (New York: Alfred A. Knopf, 1948).

Matthiessen, F.O. and Kenneth B. Murdock (eds), *The Notebooks of Henry James* (New York: Oxford University Press, 1947).

Menikoff, Barry, 'The Subjective Pronoun in the Late Style of Henry James', *English Studies*, 52 (October 1971), no. 5, 436–41.

Mull, Donald L., *Henry James's 'Sublime Economy': Money as Symbolic Center in the Fiction* (Middletown: Wesleyan University Press, 1973).

Nierlich, Edmund, *Kuriose Wirklichkeit in den Romanen von Henry James: Ein Methodischer Beitrag zur Werkanalyse in der Literaturwissenschaft*, Studien zur Germanistik, Anglistik und Komparatistik: Herausgegeben von Armin Arnold und Alois M. Haas, Band 17 (Bonn: Bouvier Verlag Herbert Grundmann, 1973).

Norrman, Ralf, *Techniques of Ambiguity in the Fiction of Henry James: With Special Reference to* In the Cage *and* The Turn of the Screw, Acta Academiae Aboensis. Ser. A Humaniora, vol. 54, no. 2 (Åbo: Åbo Akademi, 1977).

Nowell-Smith, Simon, *The Legend of the Master* (London: Constable, 1947).

Parkes, Henry Bamford, 'The James Brothers', *The Sewanee Review*, 56 (April–June 1948), no. 2, 323–28.

Perry, Ralph Barton, *The Thought and Character of William James* (Cambridge: Harvard University Press, 1948).

—— *The Thought and Character of William James: As revealed in Unpublished Correspondence and Notes, Together With His Published Writings*, vol. I, 'Inheritance and Vocation', vol. II, 'Philosophy and Psychology' (London: Humphrey Milford: Oxford University Press, 1935).

Persson, Gunnar, *Repetition in English: Part I: Sequential Repetition*, Acta Universitatis Upsaliensis, Studia Anglistica, Upsaliensia 21 (Uppsala, 1974).

Raleigh, John Henry, 'Henry James: The Poetics of Empiricism', *PMLA*, 66 (March 1951), no. 2, 107–23.

Ricks, Beatrice (comp.), *Henry James: A Bibliography of Secondary Works* (Metuchen: The Scarecrow Press, 1975).

Rimmon, Shlomith, *The Concept of Ambiguity – the Example of James* (Chicago and London: University of Chicago Press, 1977).

Samuels, Charles Thomas, *The Ambiguity of Henry James* (Urbana: University of Illinois Press, 1971).

Short, R.W., 'The Sentence Structure of Henry James', *American Literature*, 18 (May 1946), no. 2.

Siegel, Paul N.,'"Miss Jessel": Mirror Image of the Governess', *Literature and Psychology*, 18 (1968), no. 1, 30–38.

Tanner, Tony, 'The Fearful Self: Henry James's *The Portrait of a Lady*', in *Henry James: Modern Judgements* (Nashville/London: Aurora Publishers, 1970), 141–59.

—————— (ed.), *Henry James: Modern Judgements* (London: Macmillan, 1968).

—————— *The Reign of Wonder: Naivety and Reality in American Literature* (Cambridge University Press, 1965).

Tilford, John E., Jr., 'James the Old Intruder', *Modern Fiction Studies*, 4 (Summer 1958), no. 2, 157–64.

Twain, Mark, *The Adventures of Huckleberry Finn*, introd. Lionel Trilling (New York: Rinehart, 1954).

—————— *The Works of Mark Twain: Roughing It*, with an introd. and expl. notes Franklin R. Rogers; Text establ. and textual notes Paul Baender. The Iowa Center for Textual Studies (Berkeley, Los Angeles, London: University of California Press, 1972).

Ullmann, Stephen, *Meaning and Style: Collected Papers* (Oxford: Basil Blackwell, 1973).

Vivas, Eliseo, 'Henry and William: (Two Notes)', *The Kenyon Review*, 5 (Autumn 1943), no. 4, 580–94.

Wells, H.G., *Boon, The Mind of the Race, The Wild Asses of the Devil*, and *The Last Trump* (London, 1915).

Willen, Gerald (ed.), *A Casebook on Henry James's 'The Turn of the Screw'* 2nd edn (New York: Thomas Y. Crowell, 1971).

Wilson, Edmund, 'The Ambiguity of Henry James', in Willen, *Casebook*, 115–53.

Woodard, James Edwin, Jr., 'Pragmatism and Pragmaticism in James and Howells' (Diss., University of New Mexico, 1969).

Wright, Walter, 'Maggie Verver: Neither Saint Nor Witch', in Tony Tanner (ed.), *Henry James: Modern Judgements*, 316–26

Index

Critics mentioned in the Notes and References are not listed; for these see the List of Works Cited. Though it is not stated explicitly most entries refer to James and his work.

'fortunate fall', 9, 62
Freud, Sigmund, 142

Gale, Robert, 31
Grover, Philip, 67
guessing, 91, 129

Hogarth, William, 19
Howells, William Dean, 108–11, 113
Huxley, Aldous, 183
hyponymy (general), 78, 80, 90
  contracting, 51, 74, 75
  expanding, 75, 81, 88

iconicism, 77, 78, 81, 82
identification, 146–84, *passim*
  symbolic i. of opposites, 162–74,
    181–2, 205–6
identity and identicality, 161ff., 186
images, 67, 75–6, 78
improvization, 71
incongruity, 144–5
innuendo, 12, 18
insecurity, *see* uncertainty
intensity (general), 2, 4, 8–9, 12, 45,
  67, 73, 193, 201
  ambiguity, its interconnection
    with, 2, 4, 12, 15, 28, 44, 90,
    92, 131, 136, 183–4
  appearance and reality, in
    connection with, 32–3
  attention, of, 73
  emotion and ratiocination, in
    relation to, 72
  emphatic affirmation, in relation
    to, 84–6
  euphemism, in connection with,
    12–13
  form and content, in relation to, 67ff.
  hyponymy, in connection with,
    75–6
  image and metaphor, in relation to,
    75–6
  italicization, in connection with, 15
  loose period, in connection with, 79
  paradigmatic instability, in relation
    to, 112
  performatives, in connection with,
    131

  playfulness, in connection with, 76
  repetition, in relation to, 68, 71
  ritual affirmation, in connection
    with, 86–7
intersentence links, types of
  antonymy, 66, 82
  hyponymy, 66, 74, 75–6, 81
  reference, 66, 73, 75, 81, 200
  repetition, 66, 68, 69, 70, 71, 74, 75,
    81, 82, 200
  synonymy, 66, 75; *see also separate entry*
Ionesco, Eugène, 73
interchangeability of roles, 142–4,
  146–84 *passim*, 186
italicization, 59, 107, 183–4
Izzo, Carlo, 69, 76

James, Henry
  autobiography, 70
  celibacy, 161
  collusion between perpetrator and
    victim of a wrong in his fiction,
    176ff.
  dictation, 71
  dualism, 186
  early and late manner of style, 3–4
  exile, 161
  labyrinthine, 200
  masochism, 177
  negativism, 160
  parodies of, 74–5
  playwriter, as a, 88
  prefaces, 71
  relativism, 144, 158
  revisions, 70–1, 189
  self-parody, 86
  sensitivity, 188–9
  sterility, 177, 191–2
  WORKS OF
  The Ambassadors, 30, 137–8, 146,
    148, 154, 155–6
  The Awkward Age, 158–9
  The Bostonians, 160
  'Collaboration', 161
  Confidence, 6
  'The Death of the Lion', 144
  'Eugene Pickering', 129
  The Europeans, 6
  'The Figure in the Carpet', 161